Social Engineering

Social Engineering

The Science of Human Hacking

Christopher Hadnagy

WILEY

Social Engineering: The Science of Human Hacking

Published by
John Wiley & Sons, Inc.
10475 Crosspoint Boulevard
Indianapolis, IN 46256
www.wiley.com

Copyright © 2018 by John Wiley & Sons, Inc., Indianapolis, Indiana

Published simultaneously in Canada

ISBN: 978-1-119-43338-5
ISBN: 978-1-119-43373-6 (ebk)
ISBN: 978-1-119-43375-0 (ebk)

Manufactured in the United States of America

SKY10085213_091924

For general information on our other products and services please contact our Customer Care Department within the United States at (877) 762-2974, outside the United States at (317) 572-3993 or fax (317) 572-4002.

Wiley publishes in a variety of print and electronic formats and by print-on-demand. Some material included with standard print versions of this book may not be included in e-books or in print-on-demand. If this book refers to media such as a CD or DVD that is not included in the version you purchased, you may download this material at http://booksupport.wiley.com. For more information about Wiley products, visit www.wiley.com.

Library of Congress Control Number: 2018943781

My whole life that I live as a social engineer, a father, husband, boss, friend, and more doesn't happen without my amazing wife, Areesa. I love you more than words can say.

My son, Colin, watching you grow up in this world and become a security-minded young man, as well as working with me, makes all the work worthwhile. I love you.

Amaya, you have been the light of my life, my reason for smiles on dark days, and the cause of joy in my heart. I cannot put into words how much I love you and how truly proud I am of who you are as a person.

ABOUT THE AUTHOR

CHRISTOPHER HADNAGY is the CEO and Chief Human Hacker of Social-Engineer, LLC as well as the lead developer and creator of the world's first social engineering framework found at www.social-engineer.org. He is the founder and creator of the Social Engineering Village (SEVillage) at DEF CON and DerbyCon, as well as the creator of the popular Social Engineering Capture The Flag (SECTF). He is a sought-after speaker and trainer and has traveled the globe to deliver at many events including RSA, Black Hat, DEF CON, and even has debriefed the Pentagon on these topics. He can be found tweeting at @humanhacker.

ABOUT THE TECHNICAL EDITOR

MICHELE FINCHER is the Information Security Awareness Lead at a specialty chemical company. She possesses more than 20 years' experience as a behavioral scientist, researcher, and information security professional. Her specialty is understanding the psychology behind secure decision-making, particularly with respect to the area of social engineering.

Michele has been a trainer and speaker on various technical and behavioral subjects for law enforcement, the intelligence community, and the private sector in venues including the Black Hat Briefings, RSA, SourceCon, SC Congress, Interop, and Techno Security.

Michele has her Bachelor of Science in Human Factors Engineering from the US Air Force Academy and her Master of Science in Counseling from Auburn University. She is a Certified Information Systems Security Professional (CISSP).

CREDITS

PROJECT EDITOR
Charlotte Kughen

TECHNICAL EDITOR
Michele Fincher

PRODUCTION EDITOR
Athiyappan Lalith Kumar

COPY EDITOR
Kathryn Duggan

PRODUCTION MANAGER
Katie Wisor

MANAGER OF CONTENT ENABLEMENT AND
OPERATIONS
Pete Gaughan

MARKETING MANAGER
Christie Hilbrich

EXECUTIVE EDITOR
Jim Minatel

PROJECT COORDINATOR, COVER
Brent Savage

PROOFREADER
Nancy Bell

INDEXER
Johnna VanHoose

COVER DESIGNER
Wiley

COVER IMAGE
Background © Floriana /iStockphoto;
Author Photo © Amaya Hadnagy
Photography, 2018

ACKNOWLEDGMENTS

"It was just a few years ago that I was sitting with my friend and mentor, Mati Aharoni, deciding to launch www.social-engineer.org."

Those are the opening words of *Social Engineering: The Art of Human Hacking*. As I sit here and read them now, it's almost like a dream; the hazy memory makes me feel like I will wake up any minute. I reflect on the journey that has taken me through the past decade, and especially the last eight years, and it has all come to life in this book.

Over the last eight years I have worked with people like Dr. Paul Ekman, Robin Dreeke, Neil Fallon, and others. I have had the honor of interviewing people like Dr. Robert Cialdini, Dr. Amy Cuddy, Dov Baron, Dr. Ellen Langer, Dr. Dan Airely, and so many others. I have had the privilege of giving a speech with Apollo Robins and meeting Will Smith. I have been flown to the UK to train members of MI-5 and MI-6. And I have been invited to the Pentagon to debrief 35 generals, heads of state, and other officials on social engineering.

The last eight years have been an amazing roller-coaster ride. But like any project, nothing is made on an island of one. These experiences, my life, and the people I have had the honor of getting to know and work with are because of so many people that have helped me along the way.

My wife, Areesa, is one of the most patient and beautiful women I have ever met. Although she does not live in this world that I exist in, she truly supports me, loves me, and gives me a happy life that is full of laughs, adventure, and everlasting memories.

When my son, Colin, was little, he was going to be a doctor, then a writer, then a volunteer. Funny enough, he tried his hand at caregiving and writing, and he still volunteers. His positive attitude and kind spirit is an example to me.

I remember swearing that I would never let my daughter, Amaya, in this world of social engineering; I would keep her safe. She has taught me that keeping her safe means teaching her, including her, and making her a part of my life. She has given me so much more than I have given her.

Although Dr. Ekman wasn't directly related to this book, his kindness, motivation and generosity are an inspiration to me. Thank you.

I want to thank and acknowledge others who have been a continuing part of my journey:

» Ping Look is an endless and selfless supply of advice and help.

» Dave Kennedy's friendship and support mean so much.

» The Innocent Lives Foundation has become an integral part of this process, so I want to thank the following people from that organization:

  » I never would have thought I could say that Neil Fallon and I would become friends (pinch me). But now he helps guide me, direct me, and encourage me. He truly reminds me to be human.

  » Tim Maloney's support and protection have been such a big part of putting together the ILF. His friendship, faith, and support in this process is something I cannot sufficiently thank him for.

  » Casie Hall's excitement and enthusiasm to be a part of the solution is contagious.

  » I thank AJ Cook for her support with ILF and being so easy to work with in our efforts to save kids. Her dedication is exemplary.

  » Aisha Tyler's (ha! Even typing that name seems a little surreal.) work ethic, kindness, and ability to focus is a model that we should all emulate.

» My team at Social-Engineer, LLC has been great. Colin, Mike, Cat, Ryan, Amanda, Kaz, Jenn, and Karen—each has helped me improve and supported me through this process.

» I swear my editor Charlotte should be my ghost writer for a book. She captured thoughts and helped me sound more intelligent. (That is a hard job!)

» And the readers and fans of the Social-Engineer *Podcast*, SEVillages at the conferences, my other books, and SE-Events—you have held me to a high standard, haven't been afraid to call me out on stupid mistakes, and have made me constantly strive to do better. Thank you!

CONTENTS AT A GLANCE

CONTENTS

FOREWORD

When I started Apple Computers in 1976 with Steve Jobs, I did not imagine where that invention would take the world. I wanted to do something that was unheard of: create a personal computer. One that any person could use, enjoy, and benefit from. Jump forward only a short 40 or so years and that vision is a reality.

With billions of personal computers around the globe, smartphones, smart devices, and technology being embedded into every aspect of our lives, it is important to take a step back and look at how we maintain safety and security while still innovating and growing and working with the next generation.

I love getting to work with youth today, inspiring them to innovate and grow. I love seeing the ideas flow from them as they figure out new and creative ways to use technology. And I truly love being able to see how this technology can enhance people's lives.

With that said, we need to take a serious look at how we secure this future. In 2004 when I gave the keynote speech at HOPE Conference, I said that a lot of hacking is playing with other people and getting them to do strange things. My friend, Kevin Mitnick, has mastered this over the years in one area of security called social engineering.

Chris's book captures the very essence of social engineering, defining and shaping it for all of us to understand. He has rewritten the book on it again, defining the core principles of how we as humans make decisions and how those very same processes can be manipulated.

Hacking has been around for a while, and human hacking has been around for as long as humans have. This book can prepare you, protect you, and educate you how to recognize, defend, and mitigate the risks that come from social engineering.

—Steve "Woz" Wozniak

PREFACE

Social engineering—I can remember when searching for that term led you to videos on getting free burgers or dates with girls. Now it seems like it's almost a household term. Just the other day I heard a friend of the family, who's not in this industry at all, talking about an email scam. She said, "Well, that's just a great example of social engineering!"

It threw me for a loop for a second, but here we are, eight years after my decision to start a company solely focused on social engineering, and now it's a full-blown industry and household term.

If you were to just start reading this book it would be easy to mistake my intentions. You might think I am fully okay with arming the bad guys or preparing them for nefarious acts. That cannot be further from the truth.

When I wrote my first book, there were many folks who, during interviews, got very upset with me and said I was arming the malicious social engineers. I felt the same then as I do now: you cannot really defend against social engineering until you know all sides of its use. Social engineering is a tool like a hammer, shovel, knife, or even a gun. Each has a purpose that can be used to build, save, feed, or survive; each tool also can be used to maim, kill, destroy, and ruin. For you to understand how to use social engineering to build, feed, survive, or save, you need to understand both uses. This is especially true if your goal is to defend. Defending yourself and others from malicious uses of social engineering requires that you step over into the dark side of it to get a clear picture of how it is used.

I was recently chatting with AJ Cook about her work on *Criminal Minds*, and she mentioned that she often has to meet with real federal agents who work serial-killer cases to prepare herself for playing the role of JJ on the show. The same idea applies directly to this book.

As you read this book, do it with an open mind. I tried my hardest to put the knowledge, experience, and practical wisdom I have learned over the last decade onto these pages. There will always be some mistakes or something you don't like or something you might feel was not 100% clear. Let's discuss it; reach out to me and let's talk. You can find me on Twitter: @humanhacker. Or you can email me from one of the websites: www.social-engineer.org or www.social-engineer.com.

When I teach my five-day courses, I always ask the students to not treat me like some infallible instructor. If they have knowledge, thoughts, or even feelings that contradict something I say, I want to discuss it with them. I love learning and expanding my understanding on these topics. I extend the same request to you.

Finally, I want to thank you. Thank you for spending some of your valuable time with me in the pages of this book. Thank you for helping me improve over the years. Thank you for all your feedback, ideas, critiques, and advice.

I truly hope you enjoy this book.

—Christopher Hadnagy

1

A Look into the *New* World of Professional Social Engineering

*I suppose your security is your success, and your key
to success is your fine palate.*

—Gordon Ramsay

I still vividly remember sitting in front of my computer screen as I started to pen the first paragraph of *Social Engineering: The Art of Human Hacking.* It was *way* back in 2010. I am half tempted to tell you we had to write books uphill both ways back then, using a typewriter, but I don't want to get too dramatic.

In that time, when you searched the Internet for "social engineering," you got a few pages on social engineering legend Kevin Mitnick and some videos on how to pick up girls or get free burgers from McDonald's. Fast-forward eight years, and now the term *social engineering* is used almost as a household term. In the past three or four years, I have seen social engineering in security, government, education, psychology, military, and every other application you can imagine.

This transition begs the question of why. One colleague told me, "It's your fault, Chris." I think he meant it as an insult, although I felt a tinge of pride at that statement. However, I don't feel that I'm solely responsible for the near ubiquity of the term *social engineering* (SE). I believe that we see it being used by everyone and their brother now because it is not only the easiest attack vector—as it was seven years ago—but because it's now also meriting the largest payloads for attackers.

The cost to set up an SE attack is low. The risk is even lower. And the potential payout is *huge.* My team has been collecting stories in the news about SE attacks and scouring the web for statistics. I feel comfortable stating that in 2017, more than 80% of all breaches had a social engineering element to them.

The IBM "2017 Cost of Data Breach Study" states that the average cost of a breach was 3.62 million US$. When the potential for a payout is that large, it's certainly not hard to see why an attacker would want to use social engineering.

PRO TIP As of 2017, the IBM "Cost of Data Breach Study" had been produced for 12 years. You can find it at `https://www-03.ibm.com/security/data-breach/`. Or you can simply enter "Cost of Data Breach Study" in any search engine to find and download a full and current report.

I also remember one of my first interviews after my *Social Engineering: The Art of Human Hacking* book was published in 2010, when I was asked, "Aren't you worried that you are arming the bad guys?" But to me, SE is like any new type of warfare.

To help me more clearly explain this, I think about the story of Bruce Lee arriving in America in the 1960s. Racial prejudice was high, and he was doing something that no one else was doing: teaching Jeet Kune Do (an ancient Chinese martial art) to people of any race, color, or nation. He was battling in the university he went to with fellow students who felt they knew a lot about fighting. But he laid out flat opponent after opponent. Eventually, some of those opponents even became Bruce's friends or students.

What is the lesson? People had to adapt to a new type of fighting, or they would just constantly get beat. Was there a risk that a student of Bruce Lee could use his newfound skills to hurt other people and do evil? Yes, but Bruce felt it was necessary to educate people, so they could remain protected.

So, my answer to the question, "Aren't you worried that you are arming the bad guys?" is the same as it was eight years ago: I cannot control how you use this information. You can read this book and go out and attack people and steal their money. Or you can read this book and learn to be a defender for what is right. The choice is yours, but the good guys need someone to help teach them.

Learning to defend against this new style of attack takes more than just learning how to take a beating. Like Jeet Kune Do, it requires a balance of learning how to attack, learning how to defend, and knowing when to do each. As you learn how to be a social engineer, you need to be able to think like the bad guys while remembering you are the good guy. To steal another analogy, you need to be strong with the force but not walk over to the dark side.

Now you might be asking, "If not much has changed in your response, then why do we need a second edition of your book?" Well, let me tell you.

What Has Changed?

This is a fundamental question when it comes to social engineering. On the surface, the answer is, "Not much." You can go back a long way and find anecdotes about social engineering. For example, one of the first documented stories I can find is in the Bible, in the book of Genesis, and it reportedly happened around 1800 BCE. Jacob wanted the blessing that was to be given to his older brother Esau. Knowing his father, Isaac, had failing eyesight and relied on other senses to know who he was speaking to, Jacob dressed in Esau's clothing and prepared food like Esau would have prepared. Here's the best part: Esau was known to be extraordinarily hairy, but Jacob wasn't, so he fastened the skins of two young goats to his arms and the back of his neck. When Isaac reached out to touch Jacob, Isaac relied on his senses of smell, touch, and taste to tell him that he was with Esau rather than Jacob. According to the account in Genesis, Jacob's social engineering attack worked!

From the dawn of recorded history, we see one account after another of humans tricking, duping, conning, or scamming one another. On the surface, there might not be much that's brand new when it comes to social engineering, but that doesn't mean that nothing ever changes.

One example is vishing. I honestly remember using the word *vishing* for the first time. People looked at me like I was speaking Klingon. Seriously, I might as well have said *laH yIlo' ghogh HablI' HIv* (you Trekkies will appreciate that). As of 2015, though, *vishing* was added to *Oxford English Dictionary*.

PRO TIP Klingon is a fictional language, but there is an actual institute (www.kli.org) devoted to teaching, translating, and speaking Klingon. You also can find numerous translators online. To date, I have not heard a story of anyone "social engineering" any other person in Klingon.

Why is it important that *vishing* is now in the dictionary? It goes to show how much social engineering vectors have affected the world. Words that once appeared to be part of a "made up" language now are part of our everyday vocabulary.

It's not just the vocabulary that's become commonplace. Now there are services that specialize in helping the bad guys be better at being bad. For example, while I was doing work for a client, I stumbled upon a service that specialized in proofreading and spellchecking malicious phishing emails. That company provided 24/7 English-speaking support. Blend stuff like that with our BYOD (bring your own device) culture and the fact that most mobile devices are mini supercomputers, and then stir in some new-world social media addiction. What you're left with is a recipe for a whole new attack landscape—social engineer style.

In addition to the landscape changing, I have changed. When I wrote the first edition of this book, the title was *Social Engineering: The Art of Human Hacking*. I chose that name because I felt that what I was describing in that book was much like art. Art is subjective; it means different things to different people. It can be applied differently and can be used, viewed, liked, and hated for completely different reasons.

This second edition is called *Social Engineering: The Science of Human Hacking.* The Merriam-Webster dictionary gives one definition of *science* as, "The state of knowing: knowledge as distinguished from ignorance or misunderstanding." Eight years ago, much of what I did was new to the security realm, and I was learning as I went. Now I am in a "state of knowing" due to the additional years of experience on my resume.

That experience, I hope, will make this book much more meaningful to you, whether you're a security expert who's looking to understand social engineering, an enthusiast who's looking to broaden your horizons, or an educator who's looking to understand problems to include in your lessons. No matter why you are reading this book, my hope is that by thinking of these topics on a more scientific level, I can relay this information in a much more useful and complete manner.

Why Should You Read This Book?

I feel that this first chapter needs to follow the same pattern I took in my first book, so I want to spend a little time discussing why I feel that anyone should read this book. Yes, I realize I might be biased here, but humor me for a moment.

Are you a human? I am going to guess that if you are sitting in front of this book, reading this paragraph, you are either some advanced form of AI or you're human. I'll even go so far as to say that 99.9999999% of this book's audience is human. Social engineering takes the way humans are wired to make decisions and exploits the vulnerabilities in those processes.

The goal of the social engineer is to get you to make a decision without thinking. The more you think, the more likely you are to realize you are being manipulated, which of course is bad for the attacker. In episodes 7 and 70 of *The Social-Engineer Podcast*, I had the privilege of interviewing Dr. Ellen Langer. She spoke to me about something she called alpha and beta mode.

Alpha mode is when one's brain is running at 8 to 13 cps (cycles per second). It is generally characterized by "daydreaming," or what Dr. Langer called "relaxed, focused concentration."

Beta mode is when one's brain runs anywhere from 14 to 100 cps. This is when our brains are alert, observant, and aware of the things going on around us.

SEPODCAST REFERENCE

Following are the URLs where you can find the episodes of *The Social-Engineer Podcast* during which I interviewed Dr. Langer:

» Episode 7 includes my first interview with Dr. Langer, in which we discuss her research and her books: www.social-engineer.org/podcast/episode-007-using-persuasion-on-the-mindless-masses/

» Episode 70 takes place five years after my first interview with Dr. Langer. She came back on the show to tell us what she had learned over the years, what had changed, and how we have advanced: www.social-engineer.org/podcast/ep-070-thinking-with-out-a-box/

Which state benefits a social engineer more? Obviously, the answer is alpha mode because thinking and awareness are lessened. This is not just the case when it comes to malicious intentions. Manipulation and some types of influence are geared toward getting you to act without thought.

For example, you most likely have seen a commercial like this: A famous female musical artist comes on the screen, and a very sad song is playing in the background. The image changes to scenes of kittens and puppies that have been beaten, hurt, and underfed. The animals are filthy and dirty, and they look like they're at death's door. Now the artist comes back on screen; she's surrounded by healthy animals, and she's showering them with love. What's the message? For only a few dollars, those malnourished, near-dead animals can be transformed into loving pets—healthy, happy, and all yours. The images in the commercial are like what you see in Figure 1-1.

Are the producers of the commercial manipulating you for selfish means? Not entirely. What they have learned is that if they trigger your emotions, there is a greater likelihood that you will donate or take the desired action. The success rate is much greater than if they just appeal to knowledge or logic. The more emotions are triggered, the less you think rationally. The less you think rationally, the quicker you will decide based solely on the emotions triggered.

So, back to my earlier point: If you are human, then this book can help you understand what types of attacks exist. You can learn how the bad guys are using your humanity against you, and you can learn how to defend against these attacks to protect your loved ones from being victims.

Let me start by giving you an overview of social engineering.

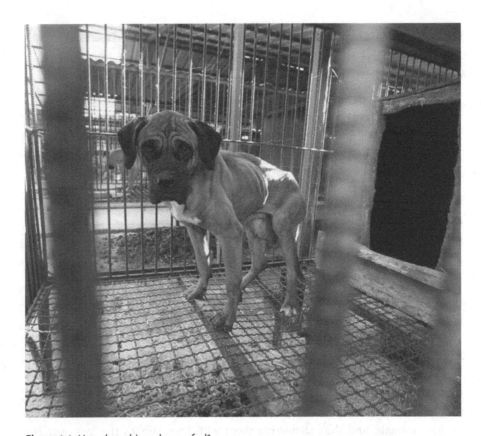

Figure 1-1 How does this make you feel?

IMAGE CREDIT TO AMAZON COMMUNITY ANIMAL RESCUE, WWW.FLICKR.COM/PHOTOS/AMAZON-CARES/2345707195

An Overview of Social Engineering

Whenever I discuss social engineering, I usually start with a definition that I have been using for the last 10 years. I've modified it only slightly over time.

But before I give you that definition of social engineering, I need to state one very important point: social engineering (SE) is not politically correct. This truth can be hard for many people to swallow, but it's real: SE takes advantage of the fact that gender bias, racial bias, age bias, and status bias (as well as combinations of those biases) exist.

For instance, imagine you have to infiltrate a client's building. To do so, you need to develop a pretext that allows you to gain entry easily. Your team is made up of a few different types of folks. If you determine that the best pretext for the job is janitorial staff, which of the following team members would be the best fit?

» 40-year-old white, blonde male

» 43-year-old Asian female

» 27-year-old Latino female

If you determine that your best pretext is intercompany kitchen work, which of the following team members would be the best fit?

» 40-year-old white, blonde male

» 43-year-old Asian female

» 27-year-old Latino female

The fact is, a skilled social engineer in any of the categories can make a go of it and succeed. But which one will lead to the least amount of thinking? Remember, thinking is the enemy of the social engineer.

With that in mind, let's get back to how I define social engineering:

Social engineering is any *act that influences a person to take an action that may or may not be in his or her best interests.*

Why is my definition so broad and general? It's because I believe that social engineering isn't *always* negative.

There was a time when you could say, "I'm a hacker," without causing normal people to run for cover, unplugging every electronic device in their path. Being a hacker used to mean someone who *needed* to know how something worked. A hacker wasn't satisfied with just base knowledge; that person wanted to dig deep into the inner workings of anything. Then, once it was understood, a hacker would see if there was any way to bypass, enhance, exploit, or alter its original purpose.

When I started my first book, I wanted to try to make sure that I could define social engineering in a way that didn't always imply that it involved a terrible scam artist or conman or grifter. The very same principles that I see the bad guys use can be applied for good purposes, and I want people to know that.

I often use this illustration: If you came up to me and said, "Hey, Chris. I want to have a princess tea party with you—you sit here, and I will paint your nails while you wear a pink scarf and we talk about Disney princesses," I would not only laugh at you, but I would slowly back away while looking for the nearest exit. Yet, I must admit that there may be some pictures floating around of this type of event.

How so? My daughter asked me to have a princess tea party with her. Now, before you say, "Hey, that's an unfair comparison—you love her!" I'll admit, that had a lot to do with my decision to join her, but think about the psychological principles that were at play for me to make that decision. To agree to a decision that I would literally refuse in a nanosecond had anyone else asked me, I had to bypass my normal decision-making in order to say "Yes."

USELESS FACT

Considering a nanosecond is one billionth of a second, and the average person speaks at a rate of 145 words per minute, I literally could not "say" the word *no* in a nanosecond. On the other hand, light, which travels at 186,000 miles per second, can travel 1 foot in a nanosecond.

When you understand how decisions are made, you can start to understand how a malicious attacker can use emotional triggers, psychological principles, and application of the art and science of social engineering to get you to "take an action that is not in your best interests."

Dr. Paul Zak appeared in *The Social-Engineer Podcast* episode 44. He wrote the book *The Moral Molecule* (Dutton, 2012). In that book and in our podcast, Dr. Zak spoke about his research into a hormone called oxytocin. His research helped us to see how closely it is linked with trust because he made one very important comment about how oxytocin is released into our blood when we feel that someone trusts us. Please understand this very vital point: your brain releases oxytocin not just when you trust someone, but also when *you feel* that someone else has given you trust. According to Dr. Zak's research, this phenomenon has been demonstrated in person, over the phone, over the Internet, and even when you can't see the person who is doing the "trusting."

SEPODCAST REFERENCE

Episode 44 of *The Social-Engineer Podcast* includes the fascinating conversation with Dr. Zak about his life's work. You can find it at www.social-engineer.org/podcast/ep-044-do-you-trust-me/

Another chemical that our brains produce is dopamine. Dopamine is a neurotransmitter produced by the brain and released during moments of pleasure, happiness, and stimulation. Blend oxytocin with dopamine, and you have a social engineering brain cocktail that can open any door you want.

Dopamine and oxytocin are released in our brains during intimate moments, but they also can be released during normal conversations. Those conversations are at the core of social engineering.

I believe we use these same principles daily—many times, unknowingly—with our spouses, bosses, fellow workers, clergy, therapists, service people, and everyone else we meet. Consequently, understanding social engineering and how to communicate with your fellow human is imperative for all people today.

In a world where technology has made it easy to communicate using emoticons or fewer than 280 characters, it has become more difficult to learn how to use conversational skills, let alone see when those skills are being used against us. Taking it one step further, social media has created a society where telling everyone everything about ourselves is acceptable, and even promoted.

When I talk about social engineering from a malicious perspective, I break it down into the following four vectors:

» **SMiShing:** Yes, this is a real thing, and it stands for SMS phishing, or phishing through text messages. When Wells Fargo was breached in 2016, I received the SMiShing attack shown in Figure 1-2.

> (wells_.fargo) Important
> message from security
> department!
> Login.-=>
> vigourinfo.com/
> secure.well5farg0card.html

Figure 1-2 This SMiShing attack trapped a lot of people.

What's crazy is that I don't even use Wells Fargo, but I still received this attack. (And no, I am not telling you what bank I use—nice try.)

With a simple click, these attacks were geared either to steal credentials or to load malware on the mobile device and sometimes both.

» **Vishing:** As I already mentioned, this is voice phishing. This has increased as a vector drastically since 2016. It is easy, cheap, and very profitable for the attacker. It is also nearly impossible to locate and then catch the attacker with spoofed numbers calling from outside the country.

» **Phishing:** The most talked about topic in the world of social engineering is phishing. In fact, the technical editor on this book, Michele, and I wrote about it in a book titled *Phishing Dark Waters: The Offensive and Defensive Sides of Malicious Emails* (Wiley, 2016). (Yes, I did just shamelessly plug one of my other books.) Phishing has been used to shut down manufacturing plants, hack the DNC, breach the White House as well as dozens of major corporations, and steal countless millions of dollars in different scams. Phishing is by far the most dangerous of the four main vectors.

» **Impersonation:** I know, we should put some form of 'ishing on this one too, but the best I could do is list it last because it's different. However, its placement in this list by no means indicates that we don't have to worry about it as much as the others. In the past 12 months, we have collected hundreds of stories of people impersonating police, federal agents, and fellow employees committing some truly horrific crimes. In April 2017, there was a story of a man who was impersonating the police and was caught. He was dealing in child pornography and using his impersonation to profit.

MORE INFO

At the time of writing, that sickening story can be found on this site: www.sun-sentinel .com/local/broward/pembroke-pines/fl-sb-pines-man-child-porn- 20170418-story.html.

Every social engineering attack you read about can be broken down into one of these four categories. More recently, we are seeing what we call the combo attack, where malicious social engineers are using a combination of these in one attack to achieve their means.

When I analyze these attacks, I start to see patterns that not only identify what kinds of tools and processes are used, but that can also help a security expert define more clearly how to perform these attacks and then use the results to educate and protect. I called this the *SE pyramid.*

The SE Pyramid

Let me just jump straight into the pyramid before I define why I came up with this and what each section means. The pyramid is illustrated in Figure 1-3.

As you can see, the pyramid is broken into a few sections, and approaches social engineering from the perspective of an SE professional—that is, not one using SE for nefarious purposes but to help clients and customers.

I'm going to define each section of the pyramid, and I'll get into the layers in more detail later in this book.

OSINT

OSINT, or Open Source Intelligence, is the life blood of every social engineering engagement. It is also the piece that should have the most time spent on it. Due to that, it occupies the first and largest piece of the pyramid. One piece of this part of the pyramid is rarely addressed: documentation. How will you document, save, and catalog all the information you find? I discuss this key factor a bit more in the next chapter.

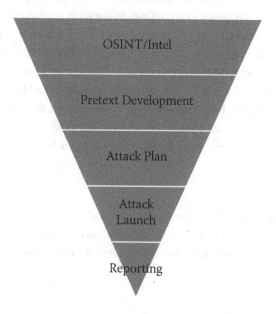

Figure 1-3 The SE Pyramid

Pretext Development

Based on all the findings from the OSINT period, the next logical step is to start to develop your pretexts. This is a crucial piece that's best done with OSINT in mind. During this phase, you see what changes or additions need to be made to ensure success. This is also when it becomes clear what props and/or tools are needed.

Attack Plan

Having a pretext in hand does not mean you are ready. The next stage is to plan out the three W's: what, when, and who.

» What is the plan? What is it we are going for and trying to achieve? What does the client want? These questions will help develop the next piece.

» When is the best time to launch the attack?

» Who needs to be available at a moment's notice for support or assistance?

Attack Launch

Now comes the fun part: launching the attacks. With the preparation done on the attack plan, you are prepared to go full steam ahead. It is important to be prepared but not to be so scripted that you can't be dynamic. I am all for having a written plan, and I think it can save you a ton of headaches down the road. The caution I have is that if you script out every word or action you feel needs to be taken, you can run into problems when the unexpected happens. Your brain realizes there is nothing on the script to help, and you begin to stutter, get nervous, and show signs of fear. This can really ruin your ability to succeed. Instead of scripting, I suggest using an outline, which gives you a path to follow but allows for artistic freedom.

Reporting

Wait—don't skip over this section. Come back and read it. Yes, reporting is not fun, but you can think of it this way: Your customer just paid you x dollars to perform some services, and most likely, you were pretty darn successful in those attacks.

But the customer didn't pay you just because they wanted to look cool. They paid you to understand what they can do to fix the problem. For that reason, the reporting phase is at the very tip of the pyramid, is the very pinnacle that the rest of the pyramid rests on.

The five phases of this pyramid, if followed, will lead to your success not only as a social engineer, but as a professional who is offering social engineering services to your customers. The fact is that, with the exception of reporting, these steps are followed by the malicious social engineers in the world.

In 2015, Dark Reading reported on an attack that involved this very pyramid. (You can read the article "CareerBuilder Attack Sends Malware-Rigged Resumes to Businesses" at www.darkreading.com/vulnerabilities---threats/careerbuilder-attack-sends-malware-rigged-resumes-to-businesses/d/d-id/1320236?.)

1. The attackers investigated attacking a few targets and while working through their OSINT phase, they found out that their targets used a popular site called CareerBuilder.

2. After completing the OSINT phase, the attackers started on pretext development. This led them to plan a pretext as a job seeker, who was looking to get hired at whatever role their targets were offering. They realized the tools they needed would be some maliciously encoded files and some realistic-looking resumes.

3. They started to plan the attacks, by answering some of those W questions.

4. They then launched the attacks by uploading their malicious documents *not* to the target but to the CareerBuilder website. The companies that posted the jobs would be notified by email that there was a new applicant, and that email would contain the attacker's uploaded attachments.

5. They did not follow through with any actionable reporting phase, but there is some actionable reporting on this attack thanks to some researchers at Proofpoint.

This attack was successful because the target would get an email with an attachment from a trusted and reputable source (CareerBuilder). Consequently, the target would open the attachment without thinking. And that is exactly the goal of the malicious social engineer: to get the target to take an action that is *not* in their best interest without thinking through the potential dangers involved.

What's in This Book?

When I started to plan this book, I wanted to make sure that I kept to the outline of the first edition of *Social Engineering* so those who benefited from its pages would benefit from this book too. At the same time, I wanted to change the book and update it to cover some of new attacks and things I never discussed in the previous book.

I wanted to make sure I took all the advice from fans, researchers, readers, and reviewers in the hopes that I could make this book much better than the first. Let me outline how this book is formatted so you know what to look forward to.

Following the path of the pyramid, Chapter 2, "Do You See What I See?," discusses OSINT and covers some of the timeless techniques used. I refrain from delving into actual tools too much, although I mention a few that have stayed in my tool chest for the last decade.

In Chapter 3, "Profiling People Through Communication," I examine a topic that I barely touched in the first edition. I delve deep into advanced communication modeling and profiling tools.

Chapter 4, Becoming Anyone You Want," is where I start to dive into pretexting. This is a topic that not many people talk about outside of social engineering. I cover tips, tricks, and many of the experiences (both successes and failures) that I have had over the years.

In Chapter 5, "I Know How to Make You Like Me," I compile information from the many podcasts, newsletters, and conversations with some of the world's greats—like Robin Dreeke—and apply the principles of rapport-building to social engineering. Robin Dreeke is the head of the FBI's Behavioral Analysis Unit and a good friend of mine. He is a master at building rapport and trust and has defined the steps to do both.

Chapter 6, "Under the Influence," applies the work of one of the leaders in the study of influence, Robert Cialdini, to the field of social engineering. The chapter takes the principles that he developed over his years of research and shows how they can and are being used by social engineers.

Chapter 7, "I Didn't Even Ask You for That," defines framing and elicitation and outlines how anyone can master both.

In Chapter 8, "I Can See What You Didn't Say," we return to one of my favorite topics: nonverbals. I dig super-deep into this topic in my book *Unmasking the Social Engineer: The Human Element of Security* (Wiley, 2014), but this chapter is a beginner's guide to get you started in the world of nonverbals.

In Chapter 9, "Hacking the Humans," I take the previous eight chapters and apply them to five different types of social engineering attacks. This chapter shows how important it is for you, as a professional social engineer, to apply the principles of this book.

As we near the end, Chapter 10, "Do You Have a M.A.P.P.?," covers prevention and mitigation. In a book about professional social engineering, it is fitting to have this chapter cover the four steps in learning to fight all social engineering attacks.

Then, like all good things, this book must conclude. So, Chapter 11, "Now What?," brings this book to an end.

Here are a few promises I have for you:

» I promise to not quote Wikipedia as a valued source, especially when mentioning research. (I learned from my mistakes.)

» I promise to tell you many stories from my experiences during the last seven or more years. Sometimes, I tell one story from many angles to help really get a few points solidly fixed for you. But I try and mix up those stories so you don't get bored.

» When I am using the research or work of some of the greatest minds in their fields, I will make sure you have references to their work, so you can look deeper into any topic you may want.

» Just as I did with the first book I ever wrote, I openly welcome all contacts, comments, suggestions, and criticism.

All I ask in return is that you read this book in the light it was intended. If you are a novice, this book can help you learn what is needed to be a professional social engineer. If you are experienced, then I hope my sharing a few stories, tips, and tricks will give you some new tools for your arsenal. If you are an enthusiast, then I want you to read this with the same excitement as I had while writing it. And if you are a skeptic, then read this with the thought that I am not claiming to be the one and only messiah of SE. I'm just a passionate social engineer with many years of experience that I want to share to try and make this world a little bit safer.

Summary

No book that I write would be complete without a cooking analogy, so here it goes. Like any great meal, there is a lot of planning, a great recipe that calls for fresh ingredients, and then artistic and scientific execution. Social engineering, although simplistic in nature, is not a recipe for a novice. It involves understanding how humans make decisions, what motivates them, and how to control your own emotions while exploiting those same processes in others.

The topic of this book is still as relevant today as it was eight years ago—maybe even more so now. In the past eight years, I have watched many people rise as professional social engineers. I have seen many malicious social engineers rise and fall too.

With the nature of attacks leaning so heavily toward the human element, it is imperative that all security professionals understand social engineering. But there is so much more to this topic. I remember when I started working as a chef (in a former life a long time ago), my mentor would take ingredients and tell me to taste little bits of each. But why?

He told me that I couldn't possibly know what it means "to taste" if I didn't really understand what each item tasted like. If I know that the recipe calls for some horseradish, and I want it to be a little spicier, then I understand that I could add a little bit more. Understanding that a certain ingredient also has a salty quality might make me adjust my salt for the recipe, so items are not overly seasoned. You get the point.

Even if you are not in the security industry, it is important to understand how each of these ingredients "tastes" so you can be protected. What does it mean to build rapport with someone, and how can that be used to get you to part with your money? (This is covered in Chapter 5.) How does influence, when sprinkled in an elicitation conversation, make someone give up a password over the phone? (This is covered in Chapters 6 and 7.)

Each of these ingredients can help you to learn the "taste." When you know them, you can recognize when someone tries them out on you, and you are more secure. You can sense something isn't right, and you can take defensive actions.

Have you ever watched any cooking competition with Gordon Ramsay? When he tastes a dish that he hates, he identifies the specific problem: "This dish has way too much pepper and they used too much oil." A novice, on the other hand, might say, "It's too spicy and greasy." Are those two descriptions the same thing? I think not. My goal is to help you become a Gordon Ramsay of the SE world—but maybe with less foul language.

With that said, let's jump into the first meaty chapter and discuss OSINT.

2 Do You See What I See?

Remember that failure is an event, not a person.

—ZIG ZIGLAR

OSINT stands for Open Source Intelligence, and it's the life blood of social engineering. Information is the starting and supporting point of every engagement. Because OSINT is so important to us as social engineers, it is vital that you understand all the different ways you can go about obtaining intel on your targets.

Regardless of how you obtain OSINT, you need to have a clear idea in mind of what you are looking for. That might seem easy to do, but it's not as easy as it sounds. You can't simply say, "I want all info on the target." Every type of information has a different value, and what is valuable can change with the type of attack you are looking to launch.

A Real-World Example of Collecting OSINT

Let me try to give you some perspective. According to the site www .worldwidewebsize.com, there are more than 4.48 *billion* indexed websites. This doesn't count anything that's not indexed, sites on the dark web or deep web, and so on. Annual worldwide Internet traffic reached 1.3 zettabytes (that is 1,300,000,000,000,000,000,000 bytes). One source even tells us that the Internet can contain up to 10 yottabytes of total data. (Writing 10 yottabytes looks like this: 10,000,000,000,000,000,000,000,000 bytes.)

> **FUN FACT**
>
> The yottabyte, which oddly enough comes after the zettabyte, was named after the *Star Wars* character Yoda. There are a few categories of numbers that are even larger and more oddly named than this one—for example, shilentnobyte and domegemegrottebyte.

Why is the amount of traffic on the Internet even remotely important to understand? Well, for example, if you are looking to send a spear-phish, your goal might be to look for personal hobbies, likes, dislikes, and things the target finds valuable. But if you are going to vish your target, then you might want to find details about the target's job, what role the person plays in the work organization, and what kinds of internal and external resources that person would expect calls from. If your goal is to get onsite, then you need to know whether the target would meet with people and who those people would be.

You have 4.48 billion potential websites to scrape through to look for data that can be helpful. So, before you start digging in, it is important to plan your OSINT engagement.

To help you establish some parameters for what you're looking for, use the lists of questions in Table 2-1.

Of course, the questions in the table only touch the surface. You can add other items about types of computers used, employee schedules, what languages are used, type of antivirus protection used, and much more.

Here's a story ripped from the 2017 headlines. (You can read one account of it at `https://gizmodo.com/this-is-almost-certainly-james-comey-s-twitter-account-1793843641`.) It is centered on former Director of the FBI James Comey. An Internet blogger and researcher wanted to see if she could locate James Comey's social media accounts. Because Comey was the director of the FBI, it wasn't public knowledge whether he had social media accounts, let alone how to locate them. That is where this OSINT story starts.

The full outline of the steps the blogger used to get to the bottom of the story is shown in Figure 2-1. Take a look, and then I'll walk you through it step by step.

First, the researcher had to establish what she wanted to uncover: Did Director Comey have social media accounts? If so, where were they?

Researching this using only the Internet proved to be very hard. In 2016, one website listed "The Top 60 Social Media Platforms." With that many platforms available—all with different rules and methods—it can be very hard to find one man.

Fortunately, one of the oldest forms of OSINT proved to be in the researcher's favor: listening. In one public appearance, Director Comey mentioned that he had Twitter and Instagram accounts.

That statement helped the researcher narrow the search from more than 60 social media platforms to just two. Two is a much easier number to manage in a search.

Table 2-1 Sample OSINT questions

Type of Organization	Questions to Ask
Corporation	How does the corporation use the Internet? How does the corporation use social media? Does the corporation have policies in place for what its people can put on the Internet? How many vendors does the corporation have? What vendors does the corporation use? How does the corporation accept payments? How does the corporation issue payments? Does the corporation have call centers? Where are headquarters, call centers, or other branches located? Does the corporation allow BYOD (bring your own device)? Is the corporation in one location or many locations? Is there an org chart available?
Individual	What social media accounts does the person use? What hobbies does the person have? Where does the person vacation? What are the person's favorite restaurants? What is the family history (sicknesses, businesses, and so on) of the person? What is the person's level of education? What did the person study? What is the person's job role, including whether people work from home, for themselves, and who they report to? Are there any other sites that mention the person (maybe they give speeches, post to forums, or are part of a club)? Does the person own a house? If yes, what are the property taxes, liens, and so on? What are the names of the person's family members (as well as any of the previously mentioned info on those people)?

After not finding any accounts directly linked to Director Comey, the researcher located the Twitter account for Brien Comey, the director's son. The researcher was able to confirm the connection of Brien Comey to Director Comey when Brien congratulated Director Comey for his ascension to Director of the FBI.

One of the things a user can do is to link multiple social media accounts together. In this case, Brien had linked his Instagram account to his Twitter account. The researcher checked the Instagram account, but Brien had locked his account from

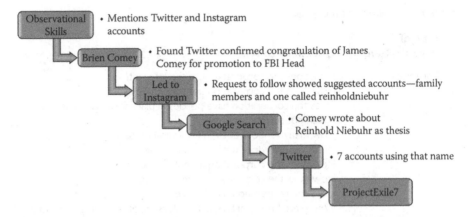

Figure 2-1 Amazing OSINT on a secure target

the public, so only those who had been granted permission to the account could see what he posted.

The researcher decided to request to follow Brien. One of the features of Instagram is that while you wait for a user to accept your follow request, you're pointed to people in the same circle, in case you also want to follow any of those people. Instagram suggested a bunch of users who were Brien's family members (not including Director Comey) and one account for reinholdniebuhr.

If you do a few Internet searches for "Reinhold Niebuhr," you quickly learn that he was an American theologian and political commentator. However, he died in 1971, so it's doubtful that he has an Instagram account. But with a little more investigation, the researcher learned that Comey wrote about Reinhold Niebuhr in his college thesis.

Armed with this information, the researcher searched Twitter and found seven accounts using that name. Out of all seven, there was one using that name publicly with the handle @ProjectExile7.

With a little more digging, the researcher found that Project Exile was the name of a program that Comey started when he was a U.S. attorney living in Richmond.

The researcher made her discoveries without accessing anything illegal, without hacking one single thing, and by looking only at open-source intelligence sources as she thought through the clues.

This is an excellent example of blending both nontechnical and technical OSINT, and it's a good lesson for all social engineers. That's the basis of the rest of this chapter: the different types of OSINT and how to utilize them as a social engineer. I've broken it down into two main sections: Nontechnical OSINT and Technical OSINT.

TO DOCUMENT OR NOT TO DOCUMENT—THAT IS THE QUESTION

Before we dive straight into the types of OSINT, I want to have a little sidebar with my thoughts on documentation.

The question is not really whether to document or not. The real questions are what do you use to document and how much do you document?

Think about what I said at the very start of the chapter: When you are searching through 10 yottabytes of data, you will find *a lot* of info on your targets. No matter how smart you are, unless you have a photographic memory, you won't be able to remember every detail. And even people with photographic memories cannot complete professional reporting by relying solely on their memories.

Now, I can't really tell you exactly how you should document, because there are too many factors. For instance, when I started down this career path and it was just little ol' me doing all the work, I used advanced notepad applications that allowed me to make a new folder or note for each client. I would then break down that note into different sections like Personal, Business, Family, Social Media, and so on. When I found a piece of OSINT, I would document it under the appropriate section, which made it easier to find that data as I was writing the report. I used little tricks like using certain colors for things I used on attacks. I used one color for moderate and another for critical finds.

Then my team started to grow, and I had many people working on one project, which made me realize that passing notepads back and forth wasn't the best solution at all. I had to come up with a solution that allowed the team members to share notes.

At first, I considered things like Google Drive. I considered cloud-based note applications and other cloud-based tools.

Those solutions presented a few problems:

» I was being tasked with obtaining Social Security numbers, banking data, and other private and personal details on people's lives. What if the solution I used got hacked? (That happened in 2013 when Evernote was breached, and more than 50 million passwords had to be changed.)

» I couldn't control the way those solutions were accessed or how the data was managed.

» The word "cloud" often caused certain clients to shudder and say "*No!*"

That led me to start building out my own servers. We obtained space in a server-hosting facility that was vetted and secure. We built our own secure VPN server and installed the software we had chosen on a server we owned that was behind firewalls, routers, and our VPN.

This meant I controlled how the data was stored, managed, backed up, transmitted, and secured. This solution let me rest easy at night because I was confident in the way we managed our clients' data.

Maybe you have a different solution. The important thing is that you take seriously how you store, manage, back up, transmit, and secure any data you collect on your clients.

Nontechnical OSINT

I consider nontechnical OSINT to be anything that does not involve *direct* inter-action between the social engineer and a computer. You might shoulder surf as a target uses a computer, but *you (the SE)* are not the one using the computer. It is information you gather using nontechnical means. There are a lot of specific methods I could go through here, but I can loosely define them all as *observational skills*, and in the following section, I give you some examples.

Observational Skills

Observational skills might seem like they're obvious and easy to use, but using them successfully is not a common skill—especially in the age of the firehose of digital media. If anything, today's marketing tactics have trained us to not pay attention to details. A 2015 study conducted by Emily Drago of Elon University (titled "The Effect of Technology on Face-to-Face Communication") makes the point that the quality of face-to-face communications has declined due to tech-nology. Sixty-two percent of individuals observed for the study used a mobile device while in conversation with others, despite knowing it would decrease the quality of that communication.

> **NOTE**   To read the full text of "The Effect of Technology on Face-to-Face Com-munication," visit www.elon.edu/docs/e-web/academics/communications/research/vol6no1/02DragoEJSpring15.pdf.

We are in a society that largely conveys messages of 280 characters and emojis, communicating through memes or social media posts. The advances that make these things possible are amazing, but they have created a situation in which peo-ple are less observant of those they are communicating with. It's also the reason that observational skills are at the top of my list in nontechnical OSINT.

You might be asking a few questions, such as these:

- » What does the term *observational skills* encompass?
- » What can you do to teach yourself these skills?
- » What should you expect to reap?

Let's discuss each of these questions and see what you can observe and learn (see what I did there?).

What Do Observational Skills Encompass?

The following scenarios give you some examples of how observational skills can be used in the real world.

Scenario 1

Your task is to gain entry to the mailroom of a large healthcare facility. You must do it in broad daylight. You can't pick locks, climb walls, or jump through windows. You're testing the front desk and security staff to see if they'll allow you into the secured area, so you must go through the part of the healthcare facility where those staff members work.

Here are just a few things you should have in your OSINT arsenal of observational skills:

» **Clothing:** This simple but sometimes overlooked piece of knowledge is important. In Chapter 1, "A Look into the New World of Professional Social Engineering," I say the goal of the social engineer is to get you to decide without thinking. If you are breaking into a place where everyone dresses casually, and you're dressed in a three-piece suit, you're going to make people take notice of you. The reverse is also true, so you want to know how employees dress so that you can dress that way, too.

» **Entries and exits:** Before you enter the building, understand where your egress points are. Is there a door where the smokers hang out? Is one entrance more heavily guarded than another? Are there shift changes that leave a certain post unmanned, or less manned?

» **Requirements for entry:** What is required to gain entry to the facility or area? Do you see employees with badges? What kind of badges? Where do they wear them? Do they have to also know a code? Do visitors get escorts? Do visitors get badges? Is there a mantrap, turnstile, security desk, or other security setup when you walk in?

» **Perimeter security:** Check out what's happening outside the building. Are there security cameras? Are there guards roaming the grounds? Are the dumpsters locked up? Are there any alarms or motion-triggered defense systems?

» **Security staff:** Are they busy looking at their mobile devices or a computer screen, or are they alert and paying attention? Do they look bored beyond belief or interested?

» **Lobby Setup:** Are keypads or security devices set up where you can shoulder-surf for passwords? (In other words, can you get close enough to peek over someone's shoulder and capture the password as it is being typed?)

Of course, there can be many more things you will want to observe, but those are some of the basics.

To help you understand why these criteria are so important, here's a true story that involves clothing, entries and exits, requirements for entry, and perimeter security. Michele (who's the tech editor on this book) and I were tasked with the very scenario I outlined at the beginning of this subsection. We had to do a fair amount of technical OSINT, which I get into later in this chapter, but there was also a fair amount of nontechnical OSINT that led to our success.

We decided to use the pretext of a pest control company that was hired to quote out an emergency spider spraying. We called our company Big Blue Pest Control and came with full Big Blue outfits and spray bottles of custom blue "poison" to kill any spiders we saw during the quoting process. This poison was actually just some blue Gatorade in a spray bottle.

FUN FACT Blue Gatorade disguised as poison is a great way to carry a replenishing and refreshing drink that can be used to quench your thirst when you're nervous about breaking into a building and sweating profusely. However, if you are taking gulps from your "poison sprayer" in the elevator when someone comes in, you might get weird looks.

We started by driving around the perimeter and noticing entrances, exits, camera locations, hangouts for the smokers, and entrances that seemed the most crowded versus least crowded. We also took note of whether the employees coming in and out had badges and how they were dressed. We then picked our initial ingress point and started to do a slow walk toward the door. The reason for the slow walk was to observe what we could of how people were being let in.

We saw two security guards overseeing people as they pressed their badges against a metal stand and were allowed in. There was also a security desk to the right that had someone manning a sign-in sheet.

We decided to try to walk right past the guards and follow the crowd in. That did not work at all. We were stopped by a security guard who asked us what we were doing and why we were there. I looked down at his name badge and saw his name, and then I started to say, "Well Andrew, we were asked to come and give a proposal for some emergency spider spraying. . . ." The guard stopped me mid-sentence by saying, "Okay, go sign in at the desk."

I thought we were in, but as we approached the desk, the man there asked for our names. As we gave our fake names, he scoured a list. When he didn't find us on the list, he said, "Sorry, you are not on our visitor list for today. You cannot come in without authorization."

We tried to explain, influence, and even use pressure and a plea for help. Nada. Shut down. We exited the front door, walked around as we discussed what we would do, and saw a few smokers outside taking a break. I told Michele to follow me, and we walked toward the smokers, acting as if we belonged and were inspecting the outside of the building. I pretended to take notes on my clipboard.

We again did a slow walk, until we saw a few people moving toward the door, so we tailgated right in behind them. Now in the building, we followed this mass of people, and I quickly noticed we were heading straight toward the front where the security guards who just rejected us were located. I saw an elevator to my right, but there were no buttons. "Darn," I thought to myself, "an elevator that is called by security." Just as I finished my thought, an elevator door opened, and I immediately stepped inside, hoping that Michele would observe and follow my lead.

Fortunately for me, Michele is pretty amazing at this type of thing and was not lost or overstressed. There was a group of people in the elevator, and Michele promptly announced so all the people could hear, "Boss, can we finish this job soon? I'm starving, and you said we can't eat 'til we're done."

I got a disapproving look from a woman on the elevator who said, "Feed the poor woman." I replied, "I want to, but we just have one more floor to inspect. The quicker we get done the quicker she can eat."

The woman sighed and said, "Well, then, let's get you where you are going. . . . ," and I butted in midsentence with "to the mailroom." The woman pulled out her badge, swiped the receiver in the elevator, hit a few buttons, and said, "Let me drop you off on the way."

Whew! Thankfully, due to Michele's great observational skills and my quick movements, we had not been caught, and we even got a nice lady to badge us to that secure floor. (And Michele was only partially faking because, really, she is *always* hungry.)

On the floor with the mailroom, we got off the elevator and discovered that the mailroom door was locked. There was a bell with a label that said, "Ring for assistance." We rang it and waited.

A woman came to the door and said, "How can I help you?" We spouted off our pretext about doing a quote and so on. The woman replied, "Well, I am going to have to call the security desk to get this approved."

Our story would have been blown if she had called security, so I said, "Well, you can if you want, but Andrew is the one who sent us down here to get this done."

She said, "Oh, Andrew sent you? Then come on in." She let us into the mailroom and said, "Just don't touch the mail." We were rummaging through ceilings by moving the ceiling tiles, network cable, and endless amounts of mail.

As you can see throughout this story, so much occurred because we made quick observations and cataloged that information for later use. (And this was just the beginning.)

I didn't know I would need Andrew's name, Michele didn't know we were going to meet a sympathetic woman on the elevator, and neither of us knew we would meet a group of disinterested smokers who didn't care that we tailgated in. But observations allowed us to use each of these for success.

Scenario 2

You are tasked to spear-phish a high-profile lawyer from a major American corporation. You're allowed to use any information you can find on her.

This story will unfold more when we get to the technical OSINT section, but to pinpoint a very valuable lesson, let me tell you how I failed miserably on this one.

Our OSINT led us to the fact that the lawyer handled some matters in Massachusetts. We discovered a recent tax law update in Massachusetts that might grab her interest and be very effective in getting her to click a link or open a malicious attachment.

I began crafting an email about the changes in the state of Massachusetts and planned every aspect of this spear. The email was written professionally, did not threaten, included the payload we wanted, gave a realistic deadline for reading and replying, and gave just enough detail to make sure she had to click to get more.

Within minutes of sending the email, we were caught and reported, and the campaign was totally blown. Did you pick out the flaw from the preceding paragraph? I will give you a few seconds to go back and look before I tell you.

Time's up!

Massachusetts is not a state but a commonwealth. This lawyer, whose attention to detail was her strong suit, received an email about changes to the *State* of Massachusetts tax law and said to herself, "Hey, they should know Massachusetts is not a state but a commonwealth!" That caused her to look at the "From" address and the URL, and to become suspicious enough that she reported it. And our cover was blown.

We did not observe the little detail in this story, and that lack of observation cost us.

The lesson of this scenario is that you need to observe everything you can. Think like the person you are social engineering. Try to understand what they would expect to see, and deliver that. Otherwise, little details can come back to bite you.

What Can You Do to Teach Yourself These Skills?

This topic is hard to cover in a short section in a book. Each person has natural ability as well as learned ability that can make learning these skills really easy or very difficult. Because I don't know you personally, all I can do here is tell you what I did to try and enhance my skills.

I would play a game that was along the lines of Capture the Flag. If I was entering a building—let's say a doctor's office—I would say to myself, "The flags are to remember the first two people I see, what color shirts they are wearing, and what magazine they are reading or what they are doing."

I would set some boundaries like these:

» They can't be the service-related folks behind the counter.

» I had to still go about my task of checking in and couldn't pause or deviate from that.

» I couldn't write anything down.

Then I would enter the building, observe what I saw, and try my hardest to remember it until I left the building. It would go something like this:

» Older woman sitting to left in blue shirt reading *Woman's Day* magazine

» Young child, male, striped T-shirt, playing with blocks on the floor

I would make a note of each of these things in my mind and try my hardest to remember them. I used little memory tricks, such as saying something to myself a couple times to try and embed it in my mind.

When I felt that I could make mental notes like this without having to think too hard, I would add some layers of complexity. Eventually, my flags list looked like this:

» Gender of X number of people

» What they were wearing

» What activities the people were engaged in when I first sighted them

» Perceived communication profile (more on this in Chapter 3, "Profiling People Through Communication")

» Body-language tells

From this, I would try to build a story in my head of why they were at the location I was at, and use the details in the story to remember them.

Honestly, this worked so well—even with my bad memory—that I can remember one office I walked into three or four years ago where I saw two women in black skirts and white button-up tops reading something on an iPad. The woman on the left did not seem to like the woman on the right, but she tolerated her, or she had somewhere else to be. I could discern these things because the woman's hips were fully bladed away from the woman on the right.

There was a man behind a counter with a security suit on—black suit, white shirt, black tie. He had a gold watch on his right wrist, which indicated he was left-handed. His hair was neat, and he had a well-trimmed beard. He was writing on a notepad with a pen. He was observant of me as well as the lobby.

There was a young man waiting in chairs in front of the counter. He was looking at a newspaper, but it appeared to me that he was faking reading. He was staring into space, and the edges of the paper were shaking. I fabricated a story that he was there for an interview and was nervous but was trying to look calm and distract himself with a paper.

It is almost as if I can see that lobby now in my mind. These little observations go a long way toward helping you achieve your goals as a social engineer. My suggestion is to look for your own weaknesses, and then start small and build up. It is important to really get the point that you must practice. Too often, I see people wanting to achieve something 100% right away, but it takes time.

Failure can teach us way more than success if we let it—which is why I need to talk about expectations.

What Should You Expect to Reap?

In the book *Unmasking the Social Engineer,* which I coauthored with Dr. Paul Ekman, I focused solely on nonverbal cues: body language and facial expressions. When I started learning how to first notice and then decipher these expressions, I felt like some kind of mind-reading superhero. I could look at a face and see emotions that the person was trying to hide, and then I blended that with body language and other actions to almost predetermine how they would react to questions or situations. The crazy part is that I found that my predictions were right more than 50% of the time. Therein began the problem. Let's say I was right 75% of the time. That means I was wrong 25%. In addition to that, it affected my perceived ability, and I felt that I could see more, understand more, and therefore SE more than I really could.

One of my most humbling lessons came from working with Dr. Ekman, who has corrected me time and time again. He said, "Chris, just because you can see the *what* doesn't mean you know the *why*."

Before I discuss expectations, I feel it's important for you to hear this repeatedly: Just because you can see the what doesn't mean that you automatically know the why. How can you make that connection between the what and the why? There are a few ways: questions, more information, and longer observation.

Here's an example: I was teaching a class, and I was talking about a social engineering story from my experience. One student suddenly got an angry look on his face. His body language shifted from being open to closed. With arms folded, he leaned back in his chair and his legs jutted out. I perceived that he was not believing what I was saying, and I began to give him more personal attention. Doing so did not seem to fix his lack of belief, and he drew back. After a few minutes, he excused himself and left the class.

I was dumbfounded. I did everything right. Why was he still mad at me?

Shortly after that, we took a break. I was walking toward the restroom, thinking about this and how I could "fix" it. The student approached me and said, "Hey, I'm really sorry I left. My boss texted me in the middle of class and said we have an emergency at work. I tried to tell him I couldn't do anything because I was in class, but he ordered me to leave and be on this ridiculous conference call. Can I make up the lesson I missed?"

I literally started laughing, which I had to explain quickly, but I told him how I misinterpreted all that I saw. I could hear Dr. Ekman in my head: "Chris, what have I told you before?" It was a great lesson for me in causality.

The same is true about OSINT and observation. Don't assume that the things I am about to show you are all the results of the "stupidity of humans." I prefer to think that people simply are uneducated to the potential dangers rather than being blatantly stupid.

Take a quick look at the picture in Figure 2-2, and make a mental note of what you observe.

Thinking like a social engineer, what do you see in this picture that could help you profile the driver of this car? Figure 2-3 is a zoomed-in version that might help.

The right side has a breast cancer support sticker. The left contains a Kids Wish Network Support sticker. Then there is a sticker that says "10-20-Life." I had no clue what this was for, so I did a quick Internet search and found that it is a sticker supporting stricter sentences for those who commit crimes using firearms.

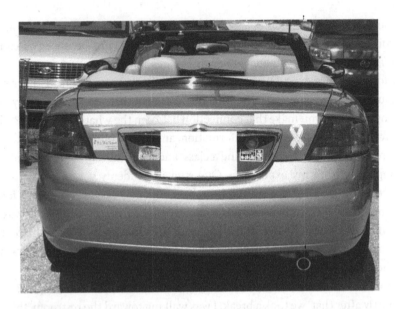

Figure 2-2 What do you see?

Figure 2-3 Is that easier to see?

What do these stickers tell you about this person? That they support charities and which ones are important to them. Could this be because they or a family member suffered from cancer or childhood sickness? Also, they feel strongly about gun laws and gun crimes. Could this be because they were a victim or know a victim of gun crimes?

Armed with these pieces of information, do you think could strike up an elicitation conversation?

Be careful! Too many times I have students who will blurt out, "We will discuss gun laws and why they are wrong," or something to that effect. But think about how hard it would be to convert *you* from one belief to another during a conversation. This person will be no different. Blend that with your goal—to have

Figure 2-4 What can you tell from this picture?

the target *not* thinking—and remember that you want to converse about their interests, not yours. I explain more about this in Chapter 7, "I Didn't Even Ask You for That," when I discuss elicitation.

Now take a look at Figure 2-4.

What do you notice here? What could you observe as a social engineer? Think of the slight details in this one simple picture:

» You can see the type of work environment.

» You can see the operating system the person uses.

» You can notice what type of tablet the person has.

» You can see the person is a fan of a certain sitcom.

» Can you notice the browser they use and mail client, too?

» Do you notice a sign that might indicate some other details about the person?

» What other details can you pick out?

This is just a cursory list; there may be much more that you picked out. Based on this, could you develop enough of a profile to work up one or two phishing emails that would trigger an emotional response?

Sometimes, however, a picture or even an in-person interaction is not enough. This is where technical OSINT can bridge that gap.

Technical Open Source Intelligence

Before you start writing a terrible review, telling the world how bad I suck because this chapter did not contain an all-inclusive list of every tool known to man for OSINTers, let me make something very clear:

This chapter does NOT contain a full list of every tool, every process, and every method of collecting OSINT from technical means.

Here is what I *can* tell you: This chapter touches on the tools and techniques I use every day in my business. There are some amazing minds out there in the OSINT world who you can delve miles deep with. Here are just a couple who I have been fortunate to come in contact with:

» **Nick Furneaux:** I flew to the UK to take Nick's four-day course and was blown away. It is truly eye-opening what can be done with APIs and an understanding of how social media applications work. Nick's website is at www.csitech.co.uk.

» **Michael Bazzell:** Michael is the man when it comes to disappearing from the web, but he's also developed an amazing set of tools for OSINT practitioners that can help them dig into social media sites and other search engines. You can find his website at inteltechniques.com.

These fine chaps are both friends of mine, and I have personally taken training, advice, and help from them. I can wholeheartedly say they are masters in the OSINT game. (Shameless plug: They both have been guests on *The Social-Engineer Podcast*. Search for *OSINT* to find the episodes.)

My focus in the world of OSINT is on the daily practical uses for the work that I do, which can be broken out into four simple topics: social media, search engines, Google, and other tools. I will touch on each of these topics to give you a flavor of how I use them, and then you can use that knowledge as a foundation for further self-education.

Social Media

No chapter on OSINT would be complete without at least a cursory mention of the topic of social media. What is odd is that I can remember a time when reading your sister's diary would have resulted in multiple beatings. Now, personal diaries are not only online, but it's an insult if you don't read them, comment on them, and like them.

Social media is basically part of our everyday existence, and it is here to stay.

Here are some statistics that will put this into order for us, according to We Are Social (https://wearesocial.com/special-reports/digital-in-2017-global-overview). As of January 2017:

» The world population was 7.476 billion.

» Internet users totaled 3.773 billion.

» There were 2.789 billion active social media users.

» There were 4.917 billion unique mobile users.

» There were 2.549 billion active mobile social media users.

This is important for you, as a social engineer, to understand. Let's consider some of the top social media platforms:

LinkedIn With over 106 million users, LinkedIn tells a person the following things:

» Your job history

» Where you got your education

» Where you went to high school

» Clubs and academic achievements you're involved in

» People who endorse your skills

Facebook With its more than 1.8 billion users, Facebook tells a person the following things:

» Your favorite music

» Your favorite movies

» Clubs you belong to

» Your friends

» Your family

» Vacations you've taken

» Your favorite foods

» Places you've lived

» Much, much more

Twitter   With its 317 million users, Twitter tells a person the following things:

» What you are doing right now

» Your eating habits

» Your geolocation

» Your emotional state (within 280 characters)

I could go on, but you get the idea. Just those three social media applications provide a ton of information for you to discover about your targets. I dare say you can build a pretty comprehensive profile on your target from this.

FUN FACT

On episode 87 of *The Social-Engineer Podcast*, we talked to Dr. James Pennebaker. He wrote a tool (www.analyzewords.com) that can analyze a person's Twitter account based on the language used. We ran Michele's Twitter account (@SultryAsian) through this tool, and she was evaluated as a spacey Valley Girl with an upbeat, in-the-moment style. Honestly, I almost spewed water when I read that because it's the opposite of Michele in real life, but it's exactly how she wanted to be viewed over social media.

Evaluating a person based on social media should not be confused with developing an actual psychological profile. As the Fun Fact mentions, there are people who communicate one way online and another in person. Even though that is true, social media is still valuable for a social engineer because many attacks occur based on the "online" personality and learning how to communicate with that aspect of the target can lead to a breach.

With hundreds of social media platforms and billions of people using them, social media is a treasure trove of data for social engineers. One of the best ways to rip information from social media platforms is by using search engines, which is the topic of the next section.

Search Engines

The Internet is constantly changing, including new and improved ways of finding information in its yottabytes of cached data. Those constant changes can be a strength for most people, but they can also become a weakness for social engineers because a search engine that works today may not work tomorrow.

I remember when Spokeo first came out. I used it almost daily. It was an amazing source of great information. As its popularity grew, so did the number of ads.

Then came the request to pay for information, and then information that was not as reliable seemed to pop up all too often.

Now, I'm not saying that Spokeo has nothing useful, but as a professional social engineer, my time is money. And if I must use another source to verify every fact I get, it can cost me a job.

In my first book, and many subsequent books after, I have found that including lists of tools is kind of useless to the reader. A few things often occur:

» The day the book is released, the tools are outdated and the ideas I gave the readers are old.

» New and better tools come along.

» A combination of the first two things.

Instead of giving you a list of websites and tools, I want to walk you through performing OSINT on a target. Yes, I will mention websites and tools that I use, but the focus will be more on how to think through this aspect of being a social engineer.

Our target is my good friend Nick Furneaux (let's hope he stays my good friend after this book comes out). It should be noted: there is no ill will toward Nick. I'm merely using him to show that even for a very aware, very alert, and very security-conscious person, the Internet holds secrets for those who know how to ask.

d0xing the Furneaux

So, what does it mean to d0x someone? The word *d0x* is a hacker term that means to work up a document on a target containing details about the target's personal life. Those details are often used to further attack the target, humiliate them, or perpetrate other crimes.

None of those are the goals here. I'm just showing you the power of OSINT and how it can be used. Often, I start at the doors of pipl.com.

Pipl (pronounced *people*) is a site I describe as what would happen if the White Pages and social media scraped sites and had a baby. What is great about this site is that you can search for a name, a user name, a nickname, or other details you may have about your target.

Just looking at the web quickly tells us that Nick's Twitter account is nickfx. Let's see what we can find by using pipl.com with that nickname. Take a look at Figure 2-5.

Figure 2-5 Do you see him?

With just a quick glance, we can see the first picture brought up the right "Nick," and only four lines down, we see Nick Furneaux associated with Chris H (I wonder who that is) and a whole new user name.

Before we get to that, let's see what happens when I click the picture that we know to be Nick. The result is shown in Figure 2-6.

With one simple click, we can see confirmation that we have the right guy as well as his location. OSINT! We know where he lives.

Now, back up one page in the results, and click that fourth link down. What does that reveal? Take a look at Figure 2-7.

We have some great OSINT here, don't we? A Facebook page and a hobby we didn't previously know that Nick had. He is a snowboarder. And he must really like that Chris H character; he seems to be everywhere.

When I click the Facebook link, I'm greeted with even more OSINT!

» He lives in Bristol, UK.

» I can see a list of friends.

» I've found a new username: nick.furneaux.1.

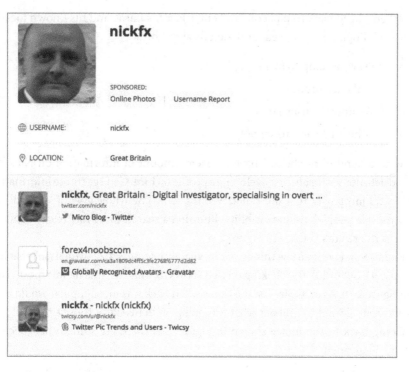

Figure 2-6 Confirmation

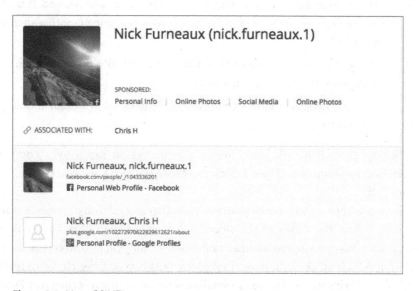

Figure 2-7 More OSINT!

When I head back to pipl.com and enter just his name and his known location of Bristol, England, I get even more details about him:

» Previous employment

» LinkedIn profile

» Yet another username

» Where he went to school

With a handful of clicks, I have a decent amount of information on Nick that would definitely be useful in developing a profile on him. Can I get more information?

Next, I jump over to a site called webmii.com. The whole goal of WebMii is to help you see people's online visibility. Running a search there for "Nick Furneaux" returns the results you see in Figure 2-8.

Right away, I notice a few things: Nick's visibility score is 4.22 (which isn't that high because it's out of 10). But clicking on that shows us *when* in time he was most visible (see Figure 2-9). As an OSINTer, the times when Nick was most popular would pique my interest—I want to find out what was going on in his life at those times.

Going back to the image shown in Figure 2-8, there are some other pieces of data to be gleaned:

» The first image links to Twitter.

» The third image links to a podcast where Nick was interviewed. It is *The Social-Engineer Podcast*, and I hear it is really amazing (another shameless plug).

» Many of the other images link to Canadian LinkedIn pages that don't pertain to the Nick Furneaux we're interested in.

» The fifth image is weird: a young man in some kind of animal onesie. What is that?

Clicking that fifth link takes me to a music video made by a company called AFB Productions. When I click the More button, I see what's shown in Figure 2-10.

The video appears to have been made by a chap named Toby Furneaux (same last name!), and the driver in the video is none other than Nick Furneaux. Of course, this discovery opens another rabbit hole of digging into who this Toby is and what AFB is all about. It doesn't take long (just two or three clicks) to realize that Toby is Nick's son, and he runs a small production company called Any Future Box (AFB for short).

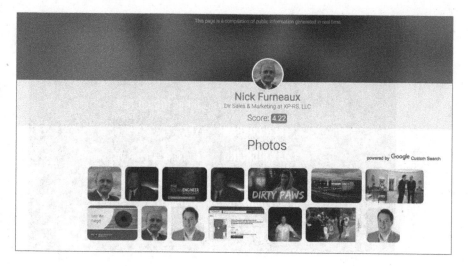

Figure 2-8 A lot more info on Nick

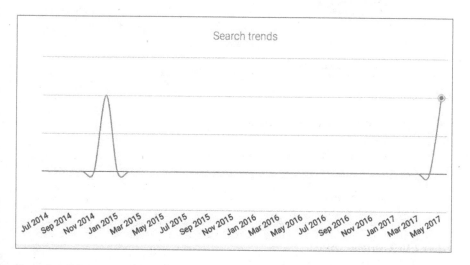

Figure 2-9 When was Nick popular?

A good OSINTer would include all of this detail in their info because family members (especially a target's children) are often great resources for attack vectors.

Refer to Figure 2-8 again. That picture of Nick has been in a few places that I stumbled upon. This picture might lead to more resources, so I grab the actual

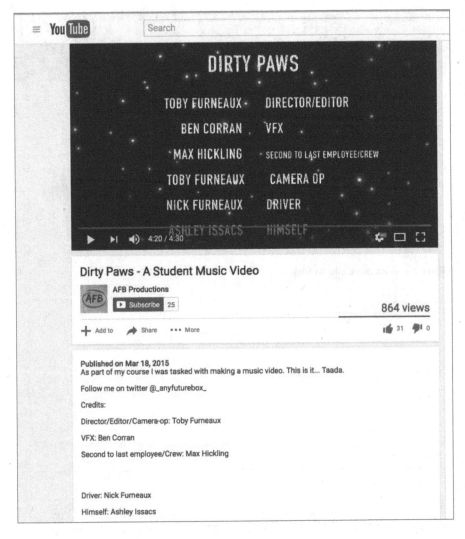

Figure 2-10 Even more OSINT!

URL of that picture and load it into a reverse image search, which you can do by following these steps:

1. Right-click on the image.

2. Click View the Image.

3. Right-click again, and then click Copy Image Location.

4. Go to www.google.com and click Images.

5. Click Paste Image by URL, and paste in the URL of the image that you copied in step 3.

You should see a page that looks like Figure 2-11.

In addition to seeing that he uses this same headshot a lot, I uncovered that Nick has a Blogspot page and wrote on a forensics page too. When I follow the link

---

Pages that include matching images

Blogger: User Profile: Nick Furneaux

https://www.blogger.com/profile/17224384959913801461 ▾

103 × 113 - Gender, MALE. Location, United Kingdom. Introduction, I've been working with computers since my ZX81, closely followed by an Oric 1 (if anyone remembers those?). In the past 11 years I've been working in the area of computer forensic investigation and research in both the Law enforcement and Corporate worlds.

CSITech - Computer Forensics

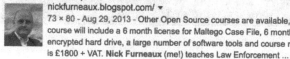

nickfurneaux.blogspot.com/ ▾

73 × 80 - Aug 29, 2013 - Other Open Source courses are available, but not like this! The course will include a 6 month license for Maltego Case File, 6 months VPN access, an encrypted hard drive, a large number of software tools and course manual. The 4 day course is £1800 + VAT. **Nick Furneaux** (me!) teaches Law Enforcement ...

nickfx on Twitter: "Its free tools time. Nick Furneaux has created a little ...

https://twitter.com/nickfx/status/11872595921?lang=en ▾

400 × 400 - Apr 9, 2010 - nickfx · @nickfx. Digital investigator, specialising in overt and covert live data acquisition and RAM analysis. UK. csitech.co.uk. Joined March 2008. Tweets. © 2018 Twitter; About · Help Center · Terms · Privacy policy · Cookies · Ads info. Dismiss. Close. Previous. Next. Close. Go to a person's profile.

Episode 039: Information Gathering on Steroids - Security Through ...

https://www.social-engineer.org/.../episode-039_information_gathering_on... ▾

80 × 104 - Nov 11, 2012 - Information is the life blood of the social engineer. "There is no such thing as bad data", is the SE Mantra. Our guest this month, **Nick Furneaux**, well known forensics expert in the UK discusses his new area of research into API Manipulation. Date Nov 12, 2012 ...

CSITech - Computer Forensics: Advanced Open Source Intelligence ...

nickfurneaux.blogspot.com/2012/.../advanced-open-source-intelligence.ht... ▾

73 × 80 - Sep 17, 2012 - Other Open Source courses are available, but not like this! The course will include a 6 month license for Maltego Case File, 6 months VPN access, an encrypted hard drive, a large number of software tools and course manual. The 4 day course is £1800 + VAT. **Nick Furneaux** (me!) teaches Law Enforcement ...

 ›

1 2   Next

Figure 2-11 That's a whole lotta Nick.

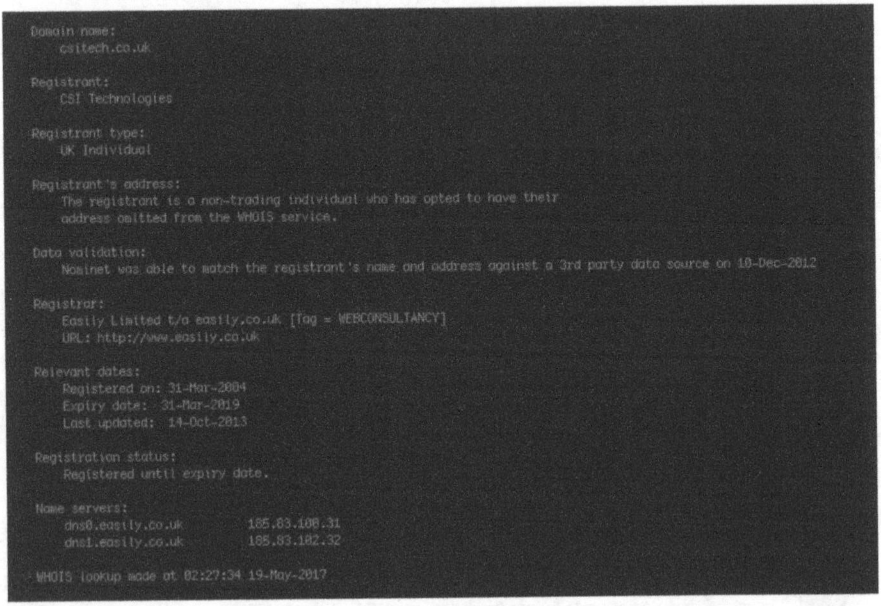

```
Domain name:
    csitech.co.uk

Registrant:
    CSI Technologies

Registrant type:
    UK Individual

Registrant's address:
    The registrant is a non-trading individual who has opted to have their
    address omitted from the WHOIS service.

Data validation:
    Nominet was able to match the registrant's name and address against a 3rd party data source on 10-Dec-2012

Registrar:
    Easily Limited t/a easily.co.uk [Tag = WEBCONSULTANCY]
    URL: http://www.easily.co.uk

Relevant dates:
    Registered on: 31-Mar-2004
    Expiry date:   31-Mar-2019
    Last updated:  14-Oct-2013

Registration status:
    Registered until expiry date.

Name servers:
    dns0.easily.co.uk          185.83.108.31
    dns1.easily.co.uk          185.83.182.32

WHOIS lookup made at 02:27:34 19-May-2017
```

Figure 2-12 Who is you?

for the forensics page, I find an interview of Nick from a few years ago, and that interview ends with his email and his website URL.

When I do a quick WHOIS lookup of Nick's website domain name, it reveals what you see in Figure 2-12.

Nick has had this website for a long time, and it's not expiring any time soon. Interestingly (and intelligently), Nick has his domain privatized. That means there is no info on the record; just his company name, which we already know, and that he is an individual in the UK.

OSINT FACT

There are multiple ways to perform a WHOIS lookup. If you use Linux or Mac, you can do it right from the terminal by typing whois *DOMAIN* (replacing *DOMAIN* with the actual domain). Or you can use a free website. There are several to choose from, but the one I use most often is http://www.whois.net.

The type of information-gathering I just walked you through is very common in the world of a social engineer. Think about why this is so. With very few clicks, I was able to uncover quite a bit of useful information on a target.

Granted, I didn't find a link to all of Nick's passwords or his private photos (thank God for that), but I did find enough information to really help if I wanted to attack Nick with a phishing or vishing attack.

Is that it, though? Absolutely not. Entering the ring is the heavy-weight champion of the world when it comes to OSINT.

Enter the Google

Google. The word alone should make a social engineer giggle with happiness. Okay, okay—that mental picture is pretty disturbing. So maybe put the idea of giggling aside and think of it more like a silent smirk of knowledge-filled happiness.

Why? Google is like an all-knowing oracle. She knows all the things you ever did, stores them, and even caches them if you try to delete them (you know, for safekeeping).

GOOGLE FACTS

Google is powerful. It owns about 88% of market share in search advertising. According to Google, the search engine has indexed more than 100,000,000 gigabytes of websites (www.google.com/search/howsearchworks/crawling-indexing).

With all this power, and trillions of indexed web pages, how can one little ol' social engineer find the tiny bits of data he or she needs? Before I can answer that, I need to give you a quick explanation of how Google (or any search engine, really) works.

Search Engine Mysteries Revealed!

There really is no mystery revealed in this section. The title is misleading. You probably already understand how search engines work, but on the off chance that you don't, here is a very quick and easy explanation of it.

Search engines use little pieces of code called spiders. Spiders "crawl" (I don't make this stuff up) through every web page on the open web and cache what they are allowed to access. There are certain files, like `robots.txt`, that stop a spider from indexing certain areas, but most other areas are indexed and cached.

That cache is put into a database, which, when you enter a search term in the search box, provides results like you see in Figure 2-13.

Let me point out a few key things in Figure 2-13. First, the search returned 105,000 results in .59 seconds. How can it search 30 trillion web pages in .59 seconds? Remember, these pages have been cached in a database, which allows for blazing-fast speeds in searching.

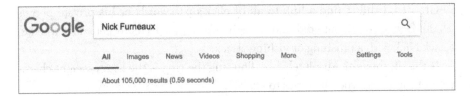

Figure 2-13 He's baaaccccckkk.

Scraping 105,000 web pages would be not only improbable but, most likely, impossible. So, let me tell you about operators.

Enter the Operators

Google has created a set of search terms called *operators* that limit what Google looks for. Think of it as being the difference between using a magnifying glass and a microscope. Both get you closer to an object you want to inspect, but if you really want to home in on the details, a microscope is the way to go. These operators are the microscope of searching.

The following two websites list all the useful operators for Google (and even some for Yahoo! and Bing):

» https://support.google.com/websearch/answer/2466433?hl=en&ref_topic=3081620

» www.googleguide.com/advanced_operators_reference.html

For your convenience, here is a list of the operators I find the most useful:

» **intext:** This operator searches for whatever follows it "in the text" of the web page or document being searched. For example, if you type **intext:csitech**, Google searches for all occurrences of that phrase.

» **site:** This operator limits your search terms to the site you list. For example, if you type **site:csitech.co.uk**, Google searches only that domain and nothing outside of it.

» **inurl:** This operator may sound similar to the **site** operator, but it limits your search to any *URL* that contains the search term you type. If you type **inurl:csitech.co.uk**, the search would also include any website that has the term **ccistech.co.uk** in its URL. For example, if there was a site called **forensicsmag.com/csitech.co.uk/interviews**, it would be returned on this search but not in the search with the **site** operator.

»   `filetype:` This operator does exactly what it sounds like—it limits your search to the file type you choose.

»   `cache:` This operator searches for the cached version of the domain, file, or other artifact you list.

»   `info:` This operator gives you info on the domain you list here.

Like most things involving software, there are rules. Google searching is no different.

»   The search term follows the operator, a colon, and no space. If you search for **site:whitehouse.gov**, for example, you limit your search to whitehouse.gov. But if you search for **site: whitehouse.gov**, you limit your search to the space after the colon (:), which is ineffective.

»   You can use a hyphen (-) before an operator to remove those results from your search. For example, if you know you want to find all csitech references but don't want any in the .com space, you can try this search to limit your results: **inurl:csitech.co.uk -site.com**.

»   If you have a search term that is more than one word, and you want all of the words included in the search, you must use quotation marks. For example, if I want to search for Nick Furneaux, I could try **intext:"Nick Furneaux"** to include both first and last names in my `intext` search.

»   According to Google (https://support.google.com/gsa/answer/4411411#requests), there is a limit to the number of search terms allowed. The default is 50, and the upper limit is 150. (But honestly, if you are searching with upward of 100 search terms, you might need help.)

Believe me, there are a lot more search terms and other goodies than what I listed here. Google is a powerful tool, and I could spend volumes delving into every little corner of it. But we need to get back to our OSINT. Let's work through some examples and see what we can find.

Limiting for the Win

When I interrupted my search for info about Nick Furneaux earlier in this chapter, I was on my way to creating a nice little profile about him. Can Google either reconfirm my findings or give even more information?

I had found some information like his name and a nickname he uses on at least one social media outlet. What if I search for those two together to see what could be found? Typing **intext:"Nick Furneaux" intext:nickfx** into the Google search box will result in what's shown in Figure 2-14.

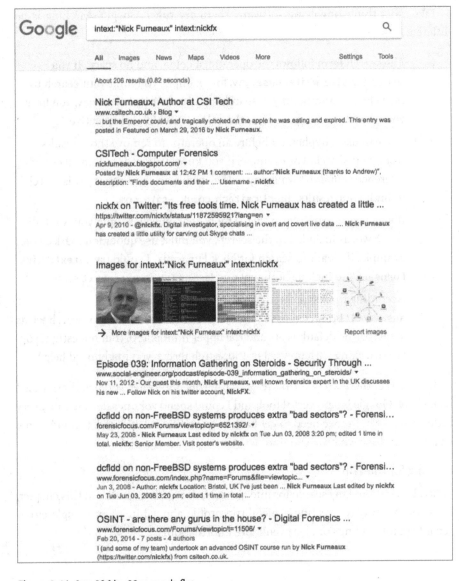

Figure 2-14   0 to 206 in .82 seconds flat

In less than one second, I have a solid 206 results on the target. One of the features of searching on Google is being able to see images related to your search. Clicking the More Images For link can show you some interesting results. In this case, the images can take me to pages that talk about Nick.

But I already know a lot of this information about Nick, so let's see what else I can find. I change the search term to **intext:"Nick Furneaux" intext:UK**. The results are shown in Figure 2-15.

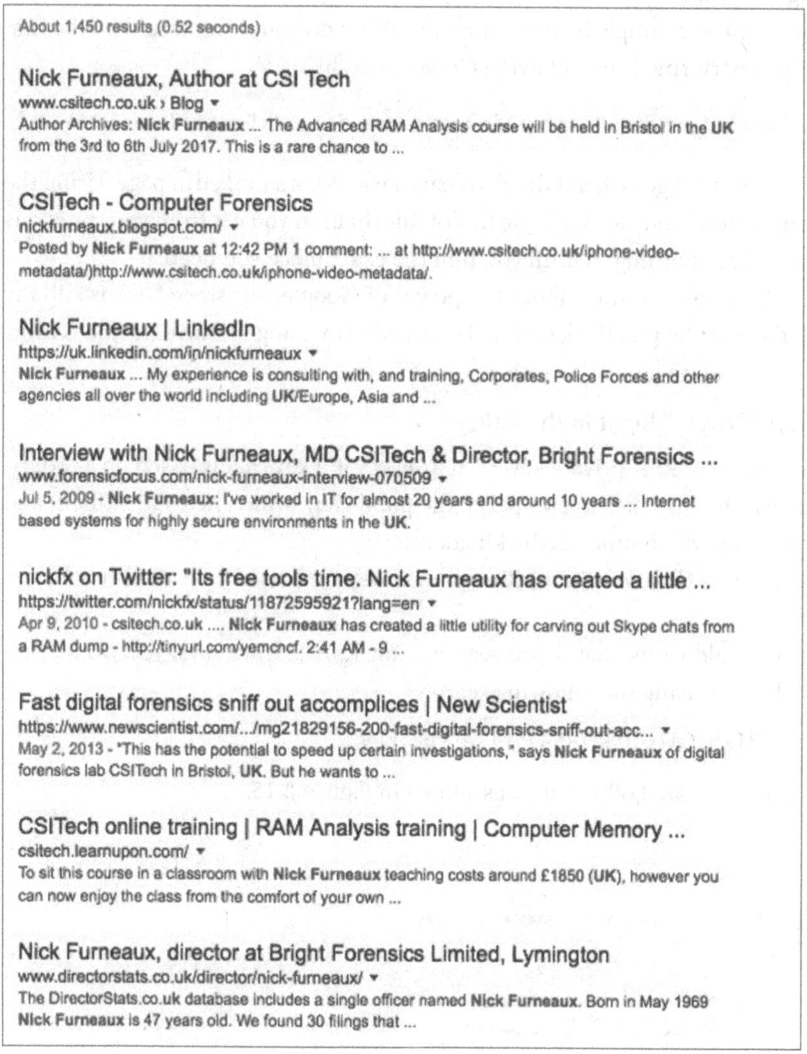

About 1,450 results (0.52 seconds)

Nick Furneaux, Author at CSI Tech
www.csitech.co.uk › Blog ▾
Author Archives: Nick Furneaux ... The Advanced RAM Analysis course will be held in Bristol in the UK from the 3rd to 6th July 2017. This is a rare chance to ...

CSITech - Computer Forensics
nickfurneaux.blogspot.com/ ▾
Posted by Nick Furneaux at 12:42 PM 1 comment: ... at http://www.csitech.co.uk/iphone-video-metadata/)http://www.csitech.co.uk/iphone-video-metadata/.

Nick Furneaux | LinkedIn
https://uk.linkedin.com/in/nickfurneaux ▾
Nick Furneaux ... My experience is consulting with, and training, Corporates, Police Forces and other agencies all over the world including UK/Europe, Asia and ...

Interview with Nick Furneaux, MD CSITech & Director, Bright Forensics ...
www.forensicfocus.com/nick-furneaux-interview-070509 ▾
Jul 5, 2009 - Nick Furneaux: I've worked in IT for almost 20 years and around 10 years ... Internet based systems for highly secure environments in the UK.

nickfx on Twitter: "Its free tools time. Nick Furneaux has created a little ...
https://twitter.com/nickfx/status/11872595921?lang=en ▾
Apr 9, 2010 - csitech.co.uk .... Nick Furneaux has created a little utility for carving out Skype chats from a RAM dump - http://tinyurl.com/yemcncf. 2:41 AM - 9 ...

Fast digital forensics sniff out accomplices | New Scientist
https://www.newscientist.com/.../mg21829156-200-fast-digital-forensics-sniff-out-acc... ▾
May 2, 2013 - "This has the potential to speed up certain investigations," says Nick Furneaux of digital forensics lab CSITech in Bristol, UK. But he wants to ...

CSITech online training | RAM Analysis training | Computer Memory ...
csitech.learnupon.com/ ▾
To sit this course in a classroom with Nick Furneaux teaching costs around £1850 (UK), however you can now enjoy the class from the comfort of your own ...

Nick Furneaux, director at Bright Forensics Limited, Lymington
www.directorstats.co.uk/director/nick-furneaux/ ▾
The DirectorStats.co.uk database includes a single officer named Nick Furneaux. Born in May 1969 Nick Furneaux is 47 years old. We found 30 filings that ...

Figure 2-15 Are we getting warm yet, Nick?

The first result tells me he is training in a town called Bristol. The last result provides the name of a company that Nick might still be a part as well as his full date of birth and even an address in—you guessed it—Bristol.

The page also includes a list of family or friends that he might be working with at that company. It's a treasure trove of information.

Changing the "**UK**" in the previous search to "**Bristol**" will lead us to information such as his postal code and even some names of other family members that might be living with him.

Here's one last example before I move on. What do you think would be the first result if you performed the following Google search?

```
intext:"Nick Furneaux" site:linkedin.com intext:Bristol
```

The first result I got when I did this search was Nick's LinkedIn page. Using the Google operators, you can add little bits of information you get from your previous searches to keep homing in until you find the exact piece you need.

I want to show you more about the power of Google, but since Nick is still my friend (or at least he was the last time I checked), I'm going to move the focus away from him and on to general searches.

But It Says "Private" Right in the Title

Have you heard of RSA private keys? An RSA key is a key that is based on a proprietary algorithm. It comes in two parts: the public key, which helps identify it, and the private key, which unlocks the kingdom.

According to this definition, RSA private keys are used to establish a secure connection.

So, you would think that if you searched for RSA private keys, you would find none, right? But using the following search

```
BEGIN (CERTIFICATE|DSA|RSA) filetype:key
```

gives you more than 3,000 results, as shown in Figure 2-16.

Figure 2-16 Why did you call it private?

But It's Marked Confidential

Often, government entities mark documents with certain classifications to indicate whether the general public should see them. Markings like "CLASSIFIED" and "TOP SECRET" usually indicate that the documents aren't for general consumption. You would assume that you can't find any of those online. (You know what they say about people who assume . . .)

But since I like living life outside prison walls, let's say we just want to see if there are any documents with passwords, which should be confidential, right?

What if I searched for `site:gov.ir intext:password filetype:xls`? This should limit my search to any `gov.ir` domain and look for only XLS files with the word *password* in them. The results are shown in Figure 2-17.

Hmm, that doesn't seem right. Why would a document in an Iraqi government server have the English word *password* in it? Ah, but what if I use the `translate.google.com` site to translate the word *password* into Persian? Does it help? Figure 2-18 shows the result.

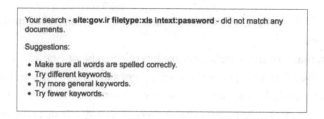

Figure 2-17 What went wrong?

Figure 2-18 Multilingual Google searches

The power of Google is truly shown here. I didn't need to know Persian or even search in Persian. I just had to tell it to look for that word, and I was able to find documents.

Webcams: It's Time to Stop Dancing in Your Underwear

There was a boom in the desire for people to have webcams hooked up in their homes. People used them for monitoring their children, babysitters, and pets; for security; and more.

Many of these cameras were sold with default settings that left them vulnerable and wide open. Sometimes the software sold with the cameras also left a lot to be desired. Easy for the user? Yes. But also easy for attackers.

One such software was webcamXP. As indicated by its name, it was made to run on Windows XP, Vista, 7, 8, 9, 10, Server 2003, 2008, and 2012. According to its website, the software's last update was in 2016. With that in mind it should not be too popular today, so you would imagine that searching for these now would not give you too much, right?

Right?!

So, I searched for `intitle:"Webcam 7" inurl:8080 -intext:8080`, and Figure 2-19 shows the result.

Granted, many of these webcams are intended to be online and are meant for the public to see. They're streaming traffic scenes or waterfronts and other areas. But there are people who set up webcams for personal use and leave them open in their yards or homes. The point is that if these webcams are not properly secured, any person with a little skill may be watching you, and you won't even know.

Other Sources of Intel

Usually when I get to this point, people react with a mixture of horror and curiosity about what else you can turn up with a Google search. I don't want to list every Google search I have done, but I can tell you some of the things that I have easily uncovered using only Google searches:

» A webcam of some guy watching his marijuana plants grow

» People's private photos from their phones

» People's shared music and movie directories

» Documents containing full passwords, dates of birth, and Social Security numbers

» Thousands of credit card numbers in files

» Fully open SQL databases loaded with info

» Open access to traffic cams

» Open access to power grids and control systems

» A number of child pornography drop spots

The list can go on and on.

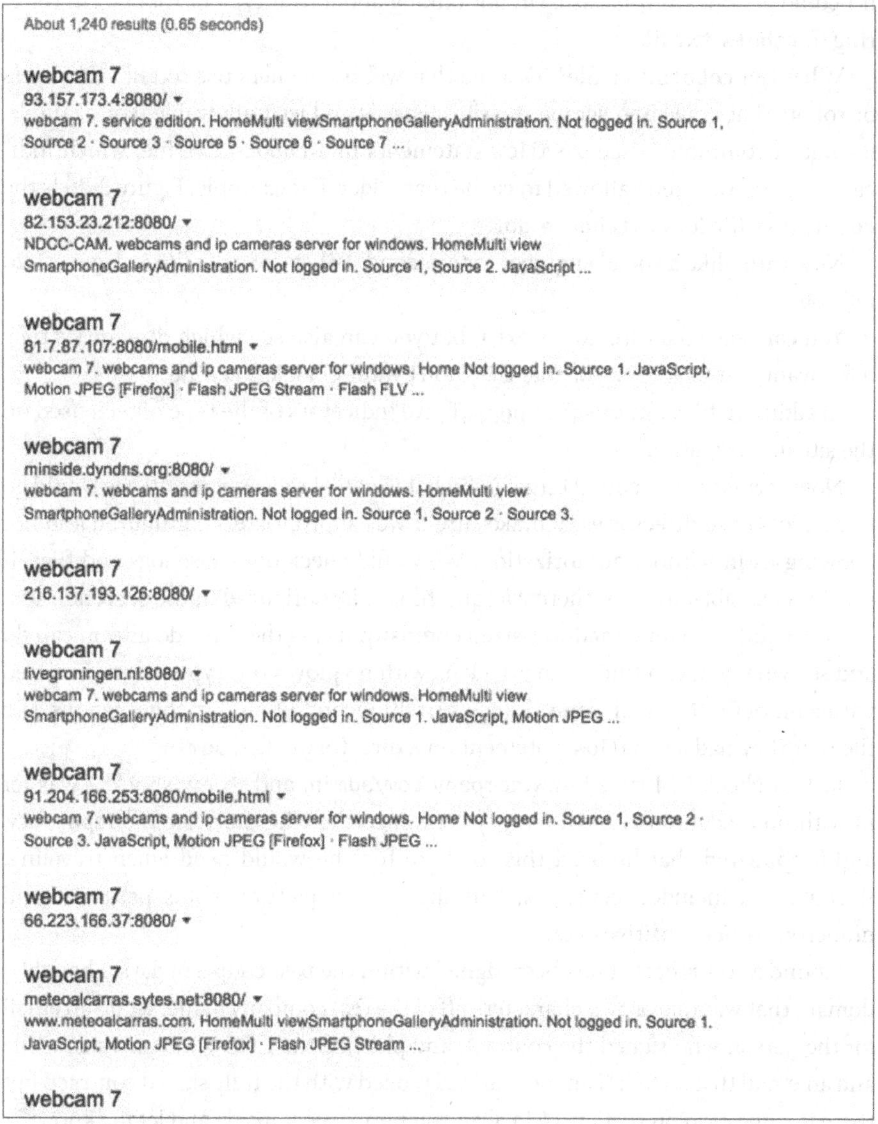

About 1,240 results (0.65 seconds)

webcam 7
93.157.173.4:8080/ ▾
webcam 7. service edition. HomeMulti viewSmartphoneGalleryAdministration. Not logged in. Source 1,
Source 2 · Source 3 · Source 5 · Source 6 · Source 7 ...

webcam 7
82.153.23.212:8080/ ▾
NDCC-CAM. webcams and ip cameras server for windows. HomeMulti view
SmartphoneGalleryAdministration. Not logged in. Source 1, Source 2. JavaScript ...

webcam 7
81.7.87.107:8080/mobile.html ▾
webcam 7. webcams and ip cameras server for windows. Home Not logged in. Source 1. JavaScript,
Motion JPEG [Firefox] · Flash JPEG Stream · Flash FLV ...

webcam 7
minside.dyndns.org:8080/ ▾
webcam 7. webcams and ip cameras server for windows. HomeMulti view
SmartphoneGalleryAdministration. Not logged in. Source 1, Source 2 · Source 3.

webcam 7
216.137.193.126:8080/ ▾

webcam 7
livegroningen.nl:8080/ ▾
webcam 7. webcams and ip cameras server for windows. HomeMulti view
SmartphoneGalleryAdministration. Not logged in. Source 1. JavaScript, Motion JPEG ...

webcam 7
91.204.166.253:8080/mobile.html ▾
webcam 7. webcams and ip cameras server for windows. Home Not logged in. Source 1, Source 2 ·
Source 3. JavaScript, Motion JPEG [Firefox] · Flash JPEG ...

webcam 7
66.223.166.37:8080/ ▾

webcam 7
meteoalcarras.sytes.net:8080/ ▾
www.meteoalcarras.com. HomeMulti viewSmartphoneGalleryAdministration. Not logged in. Source 1.
JavaScript, Motion JPEG [Firefox] · Flash JPEG Stream ...

webcam 7

Figure 2-19 Webcams galore!

Two Other Things

This section alone could be its own book. But before I move on and wrap up this chapter, I would be remiss if I didn't mention two other things.

Robots Are Cool

When I was a kid, I wanted a robot so bad. I thought R2D2 would be my best friend if I could get one. In this case, I'm not talking about *that* type of robots. I'm referring to robots.txt files.

What is a robots.txt file? It's a file that website owners use to tell the spiders or robots that crawl and scrape the sites what is and isn't allowable. For example, it's not uncommon to see Disallow statements in a robots.txt file, which indicates that robots aren't allowed to cache that folder. For example, Figure 2-20 is the robots.txt file for whitehouse.gov.

Now think like a social engineer for a second. What does the file in Figure 2-20 tell you?

You can see what directories exist, but you can also see which directories they don't want you to access—or that they don't want Google to cache.

In addition, files like mysql or pgpsql give indicators of the type of tech used on the site in its creation.

Now, if this was an actual target (which it is *not*—I repeat, it is *not*), we would go to each of those directories to make sure it was appropriately configured and not allowing us in without authorization. We would check out those logs and files, if they're accessible, to see if there was anything misconfigured in the servers.

I once did a job for a medium-sized company. It was the rare "do all you can do and see what you can find, then attack us with no gloves on" type of test. I started with a bit of OSINT and some Google searching, and I found in their robots.txt file that they had a Disallow statement on a directory called admin.

Just to check it, I typed www.company.com/admin, and to my shock, I was let in with no credentials! The directory contained the CEO's private file repository, and it appeared that he used this to share files he would need when traveling. It contained included contracts, banking data, a picture of his passport, and numerous other sensitive details.

I found a contract that had been signed within the past couple of days. I bought a domain that was one or two characters off of the real company name, set up an email for the person who signed the contract, and phished the CEO with a malicious file and an email that stated: "I am not sure if I replied with the fully signed contract, but there is a question on section 14.1a. Can you please see it inside and let me know?"

```
User-agent: *
Crawl-delay: 10
# CSS, JS, Images
Allow: /misc/*.css$
Allow: /misc/*.css?
Allow: /misc/*.js$
Allow: /misc/*.js?
Allow: /misc/*.gif
Allow: /misc/*.jpg
Allow: /misc/*.jpeg
Allow: /misc/*.png
Allow: /modules/*.css$
Allow: /modules/*.css?
Allow: /modules/*.js$
Allow: /modules/*.js?
Allow: /modules/*.gif
Allow: /modules/*.jpg
Allow: /modules/*.jpeg
Allow: /modules/*.png
Allow: /profiles/*.css$
Allow: /profiles/*.css?
Allow: /profiles/*.js$
Allow: /profiles/*.js?
Allow: /profiles/*.gif
Allow: /profiles/*.jpg
Allow: /profiles/*.jpeg
Allow: /profiles/*.png
Allow: /themes/*.css$
Allow: /themes/*.css?
Allow: /themes/*.js$
Allow: /themes/*.js?
Allow: /themes/*.gif
Allow: /themes/*.jpg
Allow: /themes/*.jpeg
Allow: /themes/*.png
# Directories
Disallow: /includes/
Disallow: /misc/
Disallow: /modules/
Disallow: /profiles/
Disallow: /scripts/
Disallow: /themes/
# Files
Disallow: /CHANGELOG.txt
Disallow: /cron.php
Disallow: /INSTALL.mysql.txt
Disallow: /INSTALL.pgsql.txt
Disallow: /INSTALL.sqlite.txt
Disallow: /install.php
Disallow: /INSTALL.txt
Disallow: /LICENSE.txt
Disallow: /MAINTAINERS.txt
Disallow: /update.php
Disallow: /UPGRADE.txt
Disallow: /xmlrpc.php
# Paths (clean URLs)
Disallow: /admin/
Disallow: /comment/reply/
Disallow: /filter/tips/
Disallow: /node/add/
Disallow: /search/
Disallow: /user/register/
Disallow: /user/password/
Disallow: /user/login/
Disallow: /user/logout/
Disallow: /experiments/
# Paths (no clean URLs)
Disallow: /?q=admin/
Disallow: /?q=comment/reply/
Disallow: /?q=filter/tips/
Disallow: /?q=node/add/
Disallow: /?q=search/
Disallow: /?q=user/password/
Disallow: /?q=user/register/
Disallow: /?q=user/login/
Disallow: /?q=user/logout/
Disallow: /?q=experiments/
```

Figure 2-20 That's a lot of disallowance!

Within 15 minutes, the CEO had the email, opened it, and was compromised. He was then emailing the fake address, saying that the contract would not open, and it just kept crashing. The penetration test (aka pen test), which was supposed to take a week, was over in about three hours.

I called the CEO, and our conversation went something like this:

CEO: Hello

Me: Hey, Paul. This is Chris over at Social-Engineer. I wanted to talk to you about the pen test. . . .

CEO: Ha! Giving up so soon, Chris? I knew we were a hard nut to crack.

Me: Well, Paul, we already have your passport, date of birth, credit cards, access to your banks, and a remote shell with admin credentials on the network. I thought I should call and see if you really want me to continue for the week?

CEO: Come on! You're making this up!! It just started a couple hours ago. Tell me, who is the loser that clicked and gave shell? I want words with him.

Me   Well, Paul. . . . *(I gulped hard, not sure if I could make the joke that was in my head.)* I wouldn't go too harsh on him; he is a pretty cool guy.

CEO: Oh yeah? Who?

Me: Paul, it's you.

I then explained every detail to him, and he realized quickly what had occurred. This particular pen test was won largely due to a `robots.txt` file and a misconfigured directory.

It's All About the Meta, Baby

According to the Oxford Dictionary, *meta* is defined as "referring to itself or to the conventions of its genre; self-referential." So, metadata is literally data about data. Very *inception*-esque, no?

Let me explain it more simply. Metadata is information about an artifact that you find in a search. Many times, that data provides some pretty interesting facts—many that might not have been put there intentionally.

Let's say I do a very benign Google search to find `.doc` files that contain information about passwords. I come upon this little document called `FinalPasswordPolicy`. What will the metadata reveal? Take a look at Figure 2-21.

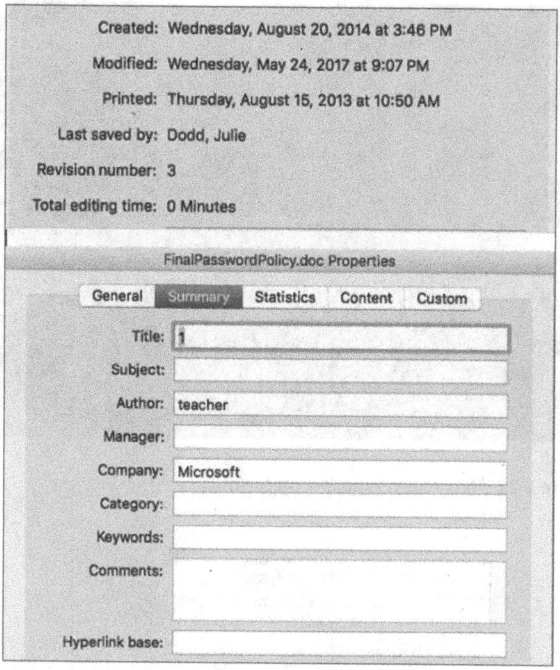

Figure 2-21 "What's-a meta you?!" (See what I did there?)

This metadata gives us the date and time it was made, the last person who saved it, the author's name/title, how many revisions the file has been through, and some other information I'm not mentioning here. You might be thinking, "So what?"

Well, just the name and the type of document that something is can be huge pieces of intel for a social engineer. Think of this: What if a social engineer were to find a new HR policy you just released? The metadata reveals when the policy was last revised (in this case, it wasn't even a month old), who wrote it, and when it was released. Of course, the policy info is in the document, too. Do you think a phishing email that seems to come from the person who wrote the policy and seemingly includes an update to the policy would get a few clicks?

Have a look at Figure 2-22.

At first, you again might be thinking, "Okay. So, are we gonna phish this guy with a coupon for hot sauce?" No. But take a look at the metadata, which is shown in Figure 2-23.

When you find a seemingly innocuous photo online, the metadata gives you information on the type of camera, the date, the time, and the GPS coordinates of

Figure 2-22 "No, really. What's-a meta you?!"

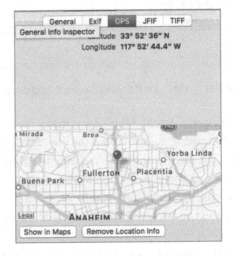

Figure 2-23 The answer is . . .

where it was taken. When you put those coordinates into Google Maps . . . well, look at Figure 2-24.

The map shows the parking lot of Pepe's restaurant, which just happens to be a pretty large user of that brand of hot sauce.

So, a guy used his smartphone to take a picture. His smartphone had GPS turned on and did not block the camera app from embedding all that metadata in the back end of the photo file. When he uploaded the picture to his social media, the file contained all this information, so it was also released to the world.

Figure 2-24 That's pretty saucy, if you ask me.

Can you see the implications yet? Imagine it's not your buddy you're eating dinner with, but one of the following:

» The CEO of a large utility company who is being targeted by a nation-state attack

» The secretary of a billionaire who has information on his banks and transfer authority

» Your 15-year-old daughter taking naughty pictures of herself

Now can you see the implications? No matter which scenario you thought of, this easily accessible information gets dangerous quickly.

I worked one job with my team in which we had been tasked to perform OSINT and then attack a high-level target in the defense space. The goal was not to compromise the man, but to test his level of willingness to take an action he should not take. For educational purposes, we were to record any calls made and any click-throughs.

Light OSINT led us to his social media pages. We hit pay dirt when we found out he was a prolific tweeter, and he loved to use his brand-new iPhone with GPS turned on. Why is this so important? Twitter allowed us to graph out his location throughout the day as he tweeted from every location he went to. In a matter of a few hours, we knew the following things:

» His favorite place to stop for coffee every morning

» The gym he went to before he went home

» Two of his favorite restaurants

» His home address

» How much he hated city traffic

There was much more OSINT, but the info in the preceding list came to be crucial in our attacks. First, we found a domain that was basically one letter different from his gym's domain. We set up a quick email that told him we were updating all accounts, and his credit card info was no longer valid. We asked him to "log in to enter his credit card info now," which prompted him to click through very quickly.

Knowing the page was going to 404 out, we waited until we saw the click, and then we called him on the phone. The conversation went something like this:

Caller: Hello. Is this Mr. Smith?"

Target: Yes, it is. Who is this?

Caller: This is Sarah over at Cold's Gym. We sent an email out earlier today about our system upgrade. Well, the email had a bad URL, so we are calling our customers to apologize. I can send you out a new link or take your credit card and update it for you. What is easier for you?

Target: No problem, Sarah, here is my card number.

Caller: Thank you, Mr. Smith! See you tonight!

This attack worked because it hit topics familiar to him, and it was believable. With just a little OSINT, one phish, and one call, we had a click, a credit card number, and another five vectors prepared in case we needed them.

Metadata is powerful and very useful to a social engineer, so I suggest that you make sure to check it on every file you obtain during OSINT.

This can be daunting, especially when you're dealing with a large number of files. I personally like to use tools like FOCA (www.elevenpaths.com/labstools/foca/index.html) and Maltego (www.paterva.com/web7) to make this job easier.

Although I promised to not get too deep into any tools in this book, I feel it is imperative to at least briefly cover these and two other useful tools, which I will do in the next section.

Tools of the Trade

As I say in Chapter 1, I decided not to focus too much on tools in this book, because tools change often.

However, there are four tools that have remained in my tool chest for the last 5 to 10 years, and I felt it would be wrong of me to not even mention them. Although these tools have stayed around for a long time, they have had interface and functionality changes. If I were to spend a ton of time going through each feature, the information would be outdated by the time you get this book. Instead, I will point you to the tools' websites where you can get tutorials and keep abreast of the latest and greatest developments. I promise, this tour will be quick, but it's an essential piece of the puzzle you won't want to miss.

SET

I can remember chatting with my good friend David Kennedy. I was telling him about my desire to have a tool that allowed me to phish someone and automatically feed them a payload, grab credentials, or clone any webpage. Dave's response was, "I think I can do that."

Not even a full 24 hours later, he had a prototype. From that moment on, Dave ran with what was called SET, or the Social Engineers Toolkit, like it was a life's mission.

He issues updates all the time—it seems like every day—and he has built-in features that make my original little ideas seem really lame. It's an amazing tool that has over two million downloads.

You can get the tool as well as instructions from `www.trustedsec.com/social-engineer-toolkit`.

IntelTechniques

Okay, this one is not really a "tool" per se as much as it's a collection of amazing search engines that my good friend Michael Bazzell has put together.

Michael is an expert at a few things, but there are two of them that he truly eats, breathes, and sleeps: finding people on the Internet and hiding from people who are looking for you on the Internet. Honestly, once Michael told me that to buy things from Amazon, I should set up a dummy company in Mexico, so I can get credit cards that don't tie back to me.

Michael has set up an amazing collection of tools that search everything from social media, phone numbers, IP addresses, and even reverse images. You can find these tools at `https://inteltechniques.com/menu.html`, and I suggest you spend some considerable time at that site.

FOCA

FOCA stands for Fingerprinting Organizations with Collected Archives. Way back at DEF CON 18 in 2010, a small group of Brazilian hackers released the tool and took the Internet by storm.

To date, there is *nothing* else like FOCA in the world. It's a Windows-only tool that has gone through some serious ups and downs over the years. At one point, I stopped using it because there had been no updates for some time, and there was no way to contact any person running it (and the tool wasn't open source).

Then the folks at ElevenPaths took over the project. They did an update and released it on their website at `https://www.elevenpaths.com/labstools/foca/index.html`. Sadly, FOCA is still Windows-only, but if you're not on Windows, it's worth setting up a virtual machine.

The speed at which FOCA grabs files and rips out useful metadata is amazing. Check it out.

Maltego: The Granddaddy of Them All

At the risk of sounding like an infomercial for Maltego, I *love* this tool. I really do. The folks at Paterva do something you rarely see: They make an amazing tool, release a smaller free version (that is just as amazing), and keep the commercial version updated, so it's always moving forward and very usable.

What is Maltego, you ask? It is a tool that helps you collect data from online sources and then gives you an interactive graph to display it. It can help you catalog, footprint, investigate, and make connections with public sources of intelligence.

Maltego makes my work much easier than it would otherwise be, and the tool is easy and fun to use. In addition, the guys at Paterva (the company that makes

Maltego) offer amazing training videos and courses. Finally, Maltego is made for every platform.

You can check it out and download it right from the Paterva website at www .paterva.com/web7/downloads.php#tab-2. I suggest you start with Maltego Classic.

Summary

Knowledge is certainly power, and there may be no better source of knowledge of your targets than OSINT. If you follow the principles in this chapter, practice, and hone those skills you can become a master and finding even the minute details hidden all over the Internet.

You have done all the OSINT. You have cataloged, collected, and documented every piece articulately. You think you have found the piece that will be your vector, and you need to start preparing your pretext. How will analyzing the data you found and looking for key indicators about the target's communication style help? That is the topic of the next chapter.

3

Profiling People Through Communication
(or Using Your Words Against You)

To effectively communicate, we must realize that we are all different in the way we perceive the world and use this understanding as a guide to our communication with others.

—TONY ROBBINS

When I wrote *Social Engineering: The Art of Human Hacking* (Wiley, 2010), I spent some considerable time talking with Chris Nickerson, owner of Lares Consulting, about communication modeling. He is quite skilled and has a deep understanding of the topic.

He really helped me to delve deep into the topic and understand some of the ways communication is used by social engineers. At the end of the day, I can boil down communication modeling to the following key points:

» There is always a source.

» There is a message.

» There is a channel.

» There is a receiver.

If you are missing one of these, you don't have communication. Whether you look at the Shannon-Weaver model or Berlo's Sender-Message-Channel-Receiver (SMCR) model of communications, they have similar principles.

Regardless of which one you are familiar with, one of the things I've learned over the years is that the exact model you use really doesn't matter. I know, I know—some of you are probably ready to start burning this book in the streets, but here is why I say this.

If you apply this book's principles regarding rapport, influence, communication profiling, and so on, and the person you are communicating with is receiving the

EXTRA INFO

In 1947, Claude Shannon and Warren Weaver developed the Shannon-Weaver model of communication, which was also called "the mother of all models." Fifteen years later, David Berlo expanded on that model and created the SMCR communication modeling tool. Later, D. C. Barnlund combined and simplified these tools, making a communication model that most of us are familiar with today. Barnlund's theory is included in *Communication Theory*, Second Edition (Routledge, 2008) as Chapter 4, "A Transactional Model of Communication."

Here is the reference: https://www.taylorfrancis.com/books/e/9781351527 538/chapters/10.4324%2F9781315080918-5]

message, it *will* work. If you use these principles the way the person you are communicating with wants to be communicated with, communication will go exactly how you want it to go.

Yes, I realize this is a bold claim, and I don't mean that it's as simple as 1 + 1 being equal to 2.

It can be complicated. Oftentimes, we get in our own way. For example, I am a very direct communicator. Because of this, I don't mind someone telling me when something I did wasn't the best—the key is that you need to tell me how to improve. I also tend to communicate that way with others, which can cause a lot of problems when I am communicating with a person who doesn't like directness.

It's not easy to just switch your communication profile on the fly, although it's easier for some people than for others. The challenge occurs when we get comfortable and relaxed because our brains trigger all the same chemical reactions we want in our targets, and those same reactions can cause us to slip back into our "comfort zone."

Let me illustrate it this way: Do you remember as a young adult (or a full-grown one) the first time you tried something new? A new type of food, let's say. Since my kids were small, my wife and I encouraged them to always try something at least once. They didn't have to like it or finish it, but we said you can't make a judgment if *you* don't try it.

One year, we traveled to Hong Kong as a family. We went into a restaurant, and my daughter spotted an item on the menu that intrigued her—it was labeled "Whole Pigeon." She asked me if she could try it. My first inclination was to say, "Really, those nasty birds?" But I quickly recalled our practice of encouraging the kids to try new things.

My daughter ordered the pigeon, and then she looked at me and said, "Well Dad, what new thing are you gonna try?" I had always been intrigued by sea cucumber, although I'm not sure I had ever wanted to eat it. Sounds harmless right?

Figure 3-1 shows my daughter chowing down on her pigeon, but I don't have an image that shows you what happened when I ate a sea cucumber. They are basically giant slugs that live in the ocean, so use your imagination.

Figure 3-1 And yes, the pigeon's head was included.

What does this anecdote about my family's eating habits in Hong Kong have to do with communication modeling? Well, as soon as I tasted the thing that was uncomfortable for me (and quite disgusting, in my opinion), I went looking for something very, very "American." Why? It was familiar and comfortable.

Communication is much like this. The first time you step out of your comfort zone to try something new, you might be uncomfortable and want to retreat to your comfort zone, especially if the experience is not amazing. It is important to not stay in your comfort zone, though. The more you try something, the greater likelihood it has of becoming part of your arsenal of tools.

FUN FACT

I've tried sea cucumber four times, and each time was as disgusting as the first. This does *not* relate to communication modeling, but I just thought you'd like to know.

To help you master communication as a social engineer, I discuss the following key components in this chapter:

» Understanding what a person is thinking upon approach

» Getting to know the DISC

» Understanding how to model your DISC style

» Using DISC to your benefit

In other chapters of this book, some skills are independent of others in the same chapter, but for this chapter, all skills tie together and are important parts of each other. Let's get started with understanding what a person is thinking upon approach.

The Approach

When I teach my five-day Advanced Practical Social Engineering course, inevitably a lot of the students have a problem with one area: the approach.

It is those first crucial seconds of interaction between you and a stranger that will set the tone for the rest of the engagement. Let me tell you a particularly embarrassing fail story to solidify this point.

After class one day, I was with my good friend Robin Dreeke and a group of students. I was challenged to show them how "easy" it can be to approach a complete stranger. Feeling pretty high because of all the positivity from the class, the dopamine flowing from teaching all day, and the adrenaline rush of the pending success, I was poised to use my glorious skill to show them all how easy it is to be a social engineer.

About seven or eight of us were standing in a lobby discussing how I would do the approach, and Robin said he would pick my target for me. I am 6′3″ tall, and Robin picked a smaller man sitting on a chair about 2 feet behind me. He was sitting on a couch reading while he waited for someone.

Now, just picture this part of the scene in your head and consider what would be the best approach for me. From behind? Heck no! That would startle the man and cause fear. Standing directly in front? No again. He would have to look up, straining his neck, and that discomfort would not encourage a conversation. How would you do it? Take a second.

Well, after Robin told me my target, I whipped around without a thought and said (in my loud New York accent): "Hey, how you doing?! Can I ask you a quick question?"

The guy was so startled by the way I whipped around and my loud introduction that he leaned too far back in his chair, lost his balance, and fell. I rushed to his side, embarrassed and worried that he was hurt. Without thinking, I said, "Let me help you up." He was much lighter than I anticipated, and I picked him and the chair up but used too much force, which sent him hurling forward on the floor.

He looked up and yelled, *"Leave me alone man! What the heck is wrong with you?!"* (But he didn't use the word *heck*, and the anger in his voice was extreme.)

I turned away from him and said, "I am really sorry, sir." I walked back toward the lobby with my head hanging in shame as the group of students mocked me. Robin was laughing so hard, he was crying, and I was defeated.

Years of experiences like this, with tons of stories just like this, helped me define something that literally changed the way I view communications. What do you think a person you are about to communicate with needs from you so they can feel comfortable and safe? Think about it.

Imagine you are standing on the street, and you see someone is obviously walking toward you and planning to interact with you. What are you thinking? My experiences have helped me identify the following four things:

>> Who are you?

>> What do you want?

>> Are you a threat?

>> How long will this take?

When you approach someone, if you can answer these four things about that person in the first 5 to 10 seconds of the exchange, you can change the way your whole interaction goes. This information sets the stage for many parts of this book, so fold or mark this page because I refer to it often. These four factors also come into play in the following topics discussed in other chapters:

>> Your pretext (Chapter 4, "Becoming Anyone You Want to Be")

>> The first words from your mouth (Chapter 5, "I Know How to Make You Like Me")

>> Body language and facial expressions (Chapter 8, "I Can See What You Didn't Say")

Figure 3-2 These four points are crucial to communications.

Figure 3-2 is a graphic to help you remember these four things.

I'm not saying that every human is literally thinking about those questions in those exact words every time another human approaches them, but they are part of the concerns, thoughts, or worries that a person has. If you (the sender of the communication) can answer these four things in your initial opening line, you can put the receiver at ease and allow that person to relax.

Conmen throughout history have known these facts and use various techniques to make their marks relax before they get to the ask (the purpose of the interaction). Understanding this can not only make you a much better social engineer, but it can also help you protect yourself when someone tries to use these techniques against *you*.

The first step is to understand your communication style. That is where we get into a very powerful but simple communication profiling tool.

Enter the DISC

In 1893, William Moulton Marston was born. At only 22 years old, he had a B.A. from Harvard; three years later, he had his LL.B. from Harvard Law School; and then only three years later, he graduated with his Ph.D. in psychology from Harvard. He took a job as a teacher at American University.

During his school years at Harvard, he was doing some research into the relationship between a person who was telling lies and their blood pressure. And in 1915, he built a machine that would measure the changes in a person's blood pressure while that person was being questioned.

In 1917, Marston published his findings, and from that—you guessed it—the polygraph was born. In the 1920s and '30s, he was very active as a lecturer and government consultant. He was unique for that time as he was not as interested in abnormal psychology as much as he was in the behavior of a population of people.

In 1928, he published a book called *Emotions of Normal People*, and in 1931, he published another book called *Integrative Psychology: A Study of Unit Response*. It was from these works that Marston derived the DISC system. He was looking for ways to measure the energy of behavior and consciousness. Although he did not develop the test that I discuss in this chapter, he developed this model and then applied it in some work he did with Universal Studios in 1930. They wanted to transition from silent pictures to movies with audio, and Marston's work was integral in helping create more-natural gestures and facial expressions.

FUN FACT

Marston was a big advocate for women's rights and the power of women. When he was studying Greek and Roman classics as a young man, he took an interest in blending that schooling with women's rights. It was these passions that led Dr. Marston to develop the heroine Wonder Woman, for which he was inducted into the Comic Book Hall of Fame in 2006.

Dr. Marston's work changed the way I look at social engineering. A lot of people were trying to figure out how to psychologically profile someone quickly, but Dr. Marston's more simplistic approach just resonated with me. I'm not a psychologist, so understanding your psych profile does little for me. But I am a social engineer, so understanding how you communicate is like having the key to a lock.

What Is DISC?

DISC in an acronym. Some people use different descriptors, but the following make the most sense to me:

D: Direct/Dominant

I: Influencing

S: Supporter/Steady

C: Conscientious/Compliant

Each of these is a descriptor of the way that style is represented. Often, DISC is represented in a shape. I use the one shown in Figure 3-3.

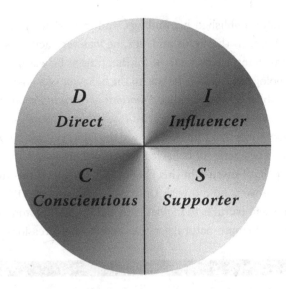

Figure 3-3 DISC simply defined

Each of these communication styles is represented in a unique way that helps us predict behavior. Using DISC, you will find that people are predictably different.

Let's say you are dealing with a *D* or direct communicator. One direct communicator may be loud and boisterous; another may be quieter and firmer; a third may be right in between. Despite those differences, they all communicate directly and in a straightforward manner. As a result, if you can profile the person quickly, you can alter your communication style to better influence the person.

There are always a few questions about this that always come up while I'm teaching my courses. Here are two of the most common ones:

Question: How do I know my preferred style?

Answer: This is a great question, but not easily answered, so I get into this in the following section.

Question: Can I be more than one style? Or a blend of a couple?

Answer: Yes, we all have strengths in more than one style, and it's possible to be strong in more than one. Some people do end up at the intersection of styles, and it's possible to change a bit over time.

Even though this assessment method is very accurate, keep in mind that any assessment like this is not always 100% (at least in my opinion). It is subject to change based on the way a person answers and by the scenario.

The way I think about it is that this is another tool in your arsenal as a professional social engineer. It helps you get closer to truly using all the skills of the pros.

Before I can even get into how you would use DISC as a social engineer, I need to discuss something that is possibly one of the most important parts of this book: understanding your own communication styles first.

To Know Thyself Is the Beginning of Wisdom

That title is not a weird riddle; it's the basis of truly understanding how communication profiling works. Before you can become a master at communicating with others, it is essential that you understand yourself first. Let me explain.

A chef has many different knives in his kitchen. I have 4-inch, 8-inch, and 10-inch knives. Each has a different shape and weight and is for a different purpose. Figure 3-4 shows a variety of knife styles. Which knife do you think is the best for chopping a head of cabbage?

Figure 3-4 Choose wisely.

I would choose the knife that's the fourth from the right because it has the weight needed to cut through a thick vegetable, and it has the length to go all the way through, which would make the cutting easier on my arms and wrist. I have seen some people choose the knives that are in the fifth or sixth position from the right to chop cabbage, and guess what happens? A few minutes into chopping, and their hands are sore and their wrists hurt—there's also a great risk of injury when you use one of those knives. By knowing which tool is best for the job, how to properly use it, and what its strengths and weaknesses are, you can choose the perfect tool for the job.

DISC is like this illustration. Some profiles work better for certain tasks than others. Knowing your style can help you truly understand your strengths and your weaknesses. It can help you to see how you can clearly communicate your thoughts and your intentions. It can also greatly increase your chance of not putting off the person you are communicating with, which, as a social engineer, is a very important part of the job.

There are a few ways I help people learn about their dominant communication styles, but mostly I use a DISC assessment tool that helps a person to learn about themselves easily. But wait! Before you go running to your Internet browser and searching for "free DISC assessment," let me tell you why that might not be the best idea.

Many online assessments that I have previewed use a method that I consider flawed. They give you a sentence and ask you to answer a predefined set of questions regarding that situation. For example:

Imagine you are Chris's manager and he just acted insubordinately. What should you do?

A. Fire him on the spot.

B. Make a few jokes about it and move on.

C. Sit him down and explain in detail why what he did was wrong.

D. Try to help him to see why his attitude is not good for the team.

The problem with questions like this on a DISC assessment is that you might not have any context for being able to answer it. What if you never managed another person? What if you never managed an insubordinate person? There are too many variables that make this a bad question and can lead to inaccurate results.

If you're going to look for an assessment test to use, I encourage you to look for one that gives you word choices and ask you to choose one that is most like you and one that is least like you, as opposed to scenario-based tests. Here's an example:

From the list of words, choose one that *you* feel describes you the most and one that describes you the least. Even if you do not have really strong feelings toward these words, one will describe you the most and the least according to your personal assessment.

MOST	LEAST
Logical	Logical
Serious	Serious
Obedient	Obedient
Free-willed	Free-willed

With sentences you are trying to imagine a situation that you never experienced, which can be really hard for many people. This is why I like to recommend assessments that use word pairs. This type of assessment allows the science at hand to work more accurately.

I often tell my students to answer each question while thinking about how they behave at *work*, which is often much different than when they are at home. As a result, I get a consistent and honest representation of their communication profiles.

Unfortunately, I haven't figured out how to administer a DISC assessment test to every reader of this book, so I must be a little creative to help you understand how powerful this is.

Look at Figure 3-5.

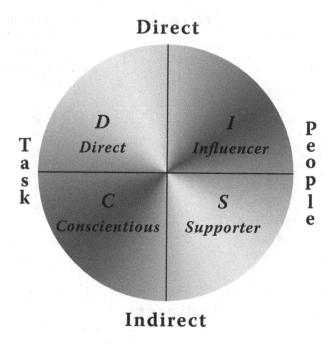

Figure 3-5 Understanding DISC

While focusing on the words *outside* the circle in the figure (i.e., ignoring the words inside the circle for now), answer these two questions about yourself:

1. Are you more direct or indirect in your communication style? *Wait!* Before you answer that, remember that I am not asking you what you think *others* think about you—I'm asking you to honestly appraise whether you are more direct or indirect. Do you get to the point quickly, or do you take your time? Do you have a problem with directness or do you enjoy it? Now, based on your answers, write down "Direct" or "Indirect" as your communication style.

2. Are you more task-oriented or people-oriented? When you are involved in a task at work, do you care more about getting it done or about the people that will help you get it done? Based on your answer to this question, write down "Task" or "People."

If I were taking this test, I would write down "Direct" and "Task." In Figure 3-5, the wedge that is between Direct and Task is labeled *D* for *direct*. See how fast that is?

Now fully assess yourself. Where did you end up? Now look at Figure 3-6 for more details.

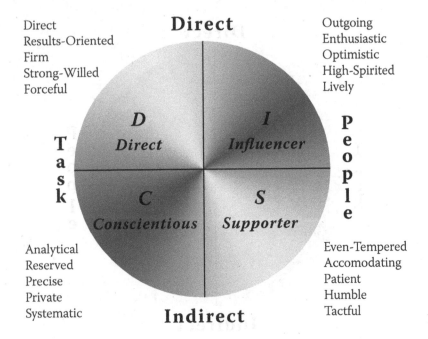

Direct
Results-Oriented
Firm
Strong-Willed
Forceful

Direct

Outgoing
Enthusiastic
Optimistic
High-Spirited
Lively

T
a
s
k

D
Direct

I
Influencer

P
e
o
p
l
e

C
Conscientious

S
Supporter

Analytical
Reserved
Precise
Private
Systematic

Indirect

Even-Tempered
Accomodating
Patient
Humble
Tactful

Figure 3-6 DISC in detail

Using myself as an example, I put myself in the *D* section and see that I am direct, results-oriented, firm, strong-willed, and forceful. That is just about a perfect description of me. (It's almost scary how accurate that is.) What does this mean, though?

I favor a direct *style of communication*. Remember, this is not a psych profile—it's a communication profile. And understanding this means you can see more clearly where you might have to alter your method of communication to better influence your target.

Now that you've answered my two test questions, you should have a pretty accurate assessment of yourself. But what does this mean when it comes to profiling other people? And how can you use that information?

Using DISC to Your Benefit

DISC profiling has been so effective that my team has used it on social media, voice calls, and even photos with alarming accuracy.

Robin Dreeke shared with me a story of a profile he built on a target by using only one photo of the guy. Let me paint the scene for you.

The photo shows a busy city street where there has been a car accident. It's not deadly—just a fender bender. The street is filled with people running toward the cars to see if everyone is okay. The target is standing with his back to the accident, not looking—his shoulders slumped down, and his hands in his pocket. That is all.

Based on the description of the scene, where would you put him on DISC diagram?

Think about those questions I asked you. Based on what I've told you about the photo, is the man more task-oriented or people-oriented? You really can't say "people-oriented," can you? So, the answer would seem to be "task-oriented."

Is he direct or indirect? While everyone else is focusing on the accident, he shows a lack of directness in that area. Robin guessed indirect.

That would put the target in the bottom-left segment, or in *C*, on the chart in Figure 3-6—which makes him analytical, reserved, precise, private, and systematic. He was heading somewhere, and that task took precedence over anything else. His body language did not scream outgoing or forceful, which lands him most accurately in the *C* region.

That ended up being a great profile for Robin to use, and if you read his book *It's Not All About "Me": The Top Ten Techniques for Building Quick Rapport with Anyone*, you can see exactly how it ended. (Hint: he was successful.)

I have been able to train people in our classes to learn how to make these kinds of assessments in a matter of minutes by just focusing on the four aspects of DISC and putting the person in the right quadrant. But what if you can't answer all of the questions perfectly?

Putting DISC to Work

Imagine if you couldn't tell whether I'm task-oriented or people-oriented, but you know whether I'm direct or indirect? You can still effectively communicate with me as a direct person, even if I'm also in the Conscientious or Supporter category.

The same would hold true if you knew I was in the Task category instead of the People category. You can communicate with me as either a *D* or *C* and be better off than if you communicate with me as an *S*. See how that works?

Here's a little test. Take a look at the Twitter page of our old friend Nick Furneaux, at `https://twitter.com/nickfx?lang=en`.

NOTE Nick is not a prolific tweeter. For that reason, you may have to think a little deeper in this exercise.

PRO TIP It is important to not get lost in retweets when doing this. Retweets do *not* give you an accurate picture of the person's communication style. I tend to look at all media and tweets that a person posts as their own.

Would you say Nick is more task-focused or people-focused? Read over his tweets and see where his comments seem to fall. I read them and think *task*, for sure. Now is his style direct or indirect? Hmm . . . this one seems a bit harder.

Take a look at the media he posted. I see very direct messages about *things*, not people. This confirms for me that Nick is more of a *D*.

Even if you cannot pinpoint someone 100%, you can get close. In the case of Nick, you can see he is definitely task-focused rather than people-focused. So guessing that he's a *D* or *C* would be okay.

Another secret of the trade is to look at some of the descriptors the person uses. Jump back to Figure 3-6 and look at the descriptor words next to both *D* and *C*. Which words describe what you see in Nick's tweets? Is he more direct, forceful, and results-oriented? Or is he precise, private, and systematic?

When I read these tweets, I certainly see more of a *D* than a *C*. Does this mean Nick is 100% a *D* communicator? Not exactly—sometimes people communicate a certain way depending on where, how, and with whom they're communicating. For instance, when I train, I tend to communicate more as an *I* than a *D*. It is better for me, the students and everyone else involved. If you wanted to influence me, you need to figure out how I communicate in the medium you are trying to influence me in.

Confused yet? Don't overthink this. Remember, this is one arrow in your quiver, and it helps you get closer to the target in the first few minutes of conversation.

Back to our example: If by now you have profiled Nick as a *D*, how do you then use this information to your benefit? To answer this, you first need to understand a little bit about how to communicate within each style whether you are in a position of authority or not.

The *D* Communicator

If you are going to communicate using an authority pretext:

- »   Be direct and straightforward
- »   Set firm boundaries
- »   Be brief and to the point
- »   Answer the *what*

If you are going to communicate using a more subdued pretext:

- »   Stress the *what*, not the *how*
- »   Give options but emphasize the result
- »   Focus on logic
- »   Agree with facts and positions, not just the person

The *I* Communicator

If you are going to communicate using an authority pretext:

- »   Be friendly and relaxed
- »   Allow the other person to do most of the talking
- »   Help their ideas get translated to action
- »   Answer the *who*

If you are going to communicate using a more subdued pretext:

- »   Stress the new and special
- »   Provide give and take
- »   Do not dominate
- »   Quote "experts" and testimonials

The S Communicator

If you are going to communicate using an authority pretext:

> » Be systematic and objective
> » Be relaxed and friendly
> » Use consistency and answer the *why*
> » Clearly define what you are asking for

If you are going to communicate using a more subdued pretext:

> » Be patient
> » Ask *how* questions
> » Make the focus about the team

The C Communicator:

If you are going to communicate using an authority pretext:

> » Be detailed
> » Be dependable
> » Provide recognition
> » Answer the *how*

If you are going to communicate using a more subdued pretext:

> » Use data and stats
> » Provide logic and facts
> » Stress reliability

Using the descriptions of each of the communication styles, let's do a little exercise. Assuming Michele is an *I* and I'm a *D*, what do I need to change to influence Michele? (You can also do this exercise by thinking about your own style and deciding what you'd need to change to influence Michele.)

I would want to be brief, factual, and to the point, but Michele prefers a friendly give-and-take exchange that not overly dominant. Do you see where the challenge comes in? I need to make sure that I can craft a pretext that allows me to hit the points that will make Michele happy and open the door for influence. To be a good influencer, you must think more about what the other person wants when communicating and less about how you prefer to communicate.

Understanding the Limitations

The great part is that this works whether you're communicating in person, on the phone, in an email, or over social media. You just need to figure out the target's communication style, your medium for delivery, and your goal for the communication. From there, the rest seems easy.

Please don't get fooled into thinking that this is a magic wand. There are factors that can add to the success or subtract from it. Just because you profile the target, make the right assessment, and craft a message that will tickle them in their communication happy zone doesn't mean you will always have 100% success. Sickness, stress, workload, and many other factors can affect someone's ability to communicate effectively. Need proof that there are limitations? Think about your kids (or the kids of people you know).

My daughter can melt my heart in a nanosecond. Despite her seemingly superhuman ability to get me to do almost anything, when I am under stress or there are too many things on my plate, I can be less patient and kind with her than I normally am. My communication method changes, which happens to everyone who's dealing with external circumstances.

Practice makes perfect though, so don't give up on this if you don't succeed the first couple dozen times. When you do get it right, it's amazing how well it works.

Here is another story: When my first book was released, I was asked to do a book signing. I hadn't expected that, and I was surprised by the nice line of people who had paid for my book and wanted me to sign it.

Many people said many nice things about my book and me—it was a little overwhelming, to say the least. One young man approached me —and talked for a solid minute about how my book changed his life. It had helped him through some rough times and even gave him a career path. I was so overwhelmed by this, I clearly remember thinking to myself, "Is this for real or another joke from Dave? Why would anyone say these things to me about *my* book?" I gave him a small smile, thanked him, and handed back his signed book. He was noticeably disappointed, but people were waiting in line behind him, so I moved on. About four or five other people came through the line, and the young man was standing over to the side with body language that clearly showed me that he wasn't happy.

Another young man came into the line and handed me his book to sign and said, "It was good, but there are about four things I saw that are really wrong, and you quoted Wikipedia four times. That is just bad as an author." I looked up at him, gave him a huge smile, and asked him to sit with me at the table so that when the line died down, he could show me where in the book he felt I went wrong.

As he came around the table to sit next to me, the first young man came running back to the table. He was very obviously angry now. He said a few expletives and then said, "I sat here and told you that you changed my life and how much of a fan I am, and you brushed me off like I don't even matter!!!! But this guy comes up and tells you that you suck, and you're his best friend???!?! What the . . . ?"

At that moment, I honestly had no response. I was dumbfounded by his anger, but I also understood it. I apologized and asked him to come sit and talk, but he was too upset. He walked out really angry.

It wasn't until much later as I replayed that whole scene in my head over and over that I clearly understand what had happened. That young man was an *I*, and he was communicating to me as an *I* would—energetic, outgoing, lively, friendly, and so on. His *I* communication style was so strong that I—as a strong *D*—didn't know how to process it, so I shut down and moved on. But when the second young man challenged me and told me how I could improve, his style resonated with me, and I wanted more.

What could I have done to fix the problem? Or better yet, what should I have done to avoid that problem altogether?

Communicate on the person's level. When the first young man came up with the flowery praise, I should have done the following:

» Asked him what part of the book really helped him

» Complimented him, if I could do so honestly and realistically.

» Actively listened and then offered to have him follow up for more conversation since the line was long

These things would have left him feeling validated and special rather than angry and tossed aside. The moral here is that even when you screw up, take the time to play it back in your head and see what you can learn from your mistakes.

Summary

DISC is a powerful tool that can get you closer to building rapport and making your target trust you and want to help you. Learn to read people quickly, and then learn how to apply your profile and adjust your style so you can communicate with your targets more easily.

Don't overcomplicate this process, though. Remember that even being able to place a person in just one half of the DISC circle will drastically up your game.

It is important to remember that DISC is not like street magic. You aren't going to become a human communication-modeling savant overnight (or maybe ever).

That shouldn't be your goal anyway. Your goal should be to keep the conversation focused on the person—not on yourself—and keep those two chemicals I mentioned in Chapter 1 (dopamine and oxytocin) flowing. By doing this, you will build trust and rapport, which makes your job as a social engineer easier.

At this point, you may be saying, "Wow, this is basically a recipe for weaponizing communications."

You aren't wrong. The fact is, many things that were not intended to be used as weapons are often weaponized. Automobiles are a good example of this.

I have a car that I love. I love driving it. It's a car I've always wanted, and now I have it. When Audi made the car, I don't think they planned on so many auto accidents being hit-and-runs. Yet according to a 2016 report by AAA Foundation for Traffic Safety, over 11% of all car-related accidents are hit-and-runs.

What's the point? The car can be a beautiful machine that is fun to drive and can take you places. It can also be a deadly weapon. It depends on the person and how they use it. Using DISC is the same.

My mantra at Social-Engineer, LLC, and during our five-day training is simple: "Leave them feeling better for having met you."

If you keep this in mind, the skills you will learn in this book will not only help you defend yourself and help you catch the attackers, but it can also help you be successful as a social engineering professional.

When you profile a person's communication style, do not look for ways to exploit them or manipulate them. Look for ways to alter your style so you can communicate with them on their level, in the way that makes them happy.

Practice what you've learned in this chapter with family and friends before you try your hand at applying it in social engineering. After you have sufficiently proven you're on the right path with the communication model, begin to put small requests for actions you want your target to take into your conversation. Test the waters.

When you see it working, you can start to move into the next topic—one that will take your skills to the next level—pretexting.

4 Becoming Anyone You Want to Be

Everything you can imagine is real.

—Pablo Picasso

If I could, I would have this chapter open with the *Mission: Impossible* theme song, but sadly we haven't figured out how to embed music into the pages of a book. But at least I have you thinking about that catchy tune, which is fitting for this chapter.

Becoming anyone you want be—which in social engineering is called *pretexting*—sounds super sexy. Some people define pretexting using words like *lie*, *falsehoods*, and other negative terms. However, I like to define pretexting in more general terms. The way I explain it in The Social Engineering Framework on my company's website (www.social-engineer.org/framework/influencing-others/pretexting) is this:

> *Pretexting is defined as the practice of presenting oneself as someone else in order to obtain private information. It is more than just creating a lie; in some cases it can be creating a whole new identity and then using that identity to manipulate the receipt of information. Pretexting can also be used to impersonate people in certain jobs and roles that they never themselves have done. Pretexting is also not a one-size-fits-all solution. A social engineer will have to develop many different pretexts over their career. All of them will have one thing in common: research.*

In one job, I had to break into seven different warehouses, and I decided to pose as a fire extinguisher inspector. In another job, we had to gain entry to the C Suite and the mail room of a company, so I pretended to be a pest control serviceman. For yet another job, I had to gain access to the security operations center (SOC) and network operations center (NOC), so I started off as an interviewee for a job, but after I gained access to the building, I had to switch to something else—so I posed as a manager from out of state. I've also presented myself as the head of human resources (HR) and a phone support rep. I could go on and on, but you get the idea: I've played lots of different roles.

The point is that there is no such thing as one pretext that fits all situations, and that is why this chapter is so important. I spend most of the chapter talking about the principles of pretexting and how you can apply them to any situation, whether you are social engineering via phone, email, social media, or in person. I take you through one job that I feel helps truly explain all these principles.

The following are the principles I discuss in this chapter:

» Thinking through your goals

» Understanding reality versus fiction

» Knowing how far to go

» Avoiding short-term memory loss

» Getting support for pretexting

» Executing the pretext

Pretexting can be one the most fun parts of the job, but it can also be one of the most dangerous. If you do not apply these principles, there can be drastic consequences. I will tell you stories of both successes and failures when it comes to pretexting.

Knowing how to pretext is vital if you want to have a career as a professional social engineer. It can truly make the difference between success and failure on the job.

The Principles of Pretexting

Before I delve into each one of the principles, I want to discuss a technique that has helped many aspiring social engineers: method acting or improvisation (aka *improv*).

Many cities offer method acting or improv classes that anyone can attend for a couple weekends. Many of the tips I give you in this book are covered in those kinds of classes, but the classes can give you something that a book can't help you with: experience.

A method acting or improv class can help you learn to step out of your comfort zone, get into character, and learn what is needed to successfully plan and execute pretexts in the wild. However, not everyone reading this book will be able to find a local class. No worries: you can purchase a DVD called *Uta Hagen's Acting Class* from Amazon.com (www.amazon.com/Uta-Hagens-Acting-Class-DVDs/dp/B0001Z3IHG). You can also find the video by searching YouTube. This excellent resource takes you through the steps of pretexting and getting into character.

However, even with a good acting class or video, you still need to know the six best tips for learning to pretext. Let's get started with the first one.

Principle One: Thinking Through Your Goals

Fire extinguisher inspector, pest control serviceman, HR manager—these are just a few of the pretexts I mentioned that I have used. How did I go about determining which one to use at each location or target?

It all starts with OSINT, where I dig into the details of the person or company and look for relevant stories, news, hobbies, likes, dislikes, events, and so on (and which I cover in more detail in Chapter 2, "Do You See What I See?"). These significant bits of data can tell me a lot about which pretext I should I focus on. But there is one other key piece of information that will determine which pretext jumps out of my arsenal into action: the goal. Understanding what it is I am trying to accomplish is more important than just understanding the business I am trying to infiltrate. Let me illustrate by telling you a story that I call, "The 18th-Floor Escapade."

I was hired to gain entry to the 18th floor of a secure building. The building was owned and operated by a property management company that was *not* my client (a company that produces online audio content). The only floor I was allowed to gain access to in this test was the 18th. Generally, this company does not allow walk-in appointments. The elevators were key-carded. And corporate headquarters was in another state.

During the OSINT phase, my team had found very little about the names and identities of the client company's employees who worked inside the target building. However, we did find a manager of the company's name as well as some of the content that manager produced there.Additionally, we located some documents on a file server that the company didn't intend to be public: a safety checklist, some internal communications newsletters, marketing material about upcoming projects, and a few other miscellaneous documents.

Based on just this information, what seems like a good pretext to you? Think about it for a second before reading on. Try to come up with at least one pretext.

Maybe you thought of an elevator repairman? That would give you reason to be in the elevator without alarming security. Maybe you thought of a rep from the company's headquarters who was at the office to conduct a surprise audit? Or maybe you thought of a different pretext that I didn't even mention here.

Here are a few other details that will help inform the pretext: My mission, if I did get inside the building and to the 18th floor, was to successfully take video and photos of exits and entryways. I was to take photos of any unlocked computers and try to get pictures of any papers or projects that were not public.

Given all those details, I had to make sure my pretext covered the ability to roam close to computers and desks, and I had to either have a camera out or be able to use a hidden camera to get the required photos.

An elevator repairman would have been a terrible pretext to accomplish the goals. Would it have gotten me in the building? Yes, but I wouldn't have gotten anywhere near my goals.

Posing as a representative from headquarters—might have gotten me into the building and onto the floor and even into offices, but there would have been limitations. I would have needed to know who worked in that office so my "surprise visit" could be fruitful.

From the safety checklist that I'd found on the file server, I learned that this company had strict guidelines about their staircase doors. They were never to be unlocked from the staircase. As a matter of fact, there weren't even supposed to be handles on the doors that were accessible from the stairwell.

Using this information, I developed a pretext that I was a third-party safety consultant. Because of a problem found in another branch, I had been sent to do quick 15-minute checks of the exits to ensure that proper policies were being followed. My visit was not announced, so the staff at the office I was visiting could be surprised and be found handling things correctly without any warning. To ensure the client that I was honest, I needed to record the whole event on my camera.

Do you see how having specific goals changed my pretext for the better? Having the full details enabled me to develop a part of the pretext that helped me achieve all my goals without causing alarm. Powerful, right?

Armed with this information, let's jump into the second principle, where I'll give you more details about "The 18th-Floor Escapade."

Principle Two: Understanding Reality vs. Fiction

This principle can be easily defined by explaining how much easier it is to remember your pretext if you base it in reality—for you and for the target. By this, I mean you should try to use pieces of your real life and use knowledge you already have or can easily assimilate. I often tell people that I think one of the hardest relationships to fake is a father-daughter relationship. I didn't understand this relationship until I had my own daughter. The way I talk about her and the emotions I feel are near impossible to fake, I think. If I didn't have a daughter but needed to build rapport with a target who did, it would be dangerous to have a pretext that includes a fake daughter. But, I can have a niece, right?

My point is that your pretext should be based on facts, emotions, and knowledge that you already possess or can easily fake. Going back to some of my proposed pretexts from the previous section, I know very little about elevators and their operation, so trying to fake my way as an elevator repairman would most likely have led to my failure if I were to be quizzed.

In addition, I tend to choose a name that I can easily answer to. Some people can answer to a name that is not theirs, but most choose to go with one that they have used or been called or that is a variation of their name.

This probably goes without saying, but generally, I try to stick with male characters for onsite, in-person social engineering. But I have pretexted as a female when doing online, social media, and even phone social engineering.

> **FUN FACT**
>
> Many companies in the United States have a policy that their support staff must never question a caller's gender. So, when someone with the name "Sally" calls in and has a voice like Barry White, you just don't ask. You risk offending the person if they have a voice that is unusual. With this knowledge, I have used the names Christina, Christine, and Laurie when making phone contact.

In terms of reality for the target, you should try to base your pretext on something that will keep your target in that alpha mode. (You might remember the discussion of alpha mode in Chapter 1, "A Look into the World of Social Engineering.")

If the subject is familiar to the target—meaning the words, titles, and context are expected—then you are more likely to leave the target in alpha mode so the person isn't alerted to potential danger.

For my "The 18th-Floor Escapade," I was using a document that I had found during OSINT. I wasn't trying to learn new skills, so I was not only in the reality zone for my targets but also in my own reality zone.

Sometimes, though, as you start to plan out the reality, you may have trouble trying to decide how much is too much.

Principle Three: Knowing How Far to Go

Knowing how far to go—without going too far—is very important. In my classes, I often have students who want to build whole lives for their pretexts. Some want to get as detailed as what they ate at their 11th birthday party.

When it comes to deciding how much detail to create, keep this in mind: people will only care about what they have to in order to complete the "social contract" you have created.

Let me elaborate on that a bit. In my safety-inspector pretext for "The 18th-Floor Escapade," what do you think the target cared about?

In this case, they didn't care about my kids' names, my dogs, or what I had for breakfast. They cared about the four questions I mention in Chapter 3, "Profiling People Through Communication":

» Who are you?

» What do you want?

» Are you a threat?

» How long will this take?

Let's think through what the target will want to know ASAP regarding my pretext:

Q: Who are you?

A: I am a safety inspector sent by corporate to do a *very* quick audit to ensure all policies are being followed.

Q: What do you want?

A: I just need about 15 minutes of your time to do this quick audit.

Q: Are you a threat?

A: There is an urgent need for me to do this, but no one is in trouble at all.

Q: How long will this take?

A: Hopefully less than 15 minutes.

The rest of the details are extras that the target doesn't need or care about. Does that mean you can go in unprepared? Not at all. You should still be prepared with some basic information about your "character" in case your target asks. So, I developed a pretext that followed a path like this:

I am Phil Williams, a 40-year-old safety inspector. I have one child. I'm married. I don't have any pets, but I love dogs and cats. I'm pretty boring; I go to work and go home. I've lived in X state for X years.

With that very basic pretext, what knowledge do I need to know to make sure I can pull it off?

- » Name of wife
- » Name of child
- » Age of child
- » The state
- » The city within that state
- » My job role and what I do for the company

That's basically it. Maybe there are a couple more tidbits that are worth planning, but for the most part, these basics are all I'd be asked to reveal.

Let me give you an example of a time when someone didn't know when to reel it in on the pretext: I was once working with a student on a homework assignment. He'd had a failure at approaching a stranger the night before, and to help him build confidence in the wake of that failure, we went to the hotel lobby so I could watch him engage with a stranger. My goal was to watch him engage to see where he was going wrong and then offer advice on how to "fix" it.

The student walked up to a woman and started off so nicely. He had a warm smile, and he was really friendly looking. The woman started to engage with him, and I saw her body language change to warm and friendly with her hips turned toward him. (You'll read more about body language in Chapter 8, "I Can See What You Didn't Say.") The student asked the woman where she was from, and she responded with a smile, "Philadelphia."

He says, "Oh really? That's amazing. Me, too!" Unfortunately, nothing was further from the truth. As I heard those words come from his mouth, I saw the train wreck starting in slow motion.

The woman replied, "Well, that's amazing! Where do you live?"

The student realized that he had just shoved not only a foot in his mouth but his whole leg. He replied, "Umm, you know. By that big bell thing . . ." His voice trailed off because he knew he was about to be hit head-on.

"The bell thing?" she asked. "You mean the Liberty Bell?"

"Oh, yeah. That is what I meant . . . ," he said sheepishly.

"First of all, I don't know what your game is, but 'bell thing'? No one from Philly would call it the 'bell thing.' And secondly, there is *no* housing near the bell thing. This conversation is over." She turned and walked away.

The student came over to me and said, "Man, that is basically my last two nights."

I asked him to tell me in detail how the last two nights' conversations went. As he described the conversations, the problem became clearer to me: he just agreed to whatever the target said without having the knowledge to back it up.

He took the lesson on "tribe mentality" (which I discuss in detail in Chapter 5, "I Know How to Make You Like Me") to mean he needed to join whatever tribe the target said they were in, and they would automatically love him.

FOR YOUR INFORMATION

So you don't have to wait until you read Chapter 5 to get the lowdown on tribe mentality, here's a brief description. Tribe mentality refers to fitting into the group (or "tribe") of people you are approaching, whether that is with your style of dress, language, culture, or other aspects of your characteristics. As a social engineer, it is preferable for you to try and fit into their tribe instead of making them try to fit into yours.

This student's experience is a good lesson in pretexting for all of us. It is important to have some knowledge of the details of your pretext. In the student's encounter with the woman from Philadelphia, all he would have needed to do to become part of her tribe was to change one sentence into a validating question, something like this: "Philly? I hear that's a great city to go be a tourist in. I've never been. What are your favorite things about Philly?" That would have told her he was listening and interested and wanted to learn more—instead of pretending that he had knowledge that he didn't.

Mastering this one concept can make a huge difference in the success you have with pretexting. After you are successful with the initial contact, people you interact with start to give you lots of details. All that detail can become hard to remember—which leads us to the next principle.

Principle Four: Avoiding Short-Term Memory Loss

It happens to all of us: you meet someone for the first time, engage in a good conversation, and then, as you are leaving, you can't remember the person's name. This can be a real deal-breaker for some folks, and it can make you appear as if you aren't interested in the person.

I have found there are more people who have a hard time remembering the details than those who have no problem at all. That is the reason this section is so important. You don't inspire confidence if you whip out a notebook mid-conversation to look at some details about your story. And it is even more concerning to the person you are speaking to if they catch you writing down details about them.

We have all heard the tips that say something like this: "Use the name as many times as you can in the first 20 seconds of hearing it, and you will remember it." That tip does work, but it doesn't always make practical sense to repeat a person's name rapidly right after hearing it. I can almost imagine meeting you for the first time, and as you exhale, you say, "Ah, Chris, Chris, Chris . . . yes Chris . . . Chris is your name. So, Chris, what were we talking about, Chris?"

Umm . . . creepy. Please don't do that when we meet.

With that said, I do find that using a person's name in some meaningful way can aid in remembering it. In "The 18th-Floor Escapade," as I entered the building and headed straight for the elevator, a security guard stopped me. She held one hand up and said, "Excuse me, where are you going?"

I stopped, knowing I would have to enter this into the report, "Oh, I'm so sorry, ma'am." I held my hand out and said, "I'm Phil Williams from *"[the name of the company, which I'd prefer not to divulge]* headquarters. We have an office here on the 18th floor."

She looked through a list she had on a clipboard and then said, "I'm sorry, Mr. Williams. I don't see your name on the list of approved visitors today."

"You are 100% right. My name won't be there. I'm sorry—I'm so rude. What is your name?" I said as I looked at her name badge. "Claire, nice to meet you."

I paused for only a second, "See, Claire, we had an incident at one of our locations due to some safety policies not being followed, and I was sent out to visit our NE offices to ensure that all policies are being followed. These need to be surprise visits, so we can ensure that the findings are legit."

"I see." Claire said.

"And one of the sections on this report is front-desk security. I'm happy to have your name, so I can report that you followed all procedures perfectly. I have your first name—and how do you spell your last name?" As I said this, I pulled out my pen, looked down at my clipboard, and wrote her first name on my own list.

She didn't even pause before she said, "Farclay. That's F-A-R-C-L-A-Y."

"Okay, Ms. Farclay. You have gotten this audit off to a great start. Thank you for that. Now, what I hope to find is that my surprise visit ends with as high marks as you will get."

She then did something I had not expected. "Well, Mr. Williams, how about I badge you to 18, and you can see if your surprise audit yields some positive results?" she offered.

"Claire! Wait, can I call you Claire?" She nodded, so I continued, "Claire, you are a genius! That is a great idea."

With pride, she walked her new friend (me) over to the elevator bays and used her security badge to open the doors and then badge me to the 18th floor. I thanked her and said, "I will see you in 15 minutes."

So, what was the key for me in that situation?

» Using the guard's name a few times in quick order

» Having as part of my pretext a reason to write everything down

For me, although these techniques work wonders, they're not always practical. For that reason, you need to have other methods in your arsenal. I employ a few different techniques:

» **The business card:** Exchanging business cards with a target is a great way to get all their details. But don't start off with this—wait until you build some rapport or are leaving.

» **Recording devices:** I sometimes record both audio and video of live engagements and audio of phone engagements to ensure I capture all the details. This can be a great tool, but make sure to get permission from the company before you record anything or anyone on their premises.

» **A partner:** I find it helpful to have someone else work with me so that person can help remember the details while I focus on other things.

All these ideas are great for keeping the details safe for the report that will follow, but they are not too useful for remembering the details while you're in the middle of an engagement.

Here are a few tips:

» **Practice.** As often as you can, practice remembering details where and when it's not part of your job to do so—family gatherings, parties, meetings at the office, sales calls, and other times when you are engaging with someone.

Challenge yourself to remember things like the color of a person's shirt, what kind of jewelry they were wearing, their full name, or other details you would not normally care about.

For me, memory works like a muscle. The more I exercise it, the better and stronger it gets.

» **Read.** I've found that spending some time reading an actual printed (hardcover or paperback) book helps my memory. There's no book in particular that I suggest you use for this purpose—just read something that's not on a screen. I don't have science to back this up this suggestion, but I can tell you that the more time I spend exercising my brain, the better it "stretches" when I need it to. I have also spent time solving math problems to enhance my ability to remember details.

My final tip for this section is that when you have short breaks, take a few minutes to record your thoughts. I do this in one of two ways: by writing down the details I need to remember or by using a voice-recording app on my phone.

When Claire badged me to floor 18 in the elevator, I whipped out my phone and hit the recording app so I could speak all the details I could remember into the program. This serves two purposes. First it helps me with my reporting later. More importantly, I find that when I say the details out loud, it helps me recall them later.

My quick recording went like this:

Claire Farclay. About 5 feet, 4 inches, blonde, medium-build security guard wearing white shirt, badge, black pants. Badge on left breast area. Pictures of two dogs at security desk. Used clipboard. Build rapport by praising that she followed procedures. Badged me to 18 using white HID badge she had clipped to a retractable lanyard on her right hip. Code she entered into elevator pad was 4381.

I just recalled those details from memory even though "The 18th-Floor Escapade" took place more than two years ago. That's how powerful this is for me now.

The next arrow to add to your quiver for successful pretexting is *support*.

Principle Five: Getting Support for Pretexting

I want you to stop and picture the pretext I have been using in this chapter: a safety auditor for a corporation. Now answer these questions:

» What would a safety auditor wear?

» What tools or supplies would a safety auditor have?

» Is there any special knowledge a safety auditor would need to have?

The answers to these questions are the basis for this section. Let's consider each one separately so we can clearly see how this principle plays out.

Q: What would a safety auditor wear?

A: I've found that these types of auditors generally wear khakis or jeans, a button-up shirt, and sneakers or work boots. They are clean-cut.

Q: What tools or supplies would a safety auditor have?

A: In my research, I discovered that they have a camera, phone, clipboard, pens and markers, paper, a checklist, and sometimes a measuring tape (depending on the job).

Q: Is there any special knowledge a safety auditor would need to have?

A: The answer to that question might require a few other questions being answered. As a safety auditor do I need to understand how fire extinguishers work? Do I need to understand how fire doors, alarms, or other aspects of the building work? Or is it okay that I am there to just check things off a list? Additionally, what should I know about the company I am trying to gain access to? What should I know about the company that I am pretending to be a part of?

I was once breaking into a building with Michele, and a security guard to whom I had given a fake business card asked me where I lived because he'd never heard of my company. I wasn't expecting that question, so I pointed to the west and said, "Oh, I live over in that direction."

The guard replied, "In the industrial sector? Where did you find housing there?"

I realized that I was about to get caught, so I said, "Oh, I meant past the industrial sector. You know, in the housing past that?"

"I am sorry, sir. I don't mean to be a jerk, but your business card says, 'Family Owned for 20 years,' and you don't even know the area where you live?" the guard questioned respectfully.

My fatal flaw here was not having enough knowledge of my pretext area that I could answer questions intelligently.

I could not have foreseen that I would be asked this question, so the guard definitely gets points for being aware, but I didn't make that mistake again. From then on, if I had a business card that said I had been there for some period, my supporting information was ready to prove that true.

More often than not, though, I'd rather make things easy, so I allow my pretext to be that I am new in the area or from out of town. That gives me freedom to not have to know everything about the location where I am.

In "The 18th-Floor Escapade," I found that having the clipboard enabled me to not just look the part, but it also allowed me to have the very thing I needed to support my detail recording. Because I looked the part, Claire had no reason to question my motives.

And that brings us to the last principle: execution. It almost seems if you follow the five preceding principles, the very last one should be easier to implement.

Principle Six: Executing the Pretext

Execution of the pretext means so much more than just applying the first five principles. By the time you're executing the pretext, nerves, unforeseen events, and— the wildcard—other humans are thrown into the mix, which means anything can happen.

I have been doing this now for close to a decade, and I still get nervous for every gig—whether it's walking into a place or picking up the phone or clicking Send on an email. Did I forget something? Will they catch me? Will I fail? These questions always race through my mind as I am starting off.

The following things help me execute the pretext more easily:

» Practice

» Stretch and breathe

» Communicate

» Do *not* use a script

It is important to remember that even with all the previous preparation there is still the unknown factor: the very observant employee, the overzealous guard, or the locked door you didn't plan for. In other words, you have to be prepared to be flexible.

Practice

If it is a phishing email, I make sure to send it to myself and some colleagues to get feedback. I also like to have my colleagues click the link or open the document to ensure everything is working. When I'm vishing, I make sure I have all supporting background sounds, information, and details ready on my screen. I also do a test call to ensure my spoofing is working. When I'm SMiShing, I send the message to another cell phone or myself to ensure it is formatted correctly and the link works. And if I'm impersonating my way into a building, I practice my opening lines and make sure I have my details solidly fixed in my mind before I even get in the car. I also ensure all my cameras and any other equipment or tools are working.

As Paul Kelly, a protégé of Dr. Ekman (who was introduced in Chapter 2), once taught me: "Perfect practice makes perfect." Practice doing it right, so your muscle memory is ready to snap into action.

Practice can make the difference between success and failure. At one of my jobs, after arriving at the location and grabbing my equipment from the trunk, I flipped the switch and discovered the camera had dead batteries. I ended up having to use the camera on my cell phone. I remember walking into that building, and all I could think about was whether my phone would work, if it would keep recording, or if it would be huge tell that I was holding my phone in a very conspicuous way.

Stretch and Breathe

This might sound silly, but I spend just a few moments taking some deep breaths and stretching. Additionally, depending on how nervous I am, I might spend a few minutes in a power pose to help build some confidence before I execute my pretext and attack. (You'll read more about power poses in Chapter 8.)

Communicate

As a professional social engineer, I make sure I communicate to the proper degree with my client. For example, the day before I launch a phishing campaign, I tell our point of contact that I am phishing the next day. (Of course, if I'm running a full black-box pen test, I only communicate this information after completion.) I do the same for vishing campaigns. This is especially important when I'm doing an impersonation gig. I will make sure my point of contact knows when it will occur, so that if there are complications, there is someone I can contact.

I got caught during one engagement. Well, that's not entirely true—the client wanted me to tell security that I was a pen tester *after* I had been successful. I told the client repeatedly that this was a terrible idea, but they insisted. It went something like this:

After successfully walking through security as a trash compactor repairman and gaining access to the whole facility unsupervised, I was leaving and said, "Sir, I just need to tell you before I leave, my name is not Paul as my ID says. It is Chris, and I am what you call a pen tester. I was testing the security of your building and the policies for entry."

As I spoke I saw the security guard's face change to anger, and his hand went to his side where he had was a stun gun. He said, "You are *what*? Am I getting fired?"

I tried to calm him down by saying, "Sir, no one is getting fired. This was just a test, so we can help your company employ new policies to tighten security."

However, he was already on his radio, calling the head of security, and he hit a button to lock the mantrap so I couldn't escape.

The head of security came out. The man I had just duped explained the situation in a very derogatory and angry way. I tried to interject, and the guard snapped, "No one is talking to you, Paul or Chris or whatever you say your name is."

I said, "I'm going to pull a letter out of my pocket that you should read." I handed them the "Get out of jail free" letter, as I like to call it. This letter is written by the client company to detail who I am, what I am doing, and that I have permission to do it. It also gives one or two contact numbers of people to back up my story.

After reading the letter, the head of security said, "How do I know this letter isn't a lie? Huh, Chris?"

"Well, that is a very good question. And to be honest, you don't. But just call one of those contact people and this will all get cleared up.", I said in my most agreeable voice.

"I am *not* calling anyone on this paper. For all I know, this number rings to your crime buddies out in the van." (I thought, "Darn, *that is a good point, and also a great idea for a future gig. Thanks Mr. Head of Security*".)

He continued, "I'm calling someone I know in corporate." He picked up the phone and dialed an extension. He rattled off the story and then asked, "Do you know anything about this?"

I could overhear the voice on the end of the line said, "I don't know anything about a pen test. Call the cops."

I was escorted to and then locked into a utility closet. (I'm not even kidding.) Fortunately, in their haste, the guards left me with my cell phone and my lock picks. In a few minutes, I was out of the closet, had unlocked the office door, and was sitting in the hallway calling my point of contact to tell him to get this fixed *now*! And am I thankful I called him the night before to ensure he was going to be in. A few minutes later, this was all squared away, and I was leaving free and un-tased.

As this story illustrates, you have to make sure you communicate with the right people about the right things at the right time. I know this is vague, but that's because the requirements and rules change per job, per task, and per client. Some clients require significantly more hand-holding than others. Just remember, you are an SE *professional*, so you must ensure your clients are happy.

Do Not Use a Script

This advice is mainly directed to you Cs on the DISC chart, who want a ton of detail and every step outlined. (Chapter 3 covers the DISC profile and what a C is in detail.) Having a script, whether for vishing or impersonation, removes your ability to be dynamic. I guarantee you one thing: nothing will go exactly as planned. Having the ability to be dynamic gives you a leg up and a higher success ratio.

Summary

I suggest you spend time reviewing the six principles of pretexting, so you can better perfect them. Remember that each principle builds on the next principle and will help you become a stronger social engineer in the process.

Planning your goals efficiently can help you come up with reality-based pretexts that keep the target in beta mode (refer to Dr. Langer's research in Chapter 1). Using reality rather than all fiction will make it easier for you to stay in pretext and make it easier for the target to believe you. Having your pretext firmly based in reality helps you determine how far you should go for that particular job, so your effort is at the right level and not too much or too little. Keeping it simple also helps boost your memory retention for not only the facts of your pretext but also whatever information you obtain (so you can recall it easier). All this planning makes it easy to decide what outfits, gear, and tech you need to support your pretext. If you have made it this far, you can easily execute the pretext.

Please remember that your pretext can make or break your whole engagement. Just imagine if you had gone with me to those warehouses, but you had shown up with a smart business suit and a briefcase. Does that fit the identity of a trash compactor repairman?

That example might be extreme, but I want you to get the point. If you start to sense that you are getting caught, you *will* get nervous. And nervousness will wreck your smoothness, your memory, and your ability to think quickly.

The pretext, when done right, helps answer those four questions I spoke about in Chapter 3: Who are you, what do you want, are you a threat, and how long will this take? But there is another purpose of those questions that needs to be addressed, which is the topic of Chapter 5, and it has to do with building rapport.

5 I Know How to Make You Like Me

Rapport is the ability to enter someone else's world, to make him feel that you understand him, that you have a strong common bond.

—TONY ROBBINS

OilHater was the nickname of a person who truly hated the oil industry. This man, who was very educated and well spoken, articulately explained on blogs and forums how awful fracking was to the environment and how it was going to ruin the earth for future generations. As his posts gained popularity and he gained a following, more and more anger was evident in his posts.

NOTE Names in this example have been changed for security.

After months of building his reputation, OilHater started to threaten violence. Posts started to discuss how blowing up fracking stations might be the way to go to stop these heinous attacks on Mother Nature. He even mentioned a few fracking stations in certain areas of Texas that he would like to target.

At this point, Paul started appearing in forums all over the Internet that spoke about the dangers of fracking. Paul was a concerned father of two young kids. A huge oil company started fracking in his area, and he wanted to know how to protect his kids from any potential harm.

The forum was full of helpful people who offered Paul advice on what to do and how to protect his family from damage to water sources and soil. Paul kept posting to the forums, asking questions that an unknowledgeable person would ask.

One day, OilHater answered a message from Paul with extensive knowledge, even correcting a few erroneous posts from other forum members. Paul thanked OilHater for helping him work through some of the confusing information he had received from multiple posters. Paul then complimented OilHater's knowledge by asking if he worked for the oil industry because he seemed to know so much about it.

OilHater explained that he was just a very concerned citizen who had spent hours educating himself on the damage the oil industry was doing. Paul asked if he could private message OilHater with some personal questions. During that private conversation, Paul shared with OilHater that he was from Texas and that he was very curious about that area and asked if it was as dangerous as OilHater had mentioned in his previous answers.

OilHater chimed right in and knew all about that area and how dangerous it was. Paul continued to probe about what could be done. It seemed as OilHater got angrier, Paul became angrier. Paul continued to treat OilHater as the expert on these matters and continued to ask questions.

Paul grew outraged that there was nothing that could be done to stop the fracking operations and save his children. He jokingly said in one conversation, "It seems like the only way to stop them is to blow them off the face of the earth. Too bad we can't."

OilHater replied, "Don't be so sure."

Paul enquired what OilHater meant by that, but OilHater went silent for a bit. Paul continued to post on the forums about how upset he was and that the area where he lived in Texas was under siege by the oil industry.

After about a week, OilHater sent a private message to Paul, saying that he had a plan to help stop fracking and that it would help Paul's kids. Paul excitedly replied that he wanted to help but wasn't sure what he could do.

OilHater told him that he had a plan but wasn't sure Paul would want to help. He then said, "It might be dangerous."

Paul said something like "I might need to take on some danger to save my kids. What do you have in mind?"

OilHater said, "Sometimes our hands have to get dirty to clean up a mess. Do you agree?"

Paul replied, "I get that. I just don't want my kids to end up with cancer or worse, and those crooks are making millions and don't care about the suffering of us little guys."

OilHater replied, "Do you remember how you said once that the only way to stop them would be to blow them off the face of the planet? We are going to make sure they can't frack for a while."

Paul said, "I'm curious now. I've never done anything like this, but my kids deserve better. What do you think we can do?"

OilHater said, "Are you familiar with Peg's Diner downtown?"

Paul replied, "Yes, I go there often."

OilHater said, "Can you meet me there Thursday night at 7:30 p.m.?"

Paul answered, "Yes, sure. But how will I know who you are?"

OilHater said, "Come to the diner and sit in a booth in the far back corner. Wear a baseball cap. I will approach you."

Paul put up some resistance at this point and said, "I'm sorry, but that seems a little weird. Can I just get your name? My full name is Paul Wilcox, and I live at 123 Main Street. I just want to know who I'm dealing with."

"Sure, sorry for being so secretive," OilHater replied, "I'm just used to being anonymous online. I'm Robert Moore. I'll meet you at Peg's at 7:30 in that booth."

At 7:30 that Thursday night, Robert was met not by Paul Wilcox but by a member of law enforcement who ensured his plans could not come to light.

If you haven't guessed by now, I was Paul Wilcox. This three-and-a-half-week project defines the very essence of what this chapter is about: how building rapport with your targets can get them to trust you. For the rest of this chapter, I will refer to this as Operation Oil.

This chapter is based on the 10 principles that Robin Dreeke outlines in his 2011 book, *It's Not All About "Me": The Top Ten Techniques for Building Quick Rapport with Anyone*. Although Dreeke was writing about everyday communications, I will show you how you can apply these principles to social engineering as well.

Before I get started with the 10 principles, I need to talk a little about something I did in Operation Oil that allowed me to start building rapport. It's something so basic but so profound that if you do not do this, you will most likely fail.

The Tribe Mentality

As a social engineer, you must establish that you are a part of the target tribe before you can even begin building rapport. A *tribe* is simply what identifies a certain group—maybe it is a style of clothing, a group task, an attitude, or shared interest. The commonality among the members of the group creates the "tribe." To establish yourself as part of a tribe, you need to figure out what aspects you need to mirror to become part of that tribe.

It might be easy to imagine how this works if you think back to high school. The clothing you wore quickly identified you in the tribe.

There's a video titled "The Tribe Mentality – THE BYSTANDER EFFECT" (https://vimeo.com/265364702) that demonstrates how important being part of the right tribe is for all of us. In the video, actors are dressed in non-business attire and lie on the ground, calling out for help, in busy subway stations where business people travel. During one session in London, the actor lay on the ground for more than 20 minutes before anyone came to his aid.

Before you judge any of the folks who passed by the actor without helping, think about the scenario. A man in jeans and a T-shirt, and a jacket, is lying on the ground in the middle of a subway station, and he's calling out for help as he holds his stomach. Now try to answer the four questions (which were introduced in Chapter 3, "Profiling People Through Communications") from the perspective of a person passing by this actor, without knowing they are an actor.

Who is this person? You just don't know. Maybe he's a drug addict? Or maybe a scam artist? Is he really sick? Can I get sick if I help him?

What does this person want? Maybe he wants money. And maybe you really want to help, but you're late for a meeting. Or maybe this man just wants you to stop so he can steal your wallet or your kidneys.

Is this person a threat? What if this man is a thief or drug addict, and when you kneel to help, he shanks you in the liver? Or what if he is really sick, and it's communicable?

How long will this take? This man isn't holding a jar for money, so this may take a while. What if you have to get this man to the hospital, and it takes all day?

There are legitimate reasons why a passerby would not be able to answer those four questions, which would make him or her hesitant to lower their shields and help the actor. Later in the video, though, the scenario is changed a bit. The same actor is dressed in a suit and lying on the ground. Guess how long it took to get help? About six seconds. When the people who stopped to help were interviewed, they said things like: "Well, he was in a suit, so I wanted to help." And, "He must have been really sick to lie on the ground in a suit."

The only thing that changed about the situation was the actor's clothing, but that one alteration allowed the passersby to have different answers to the four questions:

Who is this person? He is one of us, and he needs help.

What does this person want? He wants help, and I should give it to my fellow businessperson.

Is this person a threat?

»   Obviously not, because he is well dressed.

How long will this take?

»   It doesn't really matter, because he is one of "us" and he needs my help.

The suit and the location put the actor in the right tribe to get help. Tribe mentality is that strong. Think about it: Nothing really changed that could provide clearer answers to three of the four questions. The passersby didn't really know who the man on the ground was, how long helping him would take, or if he was a threat. They knew only that he wanted help.

In the Operation Oil scenario, I was a concerned citizen who grew angrier and more hateful toward an industry that the target already had hatred for. The more knowledge I was given, the more anger and hopelessness I exhibited, which is what put me in the same tribe as OilHater.

Both Operation Oil and the "Tribe Mentality" video support the power of the pretexting I discuss in Chapter 4, "Becoming Anyone You Want to Be." The pretext helps tremendously to get you into the right tribe. Once you are in the tribe, there are 10 principles of rapport-building that can keep your target talking to you for as long as you want.

Building Rapport as a Social Engineer

How would you define rapport? When I ask this question in my class, I get a slew of different answers. Many students use words and phrases like "developing relationships," "trust," and "making them comfortable." I really like the definition of rapport that I have been using for a few years that I combined from a few differing defintions:

> *Building a bridge for communication based on trust and common interests.*

Building a bridge is a nice mental picture for me, and the 10 principles of rapport discussed in this chapter do just that. They allow the person you're interacting with to feel comfortable as you cross over that "bridge" into their tribe. Before I tell the back story to how these 10 principles came about you need to understand why trust is so powerful.

The Moral Molecule

In episode 44 of *The Social-Engineer Podcast,* I was privileged to have Dr. Paul Zak as my guest. As I mentioned in Chapter 1, "A Look into the *New* World of Professional Engineering," Dr. Zak wrote the amazing book *The Moral Molecule: How Trust Works* (Dutton, 2012). In this book, Dr. Zak wrote about his research into oxytocin. For many years, oxytocin was ignored by researchers, but Dr. Zak decided he would figure out how it gets released into the bloodstream and what happens when it is.

Dr. Zak found many reasons oxytocin could be released into the blood, but all of them have to do with trust and the emotions involved. One anecdote he relates on that podcast is about a time when he was the victim of a classic scam called the Pigeon Drop. When he was a young man, Zak worked in a gas station. One day, a patron came in to report that he'd found a box of jewels in the bathroom. As this "good citizen" was turning over the box to Zak so he could put it in the gas station's lost and found, the phone rang. On the phone was a frantic man looking for his box of jewels. The caller was so elated that his jewels had been found, he offered a $200 reward to the honest man who had turned them in.

The man who found the jewels said he couldn't wait for the owner to arrive with the reward money, because he needed to be at a job interview. So, the caller suggested what appeared to be an amazing solution: Zak could simply remove $100 from the gas station's cash register and give it to the man who'd found the jewels. When the reward came in, Dr. Zak could keep $100 for himself and replace the $100 he took from the till. The scam-artist caller made Zak feel like he was part of a tribe by trusting him with two things: a share in the money prize for finding the "jewelry" and the responsibility of making someone else happy. He was scammed by this dynamic duo.

It wasn't until Dr. Zak was doing research for his book that he realized what that scam artist had done. When the caller made Zak feel like he was part of a trusted and special group, Zak's brain released oxytocin, which caused his brain to associate a positive feeling with the caller. So, when the caller requested that Zak give the man who found the jewels $100 out of the cash register, he happily complied.

The power of trust can make a person do something they instinctively know is not the best thing to do.

When you apply the 10 principles of rapport building that I cover in this chapter, you help the brain (both yours and your target's) release oxytocin. That release makes the target feel trust toward you. The thing that amazes me about Dr. Zak's research is that those feelings can return later just because someone thinks about or deals with the reason the oxytocin was originally released (which will be you, if you've been successful in developing rapport with your target).

Another important chemical is the neurotransmitter called dopamine. As René Riedl and Andrija Javor noted in an article titled "The Biology of Trust: Integrating Evidence from Genetics, Endocrinology, and Functional Brain Imaging" (*Journal of Neuroscience, Psychology, & Economics*, 2012, http://psycnet.apa.org/buy/2011-27428-001), dopamine is the main neurotransmitter associated with how our brains reward us. The article also notes that the combination of dopamine and oxytocin is critical in creating social settings. In essence, dopamine and oxytocin contribute to the processes that build trust as well as reinforce positive social interactions.

Are you seeing the importance of understanding the role of both dopamine and oxytocin? If you can learn how to properly use rapport and trust, you can build a bridge between yourself and your target. Developing that relationship will result in your target feeling happy (and better for having met you), which will, of course, lead to a stronger bond.

The 10 Principles of Building Rapport

For episode 20 of *The Social-Engineer Podcast*, I was out of town at a training gig. I was set up in the hotel to record the podcast, but the guest I had planned canceled on me at the last minute, which was going to ruin my record of always releasing the podcast on every second Monday of the month. I thought, "Who has joined us in the past who was a great guest and is someone I can call at the last minute to beg to be on the show?"

I shot my buddy Robin Dreeke a quick email, told him my plight, and asked if he could step in. He replied quickly with, "Yes, of course. But what topic do you want?"

Without thinking, I blurted out, "The top techniques to build rapport with anyone fast."

He said, "Give me an hour to jot down my thoughts."

An hour later, we recorded the podcast that would not only become legendary but would lead to Robin's first book. These are the 10 principles Robin covered in the podcast and later wrote about:

» Using artificial time constraints

» Accommodating nonverbals

> » Using a slower rate of speech

> » Employing sympathy or assistance themes

> » Suspending your ego

> » Validating others

> » Asking how, why, and when questions

> » Making use of quid pro quo

> » Employing reciprocal altruism

> » Managing expectations

Robin's book covers each of the principles in detail. I cover them from the aspect of a professional social engineer and, when applicable, relate them to Operation Oil.

Using Artificial Time Constraints

A time constraint is simply a constraint on your time during any engagement with another person. Adding the word *artificial* to it just means you are making up that time constraint—in truth, there is no constraint related to time. Why is this important to you as a social engineer? Think about the fourth question you need to answer for your targets: How long will this take?

An artificial time constraint does answer that question. Your artificial time constraint can be completely made up and fake, but it must be believable. When developing a time constraint, you need to consider the following things:

> » If the time constraint is too quick or too artificial, it does not hold the weight it needs to. For instance, consider this common question: "Can I talk to you for one second?" Any person you speak to will know that "one second" is not a real time constraint, so your request loses its validity.

> » The time constraint must also be realistic for the pretext you chose to use. For example, if you engage with a person in the grocery line, there is a built-in time constraint: when you get to the end of the line. You don't need to work hard to make a time constraint, you just need to work *within* the time constraint you have.

In Operation Oil, I was able to use the built-in constraints of private messaging on forums as a form of time constraints. If I had included a long diatribe of my "personal feelings," my target would have had to commit to reading them all before we developed a relationship. By keeping my messages short and to the point but emotional, I was able to limit the time that was needed for the target to reply to me, so OilHater did not feel pressured to get too involved until we built rapport. The more personal and invested our conversations got, the longer the messages became.

Accommodating Nonverbals

This principle is simple to understand, but it's hard to implement it until you practice. Accommodating nonverbals means that your nonverbal body language needs to match the pretext you are using.

Suppose that you are at your favorite department store with your young child. As you're shopping, a person who looks a little rushed approaches you and says, "I'm heading to a party, and I'm really late. It's for my nephew, who's about the same age as your son. I forgot to buy a present. Can you tell me what kids his age like?"

As you picture this scene, answer this question: Where should the person who approached you be facing? Forget about whether social engineering is involved.

Should this person be facing toward your kid? Nope—that's creepy. A person who faces your kid would probably set off all sorts of nonverbal radar flares and make you defensive.

Should the person face you? That would be less creepy, but it's not truly congruent with what said the person is saying. Therefore, it could seem aggressive.

It would make the most sense if the person was facing toward the store items or the door, because they're in a rush. That is how nonverbal body language accommodates what is being said.

When nonverbal body language matches what is being said, the target can answer the third question—"Are you a threat?"—and allow rapport to be properly built.

Here's the reason I said this principle is hard to implement: I've been doing this for more than a decade, and I still get very nervous before every vishing or impersonation job I do. If you're like me and most other folks, nervousness makes you tense. And that tension makes your muscles rigid and stiff. If your pretext doesn't involve tension or pressure, then your nonverbals will not accommodate your pretext. (Chapter 8, "I Can See What You Didn't Say," goes into more detail regarding nonverbals.)

In essence, it's hard to combat your own emotions while trying to maintain realism in your pretexts—at least for those of us who aren't sociopaths. And because I'm writing this book for those of you who are not sociopaths but are fledgling professional social engineers, controlling your nonverbal cues might not always be easy.

FUN FACT

A sociopath does have a conscience, according to Michael Tompkins, EdD, who is a psychologist at the Sacramento County Mental Health Treatment Center. But a sociopath's conscious is weak. A sociopath can easily justify the wrong he does as long as it benefits him, and he lacks empathy, which is one of the key building blocks of human communications.

I don't suggest that you script the nonverbals for your engagement, but I do suggest that you at least understand clearly what would be normal for the pretext you are choosing and then have that in mind before you launch.

This advice is not just for in-person social engineering—it also applies to any vishing you do. Poor posture can lead to tension in the muscles of your voice box or larynx, which can affect vocal quality and increase the strain on your voice. If your posture is poor or your tension is high, this can easily come across in your voice and lead to you not building rapport.

In Operation Oil, I did not have to worry about this principle.

Using a Slower Rate of Speech

What happens if you try to talk too fast about a topic that you are unfamiliar or uncomfortable with? You may stutter or stumble over words. Additionally, you may find yourself using *word whiskers*, which are expressions like "um," "like," and other short, filler words. This can cause your listeners to think you lack knowledge and confidence.

However, if you speak too slowly, listeners might view you as lacking knowledge or as being condescending. You must strike a balance between too fast and too slow.

How can you determine the perfect speed at which to talk during an engagement? It's as simple as R.S.V.P.:

R: Rhythm

S: Speed

V: Volume

P: Pitch

Try to listen to and match the person you are communicating with. The other person's R.S.V.P. will give you a good indication how you should be communicating.

WARNING When I say you should pay attention to the other person's R.S.V.P., I *don't* mean that you should try to match his or her accent. It doesn't matter how good you think you are at accents, unless you have a dialect coach at your beck and call to help you perfect the little nuances, it's better to not even try. Getting caught doing a bad accent is a rapport killer, and it's also insulting. However, you can try using colloquialisms that can make you sound a local. For example, what someone in the United States calls a *subway*, the British call a *tube*. What I call a *hoagie*, someone from Boston calls a *grinder*. Learning the local lingo can help you to blend in while you use R.S.V.P. to pick the perfect speed.

This is another principle to keep in mind as a social engineer, and it matches well with the last principle. You not only want to notice the R.S.V.P. of your target, but you should also make sure it matches your pretext. If your pretext is that you have an upcoming interview with HR, which would probably stress you out, it wouldn't really match if you seemed as calm as can be and were speaking overconfidently.

Employing Sympathy or Assistance Themes

There's a fascinating study called "Mirror Neuron and Theory of Mind Mechanisms Involved in Face-to-Face Interactions: A Functional Magnetic Resonance Imaging Approach to Empathy" that was conducted by researchers Martin Schulte-Ruther, Hans J. Markowitsch, Gereon R. Fink, and Martina Piefk (www.ncbi.nlm.nih.gov/pubmed/17651008). It discusses the effect that an empathy-based request for assistance has on a fellow human. The study makes the point that just viewing someone who's making an emotional request can trigger areas of the brain related to first-hand emotional pain experience.

In other words, if the sympathy or assistance request is handled properly, the person being asked will have a strong emotional connection to that request. That connection can make it next to impossible for the person to refuse to help.

Marketers know this, which is why many campaigns include pictures and/or background music that invoke certain emotions as requests are being made. Amazingly, this seems to work even if you are not face-to-face with the target. Although the connection is more powerful when facial expressions are involved, they're not necessary to trigger the needed emotional connection. The voice or a vivid description that causes the target to picture a scene can create an empathetic response.

This principle is very effective for social engineers. Throughout history, conmen, scammers, phishers, and—even more maliciously—serial killers have used sympathy and assistance themes in getting their targets to do things they should not do.

Here's a tip that applies to all the principles, but it's especially relevant for this principle: The level of the assistance you request must be equal to the level of rapport you have built. If someone you've just met and your lifelong best friend both ask you to help them move furniture for the day, which request are you most likely going to honor first? You're probably going to choose to assist your lifelong friend first because the level of rapport you have with a person helps you make the decision to devote time and effort to helping. If someone with whom you have no rapport requests assistance that's too personal or too great, it has the reverse effect of building rapport and can make you suspicious.

Let me use Operation Oil to help solidify these points. At first, my sympathy and assistance request merely involved going to the forums and asking for help with understanding fracking because I was worried for my kids. This request was not pointed at my target—it was a general plea for help.

After OilHater proved himself to be the "most knowledgeable" source of information on the topic, I started to make direct requests to him for assistance. The more we spoke and the stronger our rapport, the more detailed and personal my requests became. Eventually, I was able to apply a very powerful derivative of this principle, referred to as "reverse social engineering." In other words, I didn't have to apply any social engineering principles to gain compliance—the rapport I built with OilHater almost forced him into continually trsuting me and giving me more details.

Dr. Zak said that oxytocin (the trust molecule) is the strongest when you make the target feel they can trust you. It is this trust that creates the bond. It is very powerful, and it's an important factor when you're ready to make a request of a target. I was able to apply this principle during Operation Oil, and when OilHater finally trusted me enough to request my help, when his level of trust reached a point where he came to me to share his ideas—that is when our "relationship" was set in stone. By continually asking OilHater for more and more assistance in understanding the problem and potential threats and then coming to his aid when he needed help, I had developed a very strong rapport with him.

Suspending Your Ego

This one principle of rapport is so powerful, if you can master it, you might be unstoppable. But it's not nearly as easy to do as you might think.

To understand why mastering this principle can be difficult, let me first define ego suspension. True ego suspension is literally letting go of your ego—your need to be first, to be correct, or to be perceived as smart—and your knowledge of what is right and wrong. When you suspend your ego, you set all that aside for the other person, and it's not something you can easily fake.

Why is this so powerful, yet so hard to do? Often, people feel weak if they must admit they don't know something. And how are weak people often portrayed? In media, movies, music, and other forms of entertainment, people who are humble or meek are often viewed as victims. In my opinion, these general perceptions make practicing suspension of ego a difficult principle to apply. No one wants to be perceived as weak.

Here's an example to help you understand why it's hard to fake this: You're standing in a line at the grocery store, and you overhear a conversation in which someone says, "I heard from a very reliable source that if you want to cure yourself of all allergies, all you need to do is wash your face with a blend of milk, honey, and spring water three times a day."

Many people may know that statement has no scientific validity. What was your reaction when you read that statement? If you thought something like, "That is one of the dumbest things I have ever read," or "These people need to be set straight," then you weren't applying ego suspension. Suspending your ego would mean hearing someone's thoughts on a matter and reacting with, "This is their opinion, and they are entitled to have it, so let me try and understand their point of view."

Ego suspension requires you to consider someone else's thoughts, statements, and opinions as the right of that person—regardless of whether or not you agree with them. It also involves having the ability to disagree without being disagreeable.

In Operation Oil, I was able to apply the principle of ego suspension by acting like I had no knowledge about fracking and the oil industry (although I didn't have to pretend too much). Additionally, by not questioning the things OilHater said about how terrible, dangerous, and deadly the fracking industry is, I suspended my own ego and allowed OilHater to be the "boss." Any time the social engineer can suspend his or her ego and allow the target to inflate theirs, it is a perfect mix for successful rapport building.

Another factor in the successful application of this principle is having some knowledge about the topic and the ability to ask good questions. A combination of limited knowledge and good questions helps the target continue to be dominant

A PRESIDENTIAL EXAMPLE

A truly amazing example of ego suspension was exhibited by former U.S. President Ronald Reagan. During Reagan's second run for the presidency, many news outlets questioned his ability to serve another term as president of the United States, because he was "too old."

Reagan could have debated, argued, or tried to prove his critics wrong by using sound reasoning. However, arguing a point of contention can often be like adding fuel to the fire. The harder you fight it, the more it seems to prove the naysayers right—at least in their minds. Instead, President Reagan decided to be the first to bring up his age by using self-deprecating humor. He would make jokes about himself like, "I remember when a hot story broke, and the reporters would run in and yell, 'Stop the chisels!'" He would intersperse this type of humor throughout speeches and press conferences.

The press wanted to complain that Reagan was too old to serve as the president. However, by bringing up the topic before the press could, Reagan was able to take control of the situation in such a way that if the press brought up his age after he had already done so, they'd look like fools. Instead of being upset, he suspended his ego and used humor to shut down their arguments.

and allows the social engineer to display ego suspension. I used this aspect of the principle in Operation Oil by continually asking OilHater for more information and to help me get to a deeper understanding of the little bits of knowledge I had. This inflated his ego as I suspended my own.

Validating Others

This next principle goes hand in hand with ego suspension. Simply put, validation is agreeing with, complimenting, or endorsing someone else's statements, decisions, or choices. When someone feels validated by you, their brain releases dopamine and oxytocin, which in turn enables you to create feelings of trust and rapport.

Remember when I talked about using sympathy or assistance themes? The rule I mentioned there is extremely important for validation: The level of validation *must* be equal to the level of rapport.

To reinforce this point, here's an epic fail story. When I was relatively new to impersonation gigs as a professional social engineer, I entered a building that I was assigned to gain entry to and scoped out the front desk and the gatekeeper. I saw that she had about a dozen pictures of her kids, and they were facing out, not in. This indicated to me that she was proud of her family and wanted others to see them. The pictures were of various vacations they had taken, and everyone in the photos looked really happy.

I tried to think on my feet and figure the best way to build rapport, but what came out of my mouth was pretty horrendous. I looked down at one picture, pointed at it, and said, "Wow, your daughters are beautiful . . ." My words trailed off as I realized her daughters were maybe 12 and 15. I was mortified, and I could see she shared the sentiment.

She reeled back in her chair with a surprised and somewhat fearful expression that was bleeding into anger. She looked at me and said, "Thank you," but she said it sternly rather than politely. Then she added, "Who are you, and what do you want?"

As I looked at her, I probably showed every shocked, scared, and disgusted facial expression there is before I said, "Oh, I forgot something in the car. I'll be right back." But I never did go back—I had to send another team member on a different day to complete the test.

Besides hitting a 100% creep factor, I was also nowhere near the necessary level of rapport to allow me to compliment her children in that manner. A proper validation would have been more along the lines of, "Wow, that looks like a great vacation. Where did you go?" Or even, "That's a beautiful picture. I never seem to capture those great moments of my kids."

In other words, in an initial conversation with a target, your rapport level will be next to nothing. Therefore, your validation should not be too personal.

PRO TIP Make sure you understand cultural barriers when it comes to validation in the form of physical gifts or compliments. You can really ruin rapport if you cross a cultural boundary inappropriately. At the same time, understanding what may be important to the target can help you pick the right validation.

Remember when I said how powerful validation is when blended with ego suspension? That's because when you suspend your ego and allow the other person to expand his or her ego, it's validating for them. That feeling of validation can create rapport, and when a person feels validated, their brain releases those good chemicals again (dopamine and oxytocin)—and you are the reason for all this good stuff.

In Operation Oil, I was able to continually use validation by

- » Suspending my ego
- » Validating the target
- » Complimenting his knowledge
- » Listening to his advice and asking for clarifications
- » Accepting his idea for "fixing" the problem

The more times I properly validated OilHater, the stronger the rapport between us became.

Asking How, Why, and When Questions

Why are how, why, and when questions powerful for building rapport? The answer to a how, why, or when question must be more than yes or no.

That alone should help you see why validation is so important. Remember that it's validating to someone when you ask for their opinion and then listen to their response.

> **WARNING** When you employ open-ended questions, it is vital to *listen* to the response. Nothing ruins validation more than if someone is giving you their opinion, and you look as if you are bored or are not paying attention. This means you can't be thinking about your next line while they are talking.

Open-ended questions are good for keeping the conversation going. Many times, a short pause after a question while you actively listen encourages the person to keep talking.

However, be careful to not use "why" questions too many times in a row. If you do, you can come off sounding like a three-year-old child who asks "But why?... Why?... Why?" over and over. As cute as they are, three-year-olds are not the best at rapport building.

In Operation Oil, I used how, why, and when questions constantly. I would phrase things like, "Why is fracking so bad for the environment?" or "How can we really stop them from ruining my home?"

These types of questions allowed OilHater to be open and give me all his knowledge on these topics. Active listening is much easier to do online than in person because you can read the paragraphs multiple times and assimilate the information before replying. However, you still must work at being an active listener even when you're corresponding online. For example, my good friend Jim Manley gets mad at me when he sends me an eight-paragraph email detailing a problem or situation, and I read only one or two sentences and then reply with a question. He always replies with something like, "READ THE WHOLE EMAIL, HADNAGY!!" (Yes, I censored his responses drastically.) If you are like me, you need to practice active listening—even in writing.

In Operation Oil, I practiced active listening and used open-ended questions to keep the target talking.

Making Use of Quid Pro Quo

Quid pro quo is translated as "Something for something." Think of it this way: Have you ever had buyer's remorse? You spent money on something, and you were very excited. But by the time you got home and opened the package, you started to think to yourself, "Did I really spend that much on just this?"

This remorse is a result of feeling that what you got really wasn't worth what you gave. One of the worst mistakes a social engineer can make is to leave the target feeling "buyer's remorse." In social engineering terms, buyer's remorse is when the target later thinks to themself, "Man, that was a great conversation I had today with . . . Hmm, what was his name? Where was he from? Wait, I told him my full name and date of birth, showed him pictures of my kids, and even let him see my driver's license, and I don't even know his name."

That mental conversation can create fear and anxiety in the target because what you gave them doesn't feel equal to what they gave you. Now before you get carried away, I said "doesn't *feel* equal" not "doesn't equal." There is a huge difference between the two.

For one job, I was in a store and approached a target who was with his young son. I made sure I was facing toward the store shelves, and I opened by saying, "Excuse me. I'm heading to a party that I'm very late for. My wife is going to kill me because I was supposed to get the gift for my nephew, who looks like he's the same age as your son. What do kids that age like these days?"

With that opening, I established quid pro quo by giving the target the following information:

- »   I'm married.
- »   I have a nephew, so therefore I have a brother or sister with kids.
- »   I'm late.
- »   I'm heading to a party.
- »   I'm clueless about kids.

In one or two short sentences, I told the target so much that, by the time we were done and I had enough of his story, he would never feel that buyer's remorse because he "knew" me.

PRO TIP The information you give does not need to be real (name, number of kids, and so on), *but* remember that the more fake details you give, the more you must remember and keep straight. For this reason, use K.I.S.S. (Keep It Simple Social Engineer) for more success.

In Operation Oil, I used quid pro quo a few times, but most notably when OilHater had scheduled our time to meet at Peg's Diner. I gave him my full name and address first to build trust and because I hoped that he would reciprocate. He did, which allowed me to successfully stop a potential violent act.

Employing Reciprocal Altruism

Think of this principle in simplistic terms. A reciprocating saw works by the blade going back and forth, or in and out, and that's also how this principle of rapport works. You send out altruism (whether in word or deed) by giving something important to the target, and in return, the target gives something to you.

If you open the door for someone as they walk toward an entryway that has two sets doors to pass through, what will they almost always do? Hold the second door open for you. This is reciprocal altruism. How can you apply this to social engineering? If you give something of value to a person, he or she will feel indebted and want to repay that gift. *Now, here's a very important question*: Who determines the value of the gift?

The receiver determines the value, not you. The connection to what is important to the target can be made via OSINT, observation, or generalities, but however you do it, don't assume that because you value something, the target will likewise value it. On the other hand, if you find something that the target truly values, then their feelings of indebtedness will be great enough to ignore many a security protocol.

As I entered one building, I approached the gatekeeper, who looked like she had been crying. I left SE mode for a moment and said, "Are you okay?"

I was genuinely concerned, and she could see that, so she replied, "I came to work this morning wearing earrings my husband gave me for our 10th anniversary. He saved for two years to buy them, and I just lost one." She started to tear up again.

I said, "Well, maybe it's on the floor," and I got down on the floor and started looking. She did too as she said, "I've already checked, but I guess it can't hurt to check again."

The sun came in through the window, and I saw a small glimmer on her shoulder. I said, "You probably already checked this, but I see a glimmer on the back of your shoulder. Can I just check again?"

She leaned in, and I plucked a beautiful diamond earring off her sweater and handed it to her. Her tears of sorrow turned to joy as she hugged me and thanked me so many times that it got embarrassing.

She then said, "I am so terrible. I kept you here for so long. How can I help you?"

At that moment, I decided to get back into SE mode because I realized that any request I made at this point was nearly guaranteed to be honored. "Well, you were pretty upset, so I didn't want to be pushy. But I'm late for my meeting with HR, so I'll just grab my things and go." I stood up, grabbed my bag and folders, and walked toward the locked door. I walked as if I was going to go right through it, and as I got close, I heard the mechanical buzz of the door unlocking.

The gift that I had unintentionally given the gatekeeper (finding her precious anniversary earring) was worth more to her than the potential embarrassment of stopping me from my important meeting for something as silly as security protocols.

In Operation Oil, I used reciprocal altruism a couple ways. First, I listened and validated OilHater's knowledge. Second, I was willing to give up some of my time to meet with him in order to take care of the problem. Both things built trust and rapport, which led to OilHater making a decision that was *not* in his best interest.

Managing Expectations

When you use these principles, you will see doors open that you never imagined would open. It is almost like being a mind reader or a Jedi. You start a conversation, and before you know it, the person is giving you their life story. The challenge is to *not* use these principles in your everyday life—you must learn to dial it back and not always be "on." Another challenge is the sheer volume of information you may receive about people—which can be overwhelming.

The moment you are mid-engagement is when you need to apply this the most. Just as validation, trust, and rapport release dopamine and oxytocin in your target, the same happens to you. When you feel good, those same chemicals are released, and you feel the same good feelings, which can cause you to take unnecessary risks. If you go too far too soon, you can ruin rapport in a way that might be near impossible to rebuild.

The other side of this coin is managing your expectations when things don't go as you want them to. Remember this motto: "Leave them feeling better for having met you." If you notice that your efforts are leading to a lack of rapport or, even worse, negative emotions, it is best to make an excuse to leave and move on. You do not want to ruin your reputation as a serious security professional because your need to win is stronger than your desire to leave your clients feeling good.

Because these principles all work amazingly well, there's a challenge in learning to employ the principles in everyday use when not working as a professional social engineer. The challenge is not treating people as a tool for your use. Part of managing your expectations is knowing that as you use these principles in a non-pentest enviroment, you must often adjust the way you communicate.

In Operation Oil, I had to manage my expectations because it took almost two weeks before OilHater became one of the people posting to me in the forums. Then there was a period of time when he went silent, and I had to think about how "Paul" would react to this. Although I wanted OilHater to keep chatting, I had no clue if he was gone for good or just a few days. Managing my expectations and being patient resulted in a successful outcome.

The Rapport Machine

One of the questions about these skills that I often get asked is how to practice them without being a social engineer yet (i.e., when you're in training) so that they come naturally when you do begin to use them in professional SE. In this section, I give you some tips on how to practice and perfect the 10 principles.

Use the Friends and Family Plan

You don't have to wait to be on the clock to practice. Pick one principle, such as validation, and try your hand at it the next time you're at a family gathering. Observe a cousin you haven't seen for a while and then try to offer a sincere compliment. Follow that up with a question about her or his life and actively listen to the response. See how willing she or he is to answer.

At the next gathering or work event, pick another principle, such as accommodating nonverbals, and notice the different ways people react to you depending on how much or little you face them. Over time, you begin to develop a toolkit of what works and what doesn't, and you start putting the principles into practice even when you're not actively thinking about them.

Read

There are a lot of books (like Robin Dreeke's) that talk about rapport building. You can find a pretty comprehensive list on www.social-engineer.org/resources/seorg-book-list. Reading about these principles reinforces them in your mind and makes it easier for you to call upon them when you need to.

Take Special Note of Failures

When things don't work as planned, and a conversation takes a trip down the drain, don't try to hide and forget it. Instead, take special note of what happened and why.

I've learned more from my failures than from my successes, and consequently, my successes mean more because of my failures. Learning from my failures and taking special note of them enables me to be a better teacher of these skills as well as a better social engineering professional.

Summary

This chapter walked you through how to recognize, use, and benefit from the ability to build rapport with anyone. These skills are powerful when you're communicating with other people and are essential for you to become a professional social engineer.

Regardless of whether you are phishing, vishing, SMiShing, or impersonating, you need these skills to get the maximum benefit. But I have one final note: It is just as important to learn how to disengage without ruining rapport as it is to learn to build the rapport.

I've noticed that disengaging tends to be one of the most difficult skills for my students to manage after they get the principles to work, because disengaging feels bad. Your target is pouring out their life story to you and telling you everything you wanted to know (as well as some things you didn't want to know), and now you're just supposed to walk away?

Well, no. You need to learn to disengage. And if you followed the 10 principles, disengaging will be easy. Let me give you a couple examples.

If I employ artificial time constraints, I can look at my watch and say, "Oh, my! I can't believe how much time has passed. You've been so engaging, I lost track of time *[validation]*. I'm really sorry, but I have to run *[ego suspension]*."

If you employ quid pro quo and validation to build rapport, you can say, "Well, look at that! You're so fascinating to talk to *[more validation]* that I forgot I'm supposed to pick up salad makings for my wife/husband on the way home. I'd better bolt *[confirming the quid pro quo by giving the target the "personal" information that you are having salad tonight and you have a spouse]*!"

I find it helpful to plan a few exit strategies that fit the pretext I'm using. This gives me a validating and kind way to get out of the situation without having to damage any rapport I've built.

WARNING If you start using rapport-building techniques while in a closed environment—such as on a plane, train, or other public transport—be aware that you will have few exit strategies. For example, if I need to use these principles on a plane, I usually have an artificial time constraint ready, which goes something like this: "I'm about to take a nap so I can work when I land, but before I do, I wanted to ask, where are you from?" I'm telling the person my goal is to *not* engage for too long. However, after many times of failing at this and being stuck talking to someone for three hours (or nine hours on one trip!) instead of getting some much-needed sleep, I now just put headphones on and don't even make eye contact.

Rapport links you to your fellow humans. As you link to more and more people, you have the choice to make them feel better or feel worse for having met you. In each choice you make on how to use these skills you have the power to influence or manipulate the person you are talking to. That's the topic of Chapter 6, "Under the Influence."

6   Under the Influence

The secret of my influence has always been that it remained secret.
— SALVADOR DALI

This chapter covers both influence and manipulation, but for now, I want to focus on influence. How do you define influence?

I define it as "getting someone to *want* to do what you want them to do." This means that the person has the idea to do what you want them to, or at least that is the way they will remember it. Because the person perceives the idea as his or her own, it is a great idea, and the person is committed to it.

One of the greatest minds in history on this topic is Dr. Robert Cialdini. He has been researching, writing about, and perfecting the art of influence for decades now. In episode 86 of *The Social-Engineer Podcast*, I was privileged to have Bob, as he asked to be called, on the show. It was one of the most fascinating conversations I have had, and one that I learned so much from.

Bob wrote a book, which I still use today, titled *Influence: The Psychology of Persuasion* (William Morrow and Co., 1984). In it, he discusses six principles of influence that are definable, teachable, and trackable. As part of my practice, I have broken Bob's six principles into eight principles.

In this chapter, I first define these eight principles as they have been researched and studied by great minds like Dr. Cialdini. I follow the definition of each principle by tying each to social engineering.

After my discussion of each principle, I talk about framing, which is closely linked to influence. Simply put, framing is the foundation on which your beliefs, viewpoints, and thoughts are based. Later in the chapter, I discuss how you can alter those frames in your targets. I also discuss manipulation, the darker more sinister cousin to influence, and then I summarize everything, give you some tips, and send you on your way to mastering this amazing talent.

SKILLS LESSON

In my career, I've had the opportunity to use my skills to help track, trap, and stop people who exploit and hurt children. One case clearly helps define influence as stated in the chapter introduction.

For this engagement, which we will call OpRentalCar, we needed to get the home address of someone we knew was trafficking children. Authorities had proven his involvement through other means, but he bounced around so much that his home address was not clear. We knew that he was renting a car for a flight he took to a certain city. The goal was to find the place from which he rented the car and try to influence the agent to give us his home address.

My pretext was that I was the owner of a pizza restaurant in town. My story was that I had found an iPad belonging to our target in the restaurant, and I wanted to get it back to him, but it was locked. We knew that getting the address was going to be hard, so I had planned to offer free food to the rental agent in exchange for good ideas about how to track down the guy.

It took some work, but I finally found a rental agency that confirmed the car had been rented from them. Part of my conversation with the rental agent went like this:

NOTE For security purposes, I've substituted fictional names for the actual rental agent and restaurant names.

Me: Look, I'm in a bind here, so I've got a free pizza in exchange for any good ideas you might have . . .

Agent: I love Big Tony's pizza! What can I do?

Me: Well, I would ship this iPad directly back to him, but I don't have his home address. So how about if I just bring it in to you, and you ship it back?

Agent: Tony, I can't. I'm really sorry, but we have a policy that we can't be responsible for possessions that we do not find inside the car.

Me: Yeah, that makes sense. Dang. I'm not sure what to do now. What do you think I should do to get this to his house?

Agent *[thinks for a few seconds, then whispers]:* Look I'm not supposed to do this, but what if I give you his address, and you ship directly to him?

Me: Steve, you are a genius! Why didn't I think of that? You know what? When we are done, there is a $25 gift card waiting for you here.

Notice that two times in the conversation, I interjected the idea of the agent giving me the address, but then I played dumb instead of just asking for it. This is a great example of blending the principles of influence while interjecting thoughts about getting the address, which made it seem as if this was the target's idea, which in turn made it easier for him to follow through on.

As I talk about the topics in this chapter, you'll notice a lot of similarities to the principles of rapport.

NOTE I have launched a nonprofit organization called the Innocent Lives Foundation (www.innocentlivesfoundation.org), which is dedicated to saving children from the hands of predators. The foundation members are information security professionals who work closely with law enforcement in uncovering those who try to hide on the Internet while exploiting children. The skills discussed throughout this book are used extensively to expose those predators and help save children.

Principle One: Reciprocity

This principle is very much like reciprocal altruism in rapport building. It's based on the way humans want to reciprocate to those who do kind things or give us things that we enjoy. According to Cialdini, even if we don't want the item given to us, our brains are unsettled until we feel that we have paid back the giver. Marketers know this and use this principle all the time.

Reciprocity in Action

Think about the last time you were at a grocery store and got a free sample. The store or marketing company that set up that sample booth knows that most people are more prone to buying the product after receiving the free sample of it.

People are also more prone to comply with a command or ask after being complimented.

I was with my wife and daughter in London on some work. We had purchased premium economy tickets to ride home in relative comfort. Like obedient little travelers, we arrived at the airport three hours early.

I had wheeled in our luggage cart, and the overflowing luggage was teetering on the edge of destruction. I was approaching the ticket counter when I hit a little bump in the floor, and all our bags tumbled to the floor with a loud CRASH! I simply made a loud joke and said, "Accident on the M5!"

Because of my American accent, all the Brits laughed at the irony of an American using a local road name as a joke. A woman at the ticket counter looked up from her computer, smiled, and called us over. I pulled out our passports to hand them over, and my wife just started telling her how much she loved her scarf.

Now, my wife is no social engineer. She is just a naturally amazing, beautiful, and wonderful human being who truly loves people. So, she was genuinely complimenting this woman by saying things like, "Wow, you did your make up so perfectly," and, "I love how your scarf matches your eyes."

I was watching this interaction and seeing the nonverbal display of this woman, who was just beaming with pride, happiness, and all the good chemicals that a brain can release. Instantly I thought, "This is your time, Chris—make the request."

As I handed over our passports, I leaned into my wife, and I said to the woman, "My beautiful wife and I are curious—how much it would cost to upgrade us to first class for the flight home?"

This is no joke: The ticket agent started typing frantically. She gave us three first-class tickets for no extra charge, with full lounge access during the three-hour wait.

Think about it: A few compliments that were preceded by humor and followed by a request. Reciprocation for the win!

My illustration of reciprocity is in Figure 6-1.

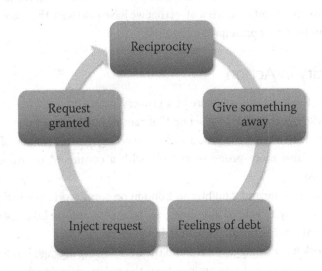

Figure 6-1 Reciprocity in action

Reciprocity works only when this path is followed. You can't interject the command or request too early. You can only make your request after you have created those feelings of debt because those feelings of debt increase the chance that the request will be honored.

Using Reciprocity as a Social Engineer

You probably have five million ideas of how to use the principle of reciprocity swimming through your head. Let me just give you a quick tip: The level of request you can make is determined by the perceived value of the gift to the receiver.

Take a moment to understand that. Remember, Cialdini said the target will feel like reciprocating regardless of whether or not that person wants the gift. If the recipient values the gift, he or she will feel more compelled to return a gift of greater or equal value.

I am part of a small group of hackers who are also whiskey enthusiasts. When we meet for gatherings, we sometimes trade bottles of whiskey. We each bring something for the other guys, so each of us goes home with something different from the others. Often, we will set a theme so that one of us doesn't bring something worth a hundred dollars while another person brings something worth much more. This keeps the principle of reciprocity under control, and no one feels less or more indebted.

As a social engineer, it is imperative that you first find out what the target person or company values. You need to prepare your pretext with that in mind. When you offer the target a chance to have something of value, you are more likely to succeed.

For example, in the assignment I spoke of earlier, OpRentalCar, I found out pretty quickly that the target really loved Tony's Pizza. Armed with that, I made the offer for free food in exchange for his great ideas. I didn't say, "If you give me *[the customer's]* address, I will give you pizza." Why wouldn't I do that?

The reason is simple: At this point, we had no rapport built. Asking for something like a customer's address before I build rapport with the target would have led the target to have all force fields raised, shields on high, and the red alert engaged.

By making an offer of free food, followed by interjecting what I really wanted, I allowed for the target to "come up" with the exact idea I needed.

FUN FACT

I didn't want the agent to go to Tony's Pizza and not receive a gift certificate. After I hung up with him, I called Tony's and bought a $25 gift certificate over the phone in his name and told them to hold them there "from Tony" for when the agent came in to claim them.

Here's another situation in which I used this principle: I had to spear phish a CEO. During the OSINT phase, I found out that he was an avid runner who loved to run marathons. I found this out because he took tons of selfies while he was running the marathons.

My spear phish came from a marketing company for a recent marathon the CEO had run. The message said something like, "During the recent Run for Kids Marathon you took a part in, we captured a few photos we would like to use for marketing and promotion. We need your approval to use these photos. Please click here to see the photos and approve." If I remember correctly, the CEO clicked the link in less than 60 minutes after he received it.

When you find what the person truly values, the target will grant the request you make with little to no thought.

Principle Two: Obligation

Obligation sounds very close to reciprocation, but there is a small difference. Whereas reciprocation is the feeling of indebtedness due to a gift or something of value that creates the action, obligation is that same feeling, but it's based on social norms or expected behaviors.

Obligation in Action

I have asked the following question of students from around the globe: If you are in traffic, and you allow a fellow motorist to merge in front of you, what is he or she obligated to do? What *must* he or she do?

The students respond that the motorist must wave, raise a finger, or give a head nod, but all those gestures mean one thing: The motorist must (or is obligated to) show some level of respect and appreciation for the kindness you just showed. What happens if they don't?

I was in Washington, DC, driving to a meeting on a beautiful four-lane highway, and traffic was being forced to merge to one lane. The traffic was coming to a screeching halt. I was determined to not let it get the best of me, so I turned up the music as I inched along. Other cars were trying to merge onto the highway from an on-ramp, and my fellow motorists where not feeling too altruistic. They were not letting people merge. So, I slowed down and flashed my lights to let in the next guy waiting to merge.

As he pulled in front of me, I looked in through his rear window for his obligatory head nod, wave, or appreciative look in his rear-view mirror. When I didn't get it, I felt my blood start to boil. My face got red, and I got more aggressive with my driving. I started to think, "No wonder everyone was being a jerk to you and not letting you in!"—as if the other motorists had some kind of sixth sense that would allow them to see this driver was going to be unappreciative.

I built a whole story line about this arrogant waste of flesh in front of me. When the other lanes opened up a few miles later, I was determined to floor it and pass the rude driver to show him who owned the road.

I laid the pedal to the floor, and all six cylinders of my super-charged sports car jumped into action. As I got next to the other driver's window, I looked over with disgust and saw . . . he had only one arm. Talk about going from anger to humility in one second flat. I quickly smiled and waved while tipping my head.

What is my point in telling you this terribly humiliating story? When I felt that the man had not lived up to his obligation to thank me, I was furious. Only when I saw that he had a valid reason for not waving did I realize my error in judgment.

Try this next time you are in a conversation with someone. As they ask you a good question, don't answer or acknowledge them. Just stare at them. If they ask if you are okay, just say, "Yep."

I can imagine most of you are letting out a nervous weird laugh or smile right now as you picture it. Why? It's awkward to think about not fulfilling the obligation of answering a question.

Obligations are powerful, especially when they relate to social norms. Figure 6-2 illustrates the cycle of obligation.

As a social engineer, you want to play into these expected reactions. Any time you don't, you reduce the chance of building rapport, because the target will be wondering why you didn't act "normal."

Figure 6-2 Obligation in action

Using Obligation as a Social Engineer

Social engineers use social situations to create a feeling of obligation for the target to act a certain way all the time. For example, it's considered rude to not hold the door for a woman or for someone carrying boxes or other cargo, and social engineers use that custom to their advantage.

For one of my jobs, I loaded a box full of heavy phones and computer parts. I waited for the lunch-hour rush and walked toward the doors of a place I was supposed to gain entry to. As I approached, some kind soul said, "Oh, let me get the door for you."

As I stepped into the building, a very stern fellow employee said, "You're supposed to see his badge before you let him in!"

I said, "He's 100% right. Hey, this box is heavy—my badge is in my front pocket if you want to grab it out." I leaned my hip toward the stern man.

He quickly snapped, "I'm not reaching my hand into your front pocket, Buddy!"

"Sheesh! Where's my brain?" I said embarrassedly. "That *is* awkward. This box weighs about 45 pounds—you want to hold it while grab my badge?"

"Just go, man—I don't have time for this!" the guy exclaimed and walked out.

The door was held out of obligation. I used the policy that the stern man stated . . . to feign offering my "pocket" out of obligation. The guy felt awkward reaching in my pocket and obliged to let me go unverified.

This scenario worked for me on more than one occasion. That is, until one day, I encountered an employee who said, "In this pocket?" as she reached toward my front right pocket.

I said, "Oh, maybe it's the other one. You can try both." I hoped the awkwardness of the situation would make her back up, but it didn't. She reached into my pocket and felt around, which, by the way, was very awkward for *me!*

After finding nothing but my keys in the first pocket, the woman said, "Give me the other side." In that pocket, she found my wallet and a knife. She looked at me and said, "Could it be in your wallet?"

I said, "I'm not sure—maybe," even though I knew full well it was not in my wallet. She snapped it open and right in the front was a picture of my infant daughter. The woman saw the photo and exclaimed, "Oh my *God*, she is so cute! What's her name?"

We then had a 15-minute conversation about my family while she held my wallet, knife, and keys, and I held this stupidly heavy box. After about 15 minutes, she just put everything back in one pocket and said, "Well, you'd better report your lost badge to security before you get in trouble. I'll see you around the office." With that, she let me go. We had developed a rapport and friendship, and she was now obligated to trust me.

Obligation is a powerful principle that can make being a social engineer much easier.

Principle Three: Concession

The *Oxford English Dictionary* defines the word *concede* as follows: "Admit or agree that something is true after first denying or resisting it."

Remember, the very definition of influence is that if a person feels ownership of an idea, then that person most likely thinks it's a great idea! Concession will help the target make it "their idea" to take the action you want.

Concession in Action

In the area where I live, the American Society for the Prevention of Cruelty to Animals (ASPCA) is very good at using concession to get people to donate. A solicitation call will go something like this:

Caller: Good morning Mr. Hadnagy. This is Carrie calling on behalf of animal lovers in Montrose. How is your dog doing?

Me: *[replying and realizing I'm talking about things close to me and smiling— oh no, how do I stop?]:* She's great. Getting up there in years though.

Caller: I'm glad she's doing good. And it is great to be chatting with a fellow animal lover. And as an animal lover, I need your help today. As you know, we need help to keep caring for all the strays in our area. We want every animal to have a loving home like your dog does. Can you help us today?

Me: *[thinking that it's almost as if I can't stop the wreck that is about to happen]:* Well, I do love animals. What do you need for help?

Caller: *[speaking with clarity and without wavering]:* We're asking for monetary help today, and many people are donating about $250 to help us.

Me: *[feeling triumphant because I'm going to shut her down]:* $250?! Wow, I'm sorry. I just don't have that much. I would love to help, but I just can't do that right now.

Caller: Oh, I get that. These are hard times, and that *is* a lot of money. How about if you help us with just $25 today, then?

Before I know it, I've pulled out my credit card. Let's look at what happened. I agreed, or conceded, to a few things:

» I'm an animal lover.

» I wanted to help.

» I would help, but the first price was too much.

When I was offered an alternative, I could not say no. What would have happened if the caller had started at $25? Donations might have ended at a much lower amount, but by starting at a much higher value, she had almost guaranteed more donations.

Law enforcement interrogators use this tactic all the time. If they can get a perp to admit to even a minor detail, to concede to one fact, it is nearly impossible for that person to go back on what he or she has said.

Check out these two alternatives. The detective could ask, "Were you at Lee's bar at 11 p.m. during the robbery?" And the perp could easily answer with, "Nope, I was never there." Or the detective could ask, "So, at 11 p.m., what did you see during the robbery at Lee's bar?" To which the perp might reply, "Well, I didn't see anything at all. It was dark." With that type of response, the interrogator knows the

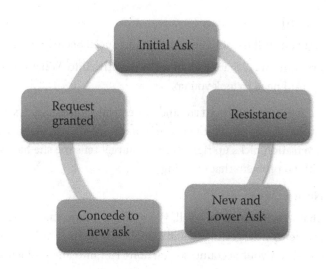

Figure 6-3 Concession in action

person being questioned was at Lee's bar at 11 p.m. The perp has made a concession! By answering the question, that person admits, or concedes, to the unasked question about whether he had been at the bar.

Figure 6-3 shows an illustration of the cycle of concession.

Using Concession as a Social Engineer

During one vishing engagement, we were tasked with getting the full name, employee ID, and Social Security number (government ID) of the employees as part of the flags. We developed two pretexts that I thought were solid, and then we started calling our targets.

The calls would go something like this:

Me: Hi, this is Paul from IT. Is this Sally Davis?

Target: Yes, it is. How can I help you, Paul?

Me: Well, last night we were flashing the bios in the firmware for the RFID badging system, and we lost some records. Did you have any problems using your badge this morning?

Target: No, it let me in just fine.

Me: That's excellent news. Well, you're lucky. Many flagged accounts had problems with getting in and using the printers. I need to verify some details on your account, so you don't run into any problems. It'll take about 30 seconds, okay?

Target: Sure, what do you need?

Me: Just your full name, employee ID, and Social Security number.

Target: Err, ummm . . . that's a lot of really sensitive info. What was your name again? I need to look you up.

Many calls followed that pattern, and we epically failed. So, I sat back and thought about the principles of influence and made one change to the pretext. The following conversation picks up right after the target tells me she had gotten into the system with no problem that morning.

Target: No, it let me in just fine.

Me: That's excellent news. Well, you're lucky. Many flagged accounts had problems with getting in and using the printers. I need to verify some details on your account, so you don't run into any problems. It'll take about 30 seconds, okay?

Target: Sure, what do you need?

Me: First, I want to make sure your name is spelled right. I have your first name as S-A-L-L-Y . . .

Target: Nope, that's a problem. There is no *E*, just two Ls.

Me: Sheesh, I'm so glad I called you. Why don't you just spell your last name, so I get it right?

From there, I would then ask for department, confirm the email address, and by the time we got down to employee ID and Social Security number, the people we called had already conceded to giving up all that info and continued. That gave us an 84% success average for that engagement—just by making that one change.

As a social engineer, remember that you don't need to go immediately for the exact flags you need. Get some minor ones to help build those feelings that will lead to the person to concede and comply.

Principle Four: Scarcity

"Going out of business sale!"

"Lowest prices ever in history!"

"Only 10 left on Earth!"

Why do these statements work on us? If something is made scarce, or less available, its value increases. How valuable was the cupcake when there were 20 of them? Now, how valuable is the last cupcake?

Scarcity in Action

For one DEF CON competition, I had this great idea to buy one of those rifles with the foam darts and hire a "sniper" who would shoot the kids in the SECTF4Kids (Social Engineering Capture The Flag 4 Kids) competition we hold each year. The competitors would have to solve a riddle and then insert a tube into a box in the back of a room that would have a sniper in it who was shooting the kids. If a competitor got hit, that person had to go back out of the room and start over.

> **FUN FACT**
>
> The competition went amazingly well, and if you want to hear how the winning team of kids actually defeated us, you'll have to ask me in person.

The rifle I bought was a Nerf CS6 Long Shot. Between the time I bought it and a few months after DEF CON, Nerf announced they were no longer making that particular model. They were replacing it with a model that many people said was inferior.

I didn't need two rifles, so I put one on eBay for the $99 I had bought it for. On the first day, the bids hit $199, then $250, then $299, then $340. The final selling price was $410. That's $410 for a plastic rifle that shoots foam darts 50 feet! (Granted, it had a scope and four clips, and we'd made some modifications, but still . . .)

I can buy a real rifle for $410, so why did a plastic rifle go for so much money? Scarcity. Because that model of rifle had been discontinued and was now unique, it became extremely valuable.

Companies often make products, food, medicines, time, jewels, and anything of value scarce to help increase the value in the consumers' eyes. Figure 6-4 shows the continuum of scarcity.

Using Scarcity as a Social Engineer

In one job, our OSINT led us to the CEO's social media accounts, where he had been posting all about his first real vacation in three years. He was taking his whole family to the Bahamas. He had pictures of the packing, pictures of the ride to the airport, pictures of his family on the plane, and one picture that said, "Now starts 2 weeks of paradise."

Armed with that knowledge as well as the name of his company's IT support company, which we had obtained from dumpster diving, I walked in the front door and approached Jane the gatekeeper. Our conversation went something like this:

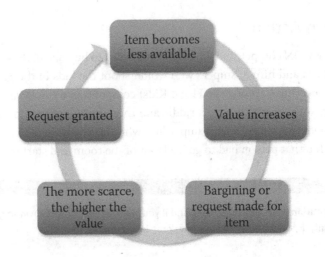

Figure 6-4 Scarcity in action

Jane: How can I help you?

Me: Hi there. I'm Paul from XYZ Company. Jeff asked me to come and take care of . . . *[looking down at my clipboard and leafed through the papers as if I was searching for something]* . . . slowness on his desktop. He thinks it's a virus.

Jane: *[looking at her organizer]*: Paul, I don't see any record of this appointment from Jeff here. I'm sorry, but you'll have to come back.

Me: Look, Jane. I don't know what to tell you. Jeff called and said he was heading to the Bahamas for two weeks and to have this fixed before he got back, or he was gonna be ticked. I had to move four other appointments around to make it here today. And I have no more time for the next month. *[I paused for a second.]* I guess that's fine. I'll email Jeff and tell him he forgot to tell you and now he has to wait for four more weeks to get it fixed.

Me: *[turning my clipboard toward Jane without pausing]*: Just sign here to acknowledge I told you that we have no openings for the next four weeks, please.

Jane: *[pausing for a second as she looked at me]*: Well, he has been complaining about his computer being slow. I don't want to tell him you can't come back for four weeks. Let's go. I'll let you in.

And with that, I was in the CEO's office without supervision and compromising everything in the building.

By making my time scarce, I had increased the value and the importance of taking the immediate time slot now. Scarcity made Jane think that turning me away could create a bigger problem down the road. That led to a full compromise of the company.

As a social engineer, you can apply scarcity to time, information, or even things you are giving away in your pretext. Scarcity will make what you have more valuable and influence the target to make decisions based on that perceived value.

PRO TIP I'm often asked, "How many people do you get fired?"

As a professional social engineer, I feel it is important to ensure my results are used for education rather than firing, unless, of course, we find an employee doing something illegal or malicious toward a company. So, I can proudly say that it's rare for anyone to get fired just because they fell for one of my pretexts.

Principle Five: Authority

When someone with the right kind of authority makes certain statements, other people take them very seriously. Here are some examples:

» If a guy in a white lab coat or doctor's scrubs says, "Drop your pants," you listen.

» If a parent, teacher, or warden says, "Don't touch that!" you listen.

» If your drill sergeant or commanding officer says, "Drop and give me 20!" you definitely listen.

All these people have one thing in common: They have authority over you. But what indicates authority? When you walk into a room, how can you tell which person has authority?

Look at Ben in Figure 6-5 and Figure 6-6. In which photo do you think Ben is showing authority, and why do you think that?

You probably think that Ben in Figure 6-6 shows authority and confidence. In both pictures, Ben is wearing the same clothing, is the same age, and has the same hair style. He's the same person in both photos. But in Figure 6-6, he is standing with his chest out, hands steepled, chin up, and no look of fear in his face at all.

Figure 6-5 What do his face and body language tell you?

All of this points to a person who is confident, and confidence makes us view the person as someone in authority. As a matter of fact, when I ask my students what indicates authority to them, they list things like confidence, loud voice, chest out, chin up, neat clothes, direct personality, and other characteristics like that.

What effect does authority have on us? It gives us a level of trust in what the person says without that person having to prove why we should obey them.

Figure 6-6 What are the signs of confidence?

Authority in Action

One of the most influential studies on this topic was done by Dr. Stanley Milgram. In 1963, Dr. Milgram examined justifications for atrocities of war that he heard during the Nuremberg Trials. During those trials, the defense that was used was, "I was following orders." In the study titled "Behavioral Study of Obedience" (www .birdvilleschools.net/cms/lib/TX01000797/Centricity/Domain/1013/AP%20 Psychology/milgram.pdf), Dr. Milgram outlines his findings.

Dr. Milgram wanted to examine whether normal, law-abiding citizens could be coerced via authority to take an action that could lead to someone's harm or death. Of course, performing this type of research would have massive limitations. How could you prove that X number of people would or would not have obeyed an authority figure who told them to harm another person?

Random citizens volunteered to be part Dr. Milgram's study. For the experiment to work, they were told that there would be a learner and a teacher and that the assignments were random, but in truth, all volunteers were designated to be teachers.

The volunteers watched as the learner was strapped to a chair, and electrodes were attached to them. The volunteers were told that wrong answers to questions would result in the learners receiving an electric shock. The learner was never really shocked—they only acted as if the shocks hurt.

The teacher (the volunteer) was shown a large box that had toggle switches that went from 15 volts to 450 volts in 15-volt increments. The volunteers even received a shock with a mere 45 volts, so they had proof of the reality of it.

Then a man in a white lab coat (the authority) sat and oversaw the teacher asking the questions. As the learner got answers wrong, the voltage went up and up on their punishment.

If the teacher objected because they heard the learner suffer, the man in the lab coat was instructed to say only one of two things:

» "The experiment must go on, please continue."

» "There is no permanent tissue damage. Please go on."

That doesn't sound too compelling, does it? But this study showed that 65% of all teachers took the learner to 450 volts!

Let that sink in. The teachers were average, working-class people. They weren't pulled from some pool of sadistic sociopaths. However, according to Dr. Milgram's study, 26 out of 40 (65%) of the volunteers continued to increase the voltage to 450 volts because someone in authority told them to continue.

Figure 6-7 illustrates the cycle of authority.

Using Authority as a Social Engineer

I always have a problem using authority directly in my social engineering pretexts. The main reason is because I often don't have the right knowledge, which means I get stuck and caught.

However, sometimes implied authority or transfer of authority is sufficient. In one job, I found an online invitation to a meeting for the financial board of our target. It happened to fall within the scope of our work, so I decided to use it. We performed OSINT on all the members invited to the meeting and found one

Figure 6-7 Authority in action

woman who seemed to be the authority figure. Aside from looking and sounding like the authority on social media, in popular employee rating sites, she had been named in a few reviews as being very hard to work for.

So, I took my partner's cell phone number and changed the name in my phone to this woman's name. (Let's call her Sally Smith.) I told my partner, "When you see me arguing with the security guard, text me this line: 'Where the heck are you? We have been waiting 15 minutes! Get back here now!'"

I grabbed a bunch of folders and papers and tried walking right past security. I knew I would be stopped, because we had determined that security was very tight. It went like this:

The security guard said briskly, "Excuse me sir! Where are you going?! STOP!"

I stopped in my tracks, turned around with a shocked look, and said, "What? Didn't you see me just walk past you and go to my car? I'm in the financial board meeting on 14. I need to go now."

"I'm sorry sir, but I didn't see you walk past. Please show me your badge," the guard requested, with a confused tone in his voice.

I let out a big sigh, "Okay, but I'm going to give Sally your name when I get up there and have to explain why I'm delayed." I started to pat my pockets and then said, "I don't know, I must have left it . . ." Then my text message notification went off.

I pulled my phone out and turned it to him. At the top of the text message screen was the name "Sally Smith" and the message underneath said, "Where the heck are you? We have been waiting 15 minutes! Get back here now!"

I said, "Do you want to call her and tell her why I'm being detained while the whole board room is waiting for these papers, or should I tell her the name of the guard who is stopping me?"

He read the text message and then looked at me and said, "I'm truly sorry, sir. I just didn't see you walk past. Please, if we can just forget this—go right ahead to the meeting."

"If you buzz me through right now, we can forget this ever happened." And with that, I was inside the fortress and roaming free.

Authority, even when it didn't come directly from me, made that security guard take an action that was *not* in his best interest. Authority is a powerful motivator!

Principle Six: Consistency and Commitment

We all want to seem consistent, which means that we want there to be agreement between what we say and what we think we are portraying. This is especially true when we commit to something. Have you ever seen a small child commit to an answer that you know is false? ("No, I did not break that lamp!") The child stays committed to the answer that's consistent with their original response even when you have provided overwhelming proof of their lie.

Why is consistency important to us? We want to—maybe we even need to—seem like we are consistent, because consistency is a sign of confidence and strength.

Consistency and Commitment in Action

I live in a pretty rural area, but recently a whole lot of oil and gas has been discovered in the ground. Now they are fracking and pumping and digging all over the county. As a result, there are a lot of trucks on my road.

I have seen a truck that's hauling tons of equipment go flying up my road at 50 or 60 miles per hour. The drivers are careless and dangerous. Some of my neighbors have taken to putting hand-drawn signs in their yards to tell drivers to slow down, be safe, and drive like their kids live in the neighborhood. If my neighbor came to me and asked to put one of these large signs in my yard, which would block my wife's beautiful flowers or my awesome car, I would decline even though I want the drivers to slow down.

In 1966, researchers Jonathan L. Freedman and Scott C. Fraser studied consistency and commitment and wrote about it in "Compliance Without Pressure: The Foot-in-the-Door Technique" (*Journal of Personality and Social Psychology*, September 1966, `www.researchgate.net/publication/17217362_Compliance_ Without_Pressure_The_Foot-in-the-Door_Technique`). They went from door to door, asking people in a neighborhood to put large, poorly lettered signs with safety warnings for drivers in their yards. The signs would have blocked some of the view of the homes. The researchers found that 83% of all homeowners declined to put the sign in their yards.

Then Freedman and Fraser made one change to their request in the next neighborhood, and they got 76% compliance! You heard me, 76% said yes! What was that change? Better lettering? Pretty signage? Payment for the sign? Renting of the space?

No, no, no, and no. The change was to the size of the sign. In the second neighborhood, they first asked homeowners to display a 3-inch sticker in their windows with the same message. Then a few weeks later, they came back around and asked homeowners to display the large, ugly sign in their yard, and 76% complied.

Freedman and Fraser called this approach "foot-in-the-door." Once they had a foot in the door (the small sticker in the window), the homeowner was more willing to comply with future requests (the large sign).

Numerous studies have been conducted since Freedman and Fraser's, and all have had the same staggering results. Compliance drastically increases when the person has agreed to something smaller first.

When you blend compliance with the principle of consistency, it is an unstoppable force. Basically, we want to be consistent and appear consistent. Our brains don't like it when we internally argue. So, we dig in our heels in and stay a course, even when we know we are wrong, if we have committed and want to remain consistent. This is represented in Figure. 6-8.

NOTE The time element for consistency and commitment doesn't need to be a lengthy period—it can be just a few seconds. As long as the person commits to the first request, they will want to stay consistent with that request.

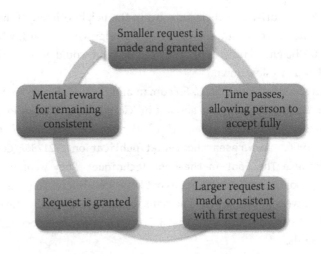

Figure 6-8 Commitment and consistency in action

Using Commitment and Consistency as a Social Engineer

One of my personal rules is *never break pretext unless you truly must.* There has to be a pretty serious situation before you break pretext. That rule came about because of the story I am about to tell you.

I was tasked with a multi-staged job in which I had to gain access to a set of dumpsters in a locked area. The dumpsters were where the company threw away their technology.

To get to the dumpsters, I had to bypass security, make my way to a secure area inside the campus, gain entry without being stopped, and be uninterrupted while I spent time looking for something of value.

I started the OSINT phase with the goal of finding the dumpster company. The target company had strict policies on giving out any info on any other vendors, but I decided to call the accounts department to see if I could talk my way to that information. The call went something like this:

Company rep:	Hi, this is Beth. How can I help you?
Me:	Beth, this is Paul from Professional Dumpster. We are relatively new to the area and are trying to get some more local business. I'm wondering if I can send you a quick quote?
Company rep:	Hi Paul. We do accept quotes from new vendors. Just send us a per-unit cost, and if the price matches, we'll request more information.

Me:	Okay, that's great. Can I have your email address to send it to please?
Company rep:	Well, you wouldn't send it to me. You'd send it to vendors@company.com.
Me:	Oh, I see. Is there a way I can cc you so I know it made it in. I've had some serious problems with people saying my quotes never showed up. I'm new to this business and not very technical.
Company rep:	Oh, okay. It is beth.p@company.com.
Me:	Beth, you're a lifesaver. Look, can I trust you with something a little personal?
Company rep:	Um, sure, I guess.
Me:	I have sold almost everything under the sun, but dumpsters is a new one for me, and I don't think I'm doing too good here. I am not even sure if our prices are competitive.
Company rep:	I'm sorry, Paul. That must be hard. Ya know . . . . Send over that proposal, and I'll personally make sure it gets looked at.
Me:	Beth, you're a lifesaver. I know this is uncool to ask, but is there any way you can just tell me who I'm going up against? *[See, by now she has committed to helping me, giving me her email address and having a conversation. But was the rapport enough for this ask?]*
Company rep:	Paul, well . . . *[sighs audibly and pauses]* I would love to, but we have a policy on this. I don't want to get in trouble, but I really wish I could.
Me:	Nah, I get it, Beth. It's just that I'm really struggling here. How about this—I'll just say some of the names, and you can cough when you hear the right name: Superior Waste, Excellent Dumpster, Waste Management *[Beth coughs]*. Beth, I hope you feel better—sounds like you're getting a cold!
Company rep:	*[chuckling]:* Thanks, I do feel like I am coming down with something. Good luck to you.

With that information, I was able to get the right costume, gain entry to the secured location, and find some undestroyed hard drives and USB devices that could have led to a full-scale compromise if they had fallen into the wrong hands.

Playing the target's desire to remain consistent to their commitments, whether physical or mental, leads the social engineer to easier compliance with all the requests they make.

Principle Seven: Liking

People like people who are like them. People like people who like them. As tongue- or brain-twisting as those two statements are, it's important to understand the deeper meaning of each.

In Chapter 5, "I Know How to Make You Like Me," I spoke about the tribe mentality. Now think about that in the context of the statement, "People like people who are *like them*." If we are similar, in the same tribe—comfortable and familiar— we will be liked, accepted, and trusted.

Now, to address the second statement, "People like people who like them," let me remind you of Dr. Zak's research into oxytocin that I mentioned in Chapter 1, "A Look into the *New* World of Professional Social Engineering." It applies here perfectly. If you like someone, or make someone feel they are liked or trusted, that person can't help but like you.

Before you say, "Well that's easy enough," let me give you a few ground rules:

The liking must be genuine.   You can't just fake liking someone and hope this works. Even if it works for the first few minutes, eventually it comes out or becomes evident that the liking was not real, and that can ruin trust and rapport beyond repair.

Do not think that compliments automatically equal liking.   For a compliment to work, it must be genuine and at the level of rapport you have built.

Nonverbals play a huge role in this.   When your nonverbals are genuine (remember my discussion of accommodating nonverbals in Chapter 5), then it is easier for someone to trust you, feel comfortable with you, and therefore like you.

The running theme of all these things is that your expression of liking must be genuine. My good friend Robin Dreeke accomplishes this by looking at each person as his or her own reality TV show. He doesn't have to like your life, or the things you do, but he has enough interest to want to find out the plot and how it unfolds. That desire to find out is genuine, and that genuineness comes across, which allows trust and rapport to be built and influence to be applied much more easily.

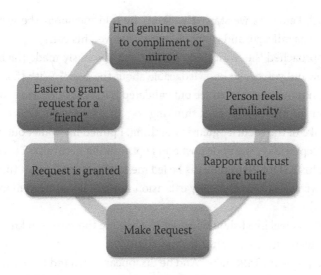

Figure 6-9 Liking in action

To help encourage this feeling, you can look for ways to give a compliment and mirror body language and/or verbal cues (without parroting) to help the person feel warm and fuzzy toward you. Figure 6-9 illustrates how the principle of liking works.

Using Liking as a Social Engineer

In one engagement, I wanted to tailgate in. As I was walking toward the front entrance, I knew I didn't have much time to come up with a solid plan.

A man was exiting his brand-new Kia and walking briskly toward the door. I picked up the pace and made sure I was within earshot of him when I asked another person who was walking toward the door, "Hey, do you know whose Kia that is?" The woman I had spoken to turned and looked at me as if I was nuts, but it didn't matter. It was enough for the owner of the car to slow down and turn around as well.

He looked at me and said, "It's mine. Is there a problem?"

I put my hand out and said, "Paul from HR." I paused long enough to pray that he was not from HR too, and then I continued: "Sorry, I'm new. My wife and I were just looking at that exact car. I'm curious what you think of it."

That was all that was needed. He wanted to show me every feature and talk about it. After a brief preview of the car, I said, "Hey, I'm late for a meeting. Do you mind if we walk and talk?"

"Not at all, Paul." As we started walking, he told me about the warranty, the comfort, the gas mileage, and so much more. He loved his car.

As we approached the front desk, I said, "You obviously made the best choice possible. How did you get so knowledgeable about the cars?" With that statement, I not only complimented his choice but validated his knowledge. He badged in and held the door for me without even thinking.

For the sake of the security guards watching, I pulled my wallet out and tapped the RFID receptacle on the door post and kept walking naturally. This guy talked to me about his Kia for 20 minutes as he led me to HR. When we got there, he said, "Well, here we are—your office. My extension is 4328. If you need more info, just let me know."

I said, "Well, I feel like I should just let you buy me the car—you know so much. Can I call you around 3 p.m. after my meeting?"

"Sure! No problem! Talk then." And he disappeared around the corner.

I liked something he liked, and I liked him for his knowledge. Those two things alone got me past security, into the building, and free from all security checks.

Liking is a powerful principle that can, literally and figuratively, open many doors for you as a professional social engineer. If you are like me, the hardest part is learning to be interested enough that your "liking" comes off as genuine.

> **PRO TIP** You don't want to be warm and friendly but then become cold and uncaring as soon as you get what you want. Those kinds of incongruent actions can cause your target to have a negative feeling.

Principle Eight: Social Proof

In 1969, Dr. Robert O'Connor performed a study called "Modification of Social Withdrawal Through Symbolic Modeling" (*Journal of Applied Behavior Analysis*, 1969, www.ncbi.nlm.nih.gov/pmc/articles/PMC1311030) The subjects of this study were young children who had social anxieties and were withdrawn in school.

The children were divided into two groups. Group 1 was shown a video that contained no level of social interaction. Group 2 was shown a video that lasted about 23 minutes and involved children being very social with positive results.

The children in group 1 had no alteration to their behavior, while the children in group 2 had marked improvement in their social interactions. Not only that, but even when the doctor returned six weeks later to observe the children, those in group 2 were now leading the pack in social interaction.

The doctor was able to modify a potentially life-long path to being socially withdrawn by using something called *social proof.* The video proved to the children in group 2 that it was good, safe, and even beneficial to be more social.

Social Proof in Action

There was a great TV program called *Candid Camera* on which they did a funny prank to show the powerful effects of social proof on different types of people. They would have three or four people who were in on the prank act like they didn't know each other, enter an elevator, and turn toward the rear. The one person who was not in on the prank would eventually turn to conform to the crowd. In one case, they even got a young man to do a full circle and remove his hat, all using social proof.

We each want to be like everyone else. Some of you might argue that you're unique and don't really fit into any group, but that in itself is a group.

When we are lost, confused, or unsure, we generally look to others to see how they are acting for cues (social proof) for what we should be doing.

> **FUNNY STORY**
>
> I showed that *Candid Camera* clip to a class I taught in Vegas. Five of my students decided to see if that would still work today. They pretended they didn't know each other and tried the test three times. In all three cases, the people who were not in on the gag would conform to the group pressure and turn in the direction the group was facing.

Figure 6-10 illustrates the cycle of social proof.

Using Social Proof as a Social Engineer

Many times, people do not want to be the first to take an action. However, I find that using social proof can ease people's minds at making the decision to take an action they are not comfortable with.

In one case, I needed to gain access to a secure area of a building, so I donned the best telephone technician outfit I could build on short notice. Instead of going directly into my target's office, I went to the building next door first. I went in and introduced myself as Paul, a local telephone technician from XYZ Telephone Company. I said I'd be servicing the area and left a fake business card.

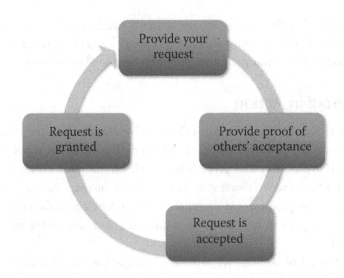

Figure 6-10 Social proof in action

I did this at the businesses on both sides of my target. Then I went into the target office. I approached the front desk and said, "My name is Paul. We are experiencing a fluctuation with the telephone lines, which is causing outages of both phone and Internet in the area. I need to check each company on the block to ensure there are no problems in the system settings." The woman at the desk started to interrupt me, but I pushed through and looked down at my clipboard as I said, "I was chatting with Beth next door, but their lines tested fine. I also ran the test on your other neighbor over here, but Fred was happy it wasn't them. So, I figured since I am out here, I should just run the tests on your system and ensure the problem is not here."

Now, instead of looking at her, I decided to scribble some imaginary notes on my clipboard order form for the other two companies. With only slight hesitation, the woman said, "Oh, I bet you made Fred's day. He's always complaining about the service."

With that, I was past the front desk and being escorted to the server room.

I have used social proof with surveys, phishing emails, vishing calls, and more. In one vishing campaign, I started each conversation with a brief introduction followed by, "I have only three more calls left for the day, and then I am done. Thankfully most people have been super pleasant today." Then I would lead right into my questions. More often than not, applying that slight social pressure worked—partially because people felt good about not being the first to give me all their information. Social proof has been one of the most powerful aspects of influence that I have used.

Influence vs. Manipulation

As I discuss the principles of influence, usually one of the questions that comes up is, "Some of the things you did sound pretty manipulative, so aren't influence and manipulation the same thing?" The fact is that influence and manipulation are similar and sometimes are confused for one another.

Let me be very clear: What I'm sharing here is my viewpoint on this topic. I am by no means saying it is the *only* viewpoint. As a matter of fact, when we had Dr. Cialdini on the podcast, I learned that his opinion on this topic differs from mine drastically.

I define influence as "getting someone to want to do something you want them to do." I define manipulation as "getting someone to do something you want them to do." The difference is that manipulation generally does not include caring about the feelings of the target. Whereas influence tends to be positive in its themes, manipulation does not stay within that boundary.

Manipulation in Action

The best way to illustrate this concept of influence versus manipulation is to tell you a story that is truly embarrassing for me, but it was also pivotal in that it changed my business.

When I started focusing on being a professional social engineer, I was stuck on this thought that I had to always win. The idea that anything less than a 100% win was failure was something I held dear. This thought motivated me to not really care much about the feelings of the client or their staff as long as I "won."

In one job, I was *not* winning. I was losing. The targets weren't clicking on any phishing emails. They were routinely shutting me down on vishing calls. My USB key drops were turned in and never inserted no matter what I labeled them. And two attempts at tailgating and using the heavy box ruse failed me.

I was frustrated, and I didn't realize this was a great time to tell the client how awesome they were. Instead, I was driven to take this to the dark side. The company had an open lunch area that was outside. I had attempted to get inside through those doors but couldn't get past the security there, but I had free access to the lunch area.

The pretext went like this: I was Frank T., the head of a new HR project to gather information for a healthcare rollout. My secretary, Marsha, was a single mom and frazzled. I was standing within earshot of a table full of employees when Marsha walked up with her head down and handed me a stack of blank papers. I look at them and in a very angry tone, I said, "What is this crap, you worthless . . ." I let out a huge sigh and said, "Look, if one simple task is too much for you to handle, maybe it's time for you to find a new job to support yourself and your kid! I'm DONE WITH YOU!"

I then slammed the papers on the table and walked away from Marsha, leaving the papers behind. Marsha sat down and started to cry.

I saw one guy making a beeline for me, but when he saw Marsha crying, he turned to her and said, "Are you okay? What was that about?"

She looked up him, scared and nervous, and replied, "Oh, I'm so sorry. I didn't mean to bother you during lunch. You know how Frank is. He is stressed."

"Frank who? No one has the right to talk to you like that. This is ridiculous." He sat down next to her.

"No, you don't understand. He's having problems at home, and he has a deadline to get these forms filled out by the end of day, and I dropped the ball and forgot. I thought I would do it during lunch, but he just freaked on me. I'm going to get fired."

"He shouldn't talk to you this way . . . this is . . ."

She interrupted, now defending her abuser, "No, it's okay. I deserve it. I was supposed to get this done last week. It's my fault. He is really a nice guy, and he took a risk on me."

"Fair or not, give me those papers!" The man, her savior, stood up and walked to every table and said, "We have until the end of day to complete this, but I want this done before you start eating lunch. When it is completed, hand it to this nice woman here."

He pointed to Marsha, who was now smiling and thanking him for saving her job and being so kind.

By the time the manager had ordered all those people in the lunch room to comply, we had dozens of forms with full names, dates of birth, network IDs, Social Security numbers, home addresses, email addresses, phone numbers, and other personal identity information.

Sure, I won—but at what cost? When the people found out it had been a ruse, do you think there was a teaching moment? What would the lesson have been? To not act like a decent human being? Don't have empathy? That is not a good lesson to be teaching.

Because I had used manipulation, I was forever known at that company as the "guy who abused his secretary." I can tell you, not only was there no learning lesson but to this day, I have not received any more work from that company.

Principles of Manipulation

Although they are negative, manipulation does have the following principles:

- » Increased susceptibility
- » Environmental control
- » Forced reevaluation
- » Removal of power
- » Punishment
- » Intimidation

The names alone should tell you why they are so negative, but there is one study that I think encapsulates why I do not like to use these principles.

In 1967, Dr. Martin Seligman and Dr. Steven F. Maier from the University of Pennsylvania performed a study to determine how some of these principles worked. They used dogs as test subjects to see how they would accept uncontrollable circumstances. Dr. Seligman and Dr. Maier wrote about the results in an article called "Learned Helplessness" (*Journal of Experimental Psychology*, May 1967, http://homepages.gac.edu/~jwotton2/PSY225/seligman.pdf).

In essence, they harnessed dogs in differing stages—either alone in a yoke or in a group—and then shocked the dogs with electricity. In some cases, the dogs had to figure out that there was a panel that, when pressed, could stop the pain. But in other cases, the lever did nothing to stop the pain of the shocks, and those dogs learned there was nothing they could do to stop the punishment—so they accepted it as part of life and lay there whimpering in pain without attempting to escape.

As disturbing as this study is to read about, it holds an important aspect to understanding the principles of manipulation. Many times, the subject will accept something they fear, that hurts, or that they know is bad simply because they don't see any other option. Fear and anger override the brain's ability to think rationally, which leaves only emotion for making decisions. As a professional social engineer, removing the option to think with logic, in most cases also removes the ability for there to be a teaching moment. After the target finds out their fears were used as a test, it leads to many negative emotions that leave the person not wanting to learn from you.

Choosing Influence or Manipulation as a Social Engineer

If you want to be a professional social engineer, you will want to ensure your client has the chance to learn from your endeavors in most cases. That means using influence rather than manipulation.

However, before you decide that there is never a time where manipulation is usable, let me tell you about a few cases where I use it and have no problem doing so.

In the Innocent Lives Foundation, we sometimes find the need to use manipulation to accomplish our goals. When we are hunting child predators or those who commit horrible crimes, whatever works is what we use.

I also use manipulation when working on nation-state attacks. Many times, when my SE team is protecting nation-state assets or infrastructure, we employ both influence and manipulation to ensure all aspects are tested.

Another situation in which I use manipulation is when a client requests it. Generally, this is when the stakes are very high, such as when the client is a large financial institution, nation-state, or infrastructure support organization that needs to test to the deepest levels possible. Sometimes a client says they need my team to use manipulation instead of influence to truly test the protocols. Typically, this request is made after numerous tests have been done, and we need to take it to the next level. When we do these additional tests, we still make sure there is a learning lesson.

For example, one of our clients needed us to test their very resilient and advanced phone-support representatives. The company protected data that was valued at millions of dollars, and the client wanted to make sure the phone-support reps would withstand the attacks they would get from real-world attackers.

After testing them a few times using influence, we decided to step it up to a pretext that involved two female agents on my SE team.

Agent 1 called the department and requested some information to complete payroll using a very believable pretext, it went like this:

SE agent 1:   Hello, this is Sarah, from XYZ Company. My payroll person just got fired, and I must do payroll today. I'm about to give birth to my first baby next week, and I need to get this done before I leave for the weekend.

Phone rep: Congratulations! How exciting! No worries—I can help you. I will just need to verify you, and then I can reset the account to let you in.

SE agent 1:	Excellent, thank you. Ouch!
Phone rep:	Are you okay, Sarah?
SE agent 1:	I don't know. I just had this weird pain. It's probably just stress. Okay, let's do this so I can head out. What do you need?
Phone rep:	Okay, I need your account number and your identification PIN.
SE agent 1:	Sir, like I said, I just had to fire my payroll person, so I don't have that PIN. She reset it, and I need to get back into this account.
Phone rep:	Oh, Sarah, I am so sorry, but I . . ."
SE agent 1:	*[going into labor and dropping the phone]:* Oh my God, oh my God, my water broke!
Phone rep:	Are you okay? Ma'am? Are you okay?
SE agent 1:	*[yelling as if to a coworker]:* You! Come over here and get this phone, and *[as if to another coworker]* YOU CALL 911!
SE agent 2:	Hello, who is this?
Phone rep:	Oh my God. Hi, this is Steve with QRS. I was just assisting Sarah with the payroll account, but I think she needs help. You should go.
SE agent 1:	*[yelling in the background]:* If you hang up that phone, I will fire you. Get the payroll information or NO ONE is getting paid next week!
SE agent 2:	*[in a very stressed tone]:* Oh, Steve, I just need to get into the account, so Sarah will let me take her to the hospital.

Amazingly enough, Steve just gave over the account number and all the information we needed.

Inventive? Yes. Manipulation? Definitely! But the company had requested that we determine whether its reps could stand up to the kind of real-world attack that was likely to come from a malicious hacker, and we had a chance to prove what would and would not work on those agents.

I haven't provided an exhaustive list of when you might be asked to use manipulation, but I've discussed some things that you need to consider if you are going to be or are presently a professional social engineer. Will you use manipulation? If so, when will you use it? How much will you use?

All the same principles of influence and manipulation work on most non-psychopathic human beings, and none of us can spend too much time on the dark side without turning dark ourselves. It is impossible to step in some mud and not get a little dirty. I find it useful to talk to my team at the Innocent Lives Foundation after we have used manipulation as a tactic, to ensure they feel okay and are not too damaged. The foundation has a psychologist on staff to ensure that our people have a safe and healthy environment in which they can unload the mental weight from any negativity.

Summary

If you take away only one important thing from this chapter, let it be this: You are human (just as I am human). Influence works—plain and simple. It works on your targets, and it works on you. It is impossible to stop it, no matter how hard you try.

Influence, when used properly, is rewarding and can alter the way someone behaves and interacts with you. When you master the ability to blend influence with rapport-building skills, you truly become unstoppable.

People will *want* to tell you everything about themselves. They will *want* to trust you. They will *want* to be your friend and help you out. This is powerful, and if you're not careful, it can go to your head, and you can abuse this power.

Keep yourself in check by constantly reminding yourself of why you chose this career path. I constantly tell myself the following things:

» I am doing this to ensure my clients maintain their security.

» I am doing this because I am good at it.

» I am doing this to help people learn about this dangerous vector.

» I am doing this to provide for my family and those I employ.

These responsibilities play a huge part in being a *professional* social engineer. And thinking this way *influences* my decisions to benefit my clients, my employees, and myself.

The principles of influence and manipulation I discussed in this chapter are used every day by marketers, advertisers, salespeople, organizations looking for donations or recruits, and everyone in between. Why should we not use these same principles to help our clients understand how dangerous they can be in the hands of a skilled conman or social engineer?

Take time to read this chapter over a few times and pick one principle at a time to work on. Try using that principle at the office or with your family in a benign way. As you master its use, it will become part of your communication arsenal—another arrow in the quiver to make you an even better social engineer.

I have two more arrows to give you for your quiver. The next chapter will take the skills I've talked about in the last two chapters over the top: Framing and Elicitation.

7 Building Your Artwork

Art and science have their meeting point in method.
—Earl Edward George Bulwer-Lytton

I decided to revert, momentarily, back to the art theme of my first book, *Social Engineering: The Art of Human Hacking* (Wiley, 2011), to clearly define why this chapter is so important. After you model your communications plan, build your pretext, master rapport and influence techniques, and are ready to go, you need to be able to put it all into action. That is where art meets the science of framing and elicitation.

As Earl Edward George Bulwer-Lytton, the 18th-century British politician and novelist, says, the *method* is where art and science meet and even cross over each other. This chapter discusses how, as a professional social engineer, you can artfully learn how to use elicitation and framing with scientifically accurate precision.

When I first started working in a kitchen, the head chef (my boss), handed me a bag of celery and said, "Julienne this bag." Being very new at that job, I had no clue what he meant. After only a few seconds, which seemed like an eternity to me, he said, "You have no clue what I am talking about, do you?"

I gave one nod, and within 60 seconds, the chef had the bag opened and a pile of celery that looked just like Figure 7-1.

"Ah, thin-sliced into strips," I said as if I was the smartest man alive. I started on my first stalk—nice and slow—while the chef observed. He said, "Good job; now I need two bags like that."

Feeling confident, I tried to imitate his speed. For the sake of those with a weaker stomach, I will not post the picture of celery and finger mixed together on the table.

Figure 7-1 Perfectly julienned celery

You're probably wondering what connection this story has to the subject of this chapter. Cooking is an art, but there is a science behind the way you use the tools—the way you wield the knife can make or break your abilities as a chef. Understanding the art of how to make food tasty is very important to a chef, and so is understanding how to prepare the food (usually minus finger parts) in a way that enhances the dish. Blending the art of food preparation and the science of putting it all together creates a perfectly balanced dish.

NOTE Over the years, I have cut my fingers so many times that they look like a creation from Dr. Frankenstein, but I have never in my career or hobby as a chef, served anyone any part of my fingers in a dish. Just thought you would like to know.

This chapter is designed to show you how to blend the art and science of framing and elicitation to bring the skills from the first six chapters to master level. If you apply what you learn in this chapter properly, you should be able to achieve at least one social engineering Michelin star.

The Dynamic Rules of Framing

Think of your house or apartment and how it is shaped. When you look at it from the outside, does one room jut out farther than the others? Do you have an odd-shaped sun room, or is it just a square? How it looks—where the walls are, where the windows are placed, the location of the doors, and so on—is determined by how the house is framed out. In other words, what you see and perceive about your house is based on how the framing was done.

Framing in the sense of communications is not so different. I consider framing, or how someone views and reacts to a certain situation, as largely based on what that person has experienced or understood throughout their life. And those frames, or viewpoints, can be altered by life experience.

When I was 16 years old, surfing and skateboarding were the center of my life. In my opinion, there was nothing else worth living for. An example of how framing is so dynamic comes from this time in my life.

One day, a group of us loaded our surfboards onto the racks of two cars, piled in, and drove in the middle of the night from the west coast of Florida to the east coast. We had heard there was a storm coming and wanted to catch some of the great waves.

We arrived at about 5:00 a.m. The sun was due to rise in an hour and a half. We unloaded all our boards and waxed up. We still had about 30 minutes before the sun would be up enough for us to clearly see, but we were anxious and 16 years old, so we decided to paddle out in the dark to catch the first wave as soon as the sun had come up. We could hear waves crashing on shore, and we could also make out the silhouette of some really large wave sets in the distance.

One by one, the six of us ran into the waves and paddled to the lineup. We sat in the water, bobbing up and down and waiting for the sun to come up. Every few minutes, we could hear what sounded like a large shotgun blast.

We didn't think anything of it as the sound seemed pretty far off and didn't sound too ominous. I started to smell something pungent, so I looked at one of my friends and said, "Hey, is it red tide?"

Red tide is a time of year when there is a really bad algal bloom that kills fish and everything else—and the smell is pretty bad. But my friend said, "No, that's not yet, not sure what that is . . ."

It was only a few minutes later, the sun was clearly over the horizon, and we were seeing beautiful peeling wave sets ready for riding. We also saw a group of fishermen on a pier pretty close to us—chumming the waters for shark! The shotgun blasts we'd heard were from the fishermen dispatching the sharks as they reeled them in. So, my friends and I were sitting in pools of chum. We laughed about it with an almost idiotic sense of humor about how dangerous it was.

I looked down and saw a giant shadow under my board. I've never been a good gauge of size, so I can't tell you exactly how long it was, but I can say it was bigger than my board.

My friends and I laughed more, and we paddled out of the chum and caught a few great waves. At the age of 16, my frame of reference was all about the surf, and danger from sharks didn't mean much to me.

As I think about that situation now, almost 30 years later, my frame of reference has certainly changed. I'm filled with fear even though I'm nowhere near water, chum, or surf. When I was that 16-year-old surfer, I had no cares in the world, and living dangerously was part of my life. Now, as the father of two, a business owner, and a person who wants to live, the idea of being in chum-filled, shark-infested waters fills me with a proper sense of dread. And by dread, I mean I want to build a time machine and go back in time to kick my own butt.

My life experiences, my age, and my internal makeup all form the frame. This point is too important to pass up. *Framing is dynamic—not static.*

Framing is a feature of how our brains work. Our minds react to the context of something rather than reacting just to the thing itself. Here are some examples:

» The moon seems to be bigger when it's on the horizon than when it's directly overhead. The reason is because our brains react to the context (the location) of the object, even though the moon is the same size in both places.

» We don't say that we kill our dogs; we say that we put them to sleep. This is a frame we use to help us deal with a painful circumstance.

» In 1974, Elizabeth Loftus demonstrated framing in a study she performed, by changing one word in a sentence. After showing people a video of a car accident, she asked one of two questions:

  » How fast were the cars going when they contacted?

  » How fast were the cars going when they crashed?

The first question always elicited a response of a slower speed than when she used the word *crashed* in the second sentence. (You can read about this study at `www.simplypsychology.org/loftus-palmer.html`.)

In a 1986 study done by David A. Snow, E. Burke Rochford Jr., Steven K. Worden, and Robert D. Benford titled "Frame Alignment Process, Micromobilization, and Movement Participation" (`www.jstor.org/stable/2095581?seq=1#page_scan_tab_contents`), the researchers defined the following four different aspects of framing.

» Frame bridging

» Frame amplification

» Frame extension

» Frame transformation

I want you to think about *frame bridging* as a social engineer. As you approach a company you see a security guard. His frame is to keep anyone who doesn't belong out. The social engineer's frame is gain access to the building.

It doesn't work too well for the social engineer to go up to the security guard and say, "Hey, I need to get in there to steal some stuff and cause general havoc." Even if you are a professional and a pentester, it won't work to say, "Look, I'm a pro and trying to help test your company to fix the holes. Let me in so I can hack your servers."

So, what builds that bridge between your frame and the guard's frame? Can you think of something I discussed earlier in this book that bridges that gap? A clue is in Figure 7-2.

The pretext bridges the gap and helps you alter the frame of the target to be more accepting of what you say and do. All the detail you put into your pretext—what you carry with you, how you look, and so on—makes framing easier, but there's more to it.

In 2004, author George Lakoff wrote the book *Don't Think of an Elephant!* (Chelsea Green Publishing). In that book, he defined four rules of framing. These four rules are essential to understand whether you want to master this art. I have adapted Lakoff's four rules to apply to social engineering.

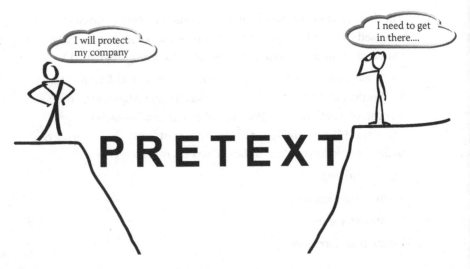

Figure 7-2 The pretext bridges the framing gap.

Rule 1: Everything You Say Evokes the Frame

To clearly grasp this rule, you need to understand how our minds work to visualize things as pictures. Great teachers and storytellers use their words to help you picture the points in the stories. Here's an example of how two different stories can be written about the same event:

> **Story 1**   As I sat on my surfboard, I saw a large wave coming toward me. I lay down and paddled, but the wave crashed, and I found myself under the water wondering just how big that shark really was.

> **Story 2**   I looked out at the horizon; the sun was just barely peeking over. Its rays not only illuminated the water but warmed my face. I saw a wave that looked like a freight train bearing down on me. Its power was easily noticeable from the speed and thickness of the wave. Its foamy head hurled toward me like an angry lion.

I lay down on my board and quickly whipped it around to face the shore. I dug into the water using every fiber of my shoulder muscles. Although fluid, I felt the water with every stroke as if I was digging through wet cement.

The wave caught my board as if a supernatural force had grabbed it. I went from standing still to dropping in on a roller coaster in a matter of seconds. I struggled to try to stand as my board wobbled and smacked the top of the water. When I turned, I saw nothing but the lip of the wave that was about to smack me in the face like an angry taskmaster.

As the wave tossed over me, I was forced underwater, and all I could do was start to imagine that living missile of a shark heading toward me. I struggled in panic and fear to make it above water. When I did, I grabbed my board in white-knuckled fear and paddled to shore.

Both stories are about the same event, but which helps you really picture it in your mind? Which helps you feel like you are there with me?

The answer is obvious: Story 2. That is why this rule is so important. Sometimes the words we choose in our daily vocabulary can create mental pictures that are offensive to targets. As a professional social engineer, I find that not only do I succeed more, but I have a higher number of return clients if I use non-offensive language than if I use language that might offend.

To keep this book PG-13, I won't go through an extensive list of words that can be offensive, but here are a few general guidelines about things you should avoid:

» **Racial Slurs**   Even said in humor, racial slurs are not funny. Not only are they not funny, they're usually seen as signs of ignorance.

» **Gender- or Sexuality-based Slurs**   These slurs have the same effect as racial slurs—they are signs of ignorance and are destructive to rapport-building.

» **Curse Words**   I find that even if my targets use coarse language, I can avoid doing so myself for the sake of those who are overhearing the conversation. Often times, by not using the same language as the target, I can effectively change their use of that language as well.

» **Bodily Functions**   These words trigger strong feelings of disgust, and therefore should be avoided.

Think about words you use in your daily vocabulary, and then decide if they might cause a target to feel one of the seven base emotions: anger, surprise, fear, disgust, contempt, sadness, or happiness. Then decide if that emotion is positive or negative. If it is potentially negative to a damaging degree, err on the side of caution before using the word.

TIP My industry does something called "penetration testing." The name alone opens itself up for a slew of non-humorous sexual innuendoes. However, more times than I care to mention, I've heard someone who has completed a pentest say, "I raped that server." Considering that in America alone, someone is a victim of sexual assault every 98 seconds, I do not find that statement funny. In fact, the negative impact of hearing a security test described as rape for a person who has been sexually assaulted could bring back the trauma all over again. *Do not use that term to describe your work!*

Rule 2: Words That Are Defined with the Frame Evoke the Frame

The other night, I walked onto my porch, and in the corner by the light, I saw a creature in a web. It was wrapping an insect into a cocoon for a later meal.

What did I describe to you? Probably what you see in Figure 7-3.

The point is that I didn't need to use the word *spider* to get you to think *spider*. I can merely describe a spider, and your brain automatically pictures it.

As a professional social engineer, my pretext automatically makes you think about the job I'm trying to tell you that I'm there for. But I can also elicit the right emotional frame by describing a situation, rather than using threats.

Figure 7-3 In case you are still guessing, yes, it's a spider.

PHOTO COURTESY OF ARTYANGEL, https://pixabay
.com/en/spider-fly-web-insect-2683918/

In one case, I sent a phish to a client that read something like this:

> *On Jan 4, your car was photographed running stop light marker*
> *XCV431. A ticket was issued and has not been paid. Failure to pay*
> *the fine can result in a negative impact.*
> *You can file a claim or verify your payment on our secure portal at*
> www.pleaseclickthisnowsoicanhackyou.com.

(Yes, the URL has been changed for safety.) Notice that I didn't need to threaten arrest. I didn't need to threaten massive fines. I just painted enough of a word-picture to trigger the emotions of curiosity and fear but then gave the recipient hope there was a way out. (And, yes, he clicked.)

Rule 3: Negating the Frame

Imagine this scene: My student was tasked with getting some personal information from a person—just the full name, date of birth, and some brief history. Even though the student was nervous about being observed by me, the conversation started off pretty good and, after a minute, sounded like this:

Student:	Wow, thank you for your help. I was wondering what to buy her for a gift, and that is a great idea. *[The student applied a very nice validation statement to an idea for a gift for his wife for her birthday.]*
Target:	Yeah, no problem. So, I gotta . . . *[She was about to say go but was interrupted by the student.]*
Student:	*[putting his hand out]:* I'm Tom, Tom Smith. *[He used a nice natural rhythm to help elicit the target's name.]*
Target:	Uh, yeah, nice to meet you, Tom. I'm Sarah.
Student:	Sarah, great to meet you. What was your last name?
Target:	Well, why do you want to know that?
Student:	Oh, no reason. Just was curious. Anyhow, so what do you do for your birthday? Are you born in July?
Target:	Hey, Tom, it was nice meeting you, but I'm not sure I want to just give that info out. Sorry.
Student:	No problem, Sarah, it's not like I am gonna *hack* you or anything!

At that last statement, the target literally leaned away from my student, looked at her watch, said she was late, and left.

What did he do? It is what we call *negating the frame*, which is defined as mentioning the very thing you do not want your target to think about, in essence causing them to think about that very thing.

What is the one thing you don't want your target to think about when you're engaging with them as a professional social engineer? How about *getting hacked*?!

If you don't want them to think about it, then don't say things like

- » "I'm not gonna use it to hack you!"
- » "It's not like I'm trying to break in!"
- » "I would never send you a phishing email."
- » "I'm not a crook!"

All of these are examples of negating the frame. Any time we mention the frame of the opposition, we negate our frame. And remember Figure 7-2—their frame is to protect.

Look for ways to augment or enhance your frame using your pretext, clothing, or other tools; therefore giving the target the ability to bypass any internal questions and doubts.

Rule 4: Causing the Target to Think About the Frame Reinforces the Frame

Any time we get someone to think about a frame, we reinforce that frame. No matter what that frame is, we reinforce it. For example, parents have the choice to reinforce positive frames or negative frames into their children, as in these examples:

- » "You are so stupid!"
- » "You're not good at sports."
- » "Can't you do anything right?"
- » "You are really pretty and smart!"
- » "You can accomplish anything you put your mind to."
- » "I know this is hard, but I know you can do it!"

As a professional social engineer, you can reinforce frames by the words, clothing, and pretexts you choose.

In one vishing job my company was doing, our pretext was that we were calling from IT and we had had a badge system corruption the night before. Our goal was to obtain full name, date of birth, employee ID, and other details from the employees we were assigned to call. It went something like this:

Target: Bob speaking. How can I help you?

SE: Bob, this is Paul down in IT. Last night, we had a badging-system corruption error, and about 100 accounts were flagged. You're a lucky winner. Did you have problems getting into the building today?

Target: No, it worked. Who is this?

SE: Paul, Paul Williams in IT. I work with Tony R. Look this will only take a minute. As you know, our badge system is tied in with pay-roll, so we don't want to delay in fixing any errors.

Target: Ha, that's true. Well, what do you need?

SE: I need to verify your full name. Can you spell your last name for me?

Target: Um, seriously? It's *S-M-I-T-H*. Not too hard.

SE: Wow, thank God I called. IT had Robert Jones in this record for this extension. That would have messed up payroll for sure. I guess when the corruption algorithm was run, it tried to relink the ta-bles and misaligned the database counters. *[I said this knowing it meant nothing, but I took a gamble that Bob from accounting was not really a geek.]*

Target: Yeah, I don't want anyone else getting my paycheck. Let's check the rest.

From there on out, it was a series of using deliberate false statements and positive reinforcement to get his full name, date of birth, employee ID, and even the last four digits of his Social Security number. My words and the pretext all reinforced my frame; therefore, the target more easily accepted it.

Keep the target thinking about your frame throughout your opening words, and it will make moving on to the next section so much easier. And we call that *elicitation*.

Elicitation

How would you define *elicitation*?

I define it as "getting information you never ask for." In essence, elicitation looks and sounds like a conversation. In that conversation, a skilled elicitor is steering the conversation in a certain direction to obtain information without you having asked for it.

Elicitation has some natural rules and principles that are inherent to its success. Each of these is a powerhouse unto itself, but when you combine them, you will master the art of conversation, and as a professional social engineer, that can make you a force to be reckoned with.

As I go through the four rules of elicitation. keep in mind this one important point: If done right, elicitation should look and feel like a normal, non-forced conversation with your target.

Ego Appeals

In Chapter 5, "I Know How to Make You Like Me," I talk about ego suspension, and this principle is the very *opposite* of that. In this case, you're focused on the target's ego rather than thinking about your own.

What is the ego? The *Oxford English Dictionary* defines it as, "A person's sense of self-esteem or self-importance." This is important to understand because when we hear this, we may automatically assume we have to inflate the target's ego, but that is not what I am saying. I'm saying you have to *appeal* to their ego.

Appealing to the target's ego needs to be done with the following three things in mind:

» You have to use sincerity.

» You have to have the proper level of rapport.

» You have to be realistic.

"Suppose I've never met you before just meet you, and I walk up to you and say, Wow, you are one of the most attractive people I have ever seen." If I then try to start a conversation with you, what might you be thinking? Probably one or more of the following:

» "Creep!"

» "What do you want?"

» "Um, what's the scam?"

» "Of course, I am. Now go away!"

Whatever you think at that moment, that appeal to your ego was not done with sincerity, realistically, and at the level of rapport we have built, so it will not result in a good elicitation.

Here's a story from the real life of my wife, who's one of the best elicitors I have ever seen. We were in New York City. I had taken her and the family to see my old stomping grounds. At one point, we were on the subway going uptown. If you've ever been in the subway, you know that people just stay to themselves. People aren't rude, but they also aren't friendly. Everyone has somewhere to go and is stressed or tired. You stick to yourself and go about your business.

My wife was sitting across from this older African-American woman who looked like she was going to catch some sleep before her stop. My wife leaned over into her space, grabbed her scarf to feel the material, and said, "Wow, this is truly beautiful and so soft. Can I ask you where you purchased this?"

Now we were on the subway in NYC, and my wife leaned across personal, ethnic, and space boundaries—and yet, those two became best friends in seconds. Why? What was the ego appeal?

Not only did my wife validate the woman's choice of clothing, but she asked this woman to educate her on where to get it. And this was no scam—my wife was sincerely interested, and that sincerity was easy to see.

Thanks to all of that, a 20-minute conversation ensued about where to get great clothing in NYC. As annoyed as I was because I realized I was now going to be spending more money, I could not help but marvel at my wife and watch and learn as she taught me how to be a master elicitor.

Now, how can you become a master like Areesa? What is the secret sauce? Here are a few hints:

» She really does love people and is interested in them.

» Her intentions are altruistic.

» She is adorable and has a great smile.

But what do you do if you're not a people-loving, friendly, adorable, smiley, tiny Asian woman like my wife?

First, practice observing some things about people—let's say your family. When you come home from work tomorrow, take notice of things: Did your daughter do the dishes? Did your son take out the trash? Is their homework done? Did your wife have a long stressful day, too?

Try simply saying something like, "Wow, I noticed the dishes were done when I came home. Thank you." Or "Hey, honey, you look super tired. Was your day okay?"

Then watch what happens. A person's body language will soften. They will open up and become friendly and more talkative. Why? You validated them and appealed to their ego.

After you've practiced on your family, take it outside the home and try it with strangers. This will be much more difficult. You have to observe without being creepy, and make your approach with all the lessons of Chapter 5. Then you start appealing to their ego.

Imagine this scenario: You're behind your target in the line at Starbucks. He is a 34-year-old tall male. He is neatly dressed and has a preppy but nerdy style. You see him pull out a brand-new iPhone and type a text on it. With just this information, what could be your ego appeal that would start a conversation? Think about it for a second before you read on.

I would try something like this: "Excuse me. I saw you have one of those iPhones. I was thinking of switching over. Do you like it so far?"

If he just spent $1000 on a phone, then he is going to have an opinion. No matter what opinion he gives you, you can validate and appeal with, "Wow, you really helped me out here. I am never good with these decisions, but you made it much easier. My name is Chris, Chris Hadnagy . . ." as I put my hand out to shake his.

And now a conversation is started.

Mutual Interest

There are a lot of really hot topics in the world today. Many of them seem to not just separate people but cause rifts the size of a small state. Some of these polarizing topics can create such passion that some people even get violent if there are disagreements.

It is important for a professional social engineer to not only understand this but to have the ability to put aside their own thoughts on these hot topics and find mutual interest.

Let me give you an example from my experience. I won't tell you which side of the fence I am on. Imagine the situation as if you were there.

I walked into an office-building lobby that I had been tasked to try to gain entry to, and I found a bunch of people standing around a TV. There had been a horrible incident—a school shooting. Children were dead and wounded. The shooter killed himself. It was truly a horrible situation.

One man said, "If I was there, I would have had my gun, and he would be dead before he even got off his first round."

Another person replied, "This is the problem! It's because guns are so easy to buy that these things keep happening!"

You could tell the room was getting divided and there were clearly two camps. The atmosphere in the room was tense as people spouted their opinions on where they stood on this matter. One person looked up to see me there and didn't even ask who I was. She just said, "Did you hear the news? Look, this is just awful."

I replied, "No, I didn't hear 'til I walked in. It sounds truly terrible. Do you have any family or friends in that area?"

"Thank God, no," she replied. Then without even a breath, she said, "But, it's okay. Bill has the solution—he will just give out handguns to everyone in the country, and we can return to the Wild West."

Bill, who I could see was getting physically upset, said, "Or we can just take your idea and sit around singing and praying while everyone kills our kids."

Ouch. This was going downhill fast. I realized that it really wasn't the time to be a professional social engineer, but I could try to defuse the situation. Since both of their comments were pointed toward me, when Bill got done speaking, they both glared at each other and then at me, almost as if to say, "So, which side are you taking?"

Knowing that if I took any side I would be alienating half the room, I said, "Oh, my. Those poor families. I have two kids of my own. I can't imagine having to deal with the news of one of them being killed. This is truly a sad day."

Suddenly the rift closed. There was no more gap. They all looked at each other and remembered it wasn't about being pro- or anti-gun. It was about our children. It doesn't matter if you are for guns or you hate them—children getting shot in school is a topic we can all agree is terrible.

When your task is to social engineer someone or a group, and the topic may be challenging or the people may not be your favorite, look for the common ground. There usually is one thing that you can find that will allow you all to be on common ground and start a conversation.

The preceding example is a serious one, but this works even in minor cases, too. Here are some topics that generally can help you start a conversation that establishes common ground:

Weather   Especially if there is some odd weather—a heavy snow storm, too much rain, unseasonably hot or cold spells—the weather can provide quick opening topics to break the ice.

Technology   Asking for advice on tech the target has (cell phone, laptop, smart watch, etc.) that you have observed can be a great way to get them talking.

Children   As long as you ask questions at the appropriate level of rapport—and you are asking general questions about kids, not about their kids specifically—this can really get people talking.

Pets   People love to talk about (and share photos of) their pets.

Sports   Although not everyone is interested in sports, if you notice someone wearing a particular team's jersey or hat, it can be a great topic. As long as you don't say something like "Ah, Cowboy's fan, huh? Sorry."—which is not a very good opener.

I suggest you avoid topics like politics, health care, religion, other very deeply personal choices, or any violent news story. These topics can create a giant rift between you and your target.

Through observation of the target and their surroundings (whether through OSINT or physical observation), find the topic that can be of mutual interest, then use that topic to start a conversation.

Deliberate False Statement

The principle of deliberate false statement is so powerful that you have to try it. What happens to you when you are in a grocery store and you hear someone in the line say something you know is false?

I have heard and seen everything including someone making noises under their breath (like "hrmph" or "yeah, right") to someone correcting a complete stranger.

Why do people react this way? We have the need to be right and to correct things that are wrong. When we hear something we "know" is wrong, we generally correct it, even if it is just in our own head first. Depending on who we are, where we are, and our passion for the topic, we might let the idea out of our head and into the open.

Here is an example that even shocked me as to how well it worked. I was sitting in a restaurant with Robin Dreeke, and we had planned out this conversation to see how deliberate false statement would work. It was a small restaurant with tables that were close to each other. It wasn't hard for diners to hear others' conversations if they wanted.

Robin said, in a pretty loud voice, "Hey, did you see that article in the *Times* that said over 80% of the people use their date of birth as their ATM pin?"

This study did not actually exist, the article that Robin was referring to wasn't real, and for the love of all that is holy, I hope that statistic is really, really off.

I chimed in, "No, that's not true. I use a combination of my wife's and my date of birth, so its 0411."

Robin said, "Well, I think it's true, because I do."

Then we both just got silent for a couple seconds, and as if on cue, the couple next to us looked over, and the husband said, "I tell her all the time to not use her date of birth for that PIN, but she tells me it's easy to remember." Amazingly enough, his wife said, "Well, how can you not remember 0660, right?"

Whoa, did this woman just give us—complete strangers in a restaurant—her PIN number? I wish I could say it stopped there. But it did not! The man to the other side of us turned to the woman he was with and said, "So, what kind of a PIN do you use?"

And without hesitation, she replied, "My bank lets me use six digits, so I actually use my daughter's whole date of birth: 031192."

The waitress who was overseeing all this said, "My bank lets me choose an actual word, which I type out using the keypad. My son named his first pet *Samson*, so I just use that."

Here I was, sitting in a public restaurant, collecting everyone's dates of birth, pets' names, and, scarily enough, bank card PINs because of one deliberate false statement.

I was so enamored by this principle that I started using it everywhere and teaching it. Then I had a student who became my teacher. I told this story in class, and he said, "Whoa, I have an idea of some things I want to try."

Later in the class, I was observing him out in public interacting with some targets. He walked up to a woman who was sitting at a table eating a bowl of strawberries. With no introduction, no rapport, he had this conversation:

Student: Hey, you like strawberries. You must be born in February!

Target: Umm, no, actually I was born in July.

Student:	Oh, like on the fourth, with the holiday?
Target:	No, the 11th. Why? *[She gave him a confused look.]*
Student:	Okay, cool. Bye.

And then he walked away. I said, "There's no way that would work again." But he went up to one complete stranger after another and threw out the weirdest deliberate false statements. Every time, people gave him information.

The flaw with this method was there was no rapport. So, when he was done, his targets were left confused and wondering what had just happened. They definitely were not left "feeling better for having met him."

Be careful with deliberate false statement, and use these guidelines:

> » Using deliberate false statement too many times in a row can make you come across as unknowledgeable, and that can make your target lose faith in you.

> » Don't confuse deliberate false statement with negating the frame. If you don't want the target to think about hacking, don't mention "hacking" in your deliberate false statement.

> » Deliberate false statement works much better after you have built some level of rapport with the target.

> » The deliberate false statement must have a ring of truth to it. If my student had approached the first woman and said, "Oh, you like strawberries—you must fly dragons," he would have had nowhere to go with that; confusion would have been the result, not the need to correct.

I truly do challenge you to try deliberate false statement. You'll be amazed at how well it works, and how much information you will receive.

Walking up to a complete stranger and asking for his or her PIN, date of birth, or other personal information will result (most of the time) in all sorts of alarms being raised. But by employing a deliberate false statement, you can work all those personal details right into a conversation.

Having Knowledge

Don't confuse having knowledge with being a know-it-all. The two things are completely different. Having knowledge on the topic you will cover with your target

FALSE STATEMENTS PLUS QUID PRO QUO

I tried my student's method in one elicitation engagement, and it worked like magic. Then I followed up with, "Ah, August 12th. That's funny, my sister was born in August, too."

Giving some quid pro quo helps the target feel at ease with what they just gave up in the elicitation. I added, "My grandma used to say that August babies were more artistic and creative. Do you have any musical talent?"

With a chuckle the woman said, "No, I am more of a math geek. That's why I'm an accountant. I guess grandmas aren't always right, are they?"

I said, "Ha, I guess not. But don't tell her. My Italian grandma will grab your ear and yell at you!"

The woman replied, "Oh, I know how that is. My family came over from Ireland. They didn't pinch as much as punch!"

"Ouch! Sounds like . . . um . . . fun. So, do you have a really Irish-sounding last name?" I thought this might be a great segue to getting more personal info.

"You can't get more Irish than my name: Mary O'Donnell," she said, putting an Irish lilt on it.

I replied, "Oh, you have a very cool little accent. Sadly, I've lost all my Italian except for the curse words."

"Well, that may come in handy still."

Notice that with one deliberate false statement and some quid pro quo, I was able to obtain this woman's full name, date of birth, job function, and other details about her life and family.

can go a long way during elicitation. Time for another fail story, and this one led to a failure on the job.

My company was tasked to gain entry to the server room of a university. In scoping out the building that the server room was in, we noticed one professor would go into the building at about 7:00 a.m. No other staff was in the building at that time, so we thought it would be a great time to gain entry. The doors all used RFID locks, and because this was an SE job, we thought we would try the human angle first.

We did OSINT on the professor and saw he wrote a paper on something to do with quantum physics and some other large words that I don't understand. With my infinite wisdom and skill (heavy dose of sarcasm here), I memorized the name of the paper, and the next morning, I planned to approach the professor.

As he briskly walked toward the building, my plan was to start a conversation about the paper, and we would walk into the building together, and when we parted ways, I would break into the server room area.

I started off, "Good morning, sir. My name is Paul Williams. You're professor Smith, right?"

"Yes, I am. How can I help you?" the professor asked, without stopping his walk toward the building.

"I wanted to ask you some questions about the paper you wrote on quantum physics," I said as I rattled off the title of the paper with effortless ease.

There was a slight pause, and he said, "Okay. What questions do you have?"

Oh no! My brain raced. How did I not think past this part? We still walked toward the door, but it seemed to be miles away now. I truly tried to think of one intelligent thing to say, and my best response was, "Um, so, what made you write that paper?" My voice trailed off at the end in uncertainty.

For the first time since I approached him, the professor stopped, turned toward me fully, and said, "I'm not sure what kind of game you are playing, Son, but come back when you've actually read it." He then turned and walked even more briskly toward the door.

Sure, I could have read the paper, but even if I had read that paper a few dozen times, I doubt I could have come up with even one or two intelligent questions on that topic. Or I could have found someone who understood the topic to help me formulate questions that were intelligent. However, neither of those solutions would have kept things simple. The simplest path would have been for me to have used a pretext that fits the knowledge I have. Maybe I could have been a student who was looking to take this professor's class, and I wanted to know what papers or books I should read to make his class more enjoyable.

When I approached him, I should have had knowledge of the university, what courses and teachers I would be interacting with, and what programs exist. Having this knowledge doesn't mean I would have had to use it and blurt it all out from the get-go just to prove my point, but having that knowledge would have made the way I talk and the things I said more believable. That way, if a question like "What courses are you in now?" had come up, I would have had that knowledge handy so I could remain believable.

The more believable you are, the easier it is for the target to assume you are who you say you are.

The Use of Questions

Questions are a natural part of conversation. From the moment we begin to speak, we use questions to send and receive data. This is why understanding the four different types of questions—as well as how to use them—is essential to becoming a good elicitor. That is what this next section will cover.

Questions are powerful parts of communication. As soon as we hear a question, our brains start to formulate a response. Even if that answer is never spoken, forming a response is unavoidable.

Skillful use of questions gets the target invested in the conversation. Each type of question can be used by a skilled social engineer to elicit both information and emotions from targets.

To help you understand how you can use different types of questions for social engineering, here's a story from my own experience, which I refer to as OpOfficeSpace.

My task was to gain entry onto the 16th floor of an office building, but the company that occupied that floor didn't own the whole building. I came up with the pretext that I was sent from corporate to conduct a surprise inspection to see if workspace safety policies, such as keeping exits unblocked, were being followed.

I based the pretext on some OSINT we had found about new policies and bad press that this company had received for having poor employee working conditions. Publicly, the company had vowed to fix those problems and claimed that they sent strong messages to all satellite offices with instructions about what to do.

I made a badge that had the corporate logo on it and "Safety Inspector" in bold letters across the top. Armed with my clipboard, camera, and some other tools, I entered the front doors and walked right past the security desk.

The woman behind the front desk popped to her feet and asked, "Excuse me sir, where are you going?"

I barely slowed down while answering, "I am going to 16."

"Um, please stop. I need to get your ID since you don't have the right badge to use the elevator."

"Oh, I'm sorry. Let me explain. What is your name, ma'am?"

"I'm Alicia Smith," she said as she pointed to her badge.

"Nice to meet you, Alicia. I work for ABC Corporation on 16, and due to recent incidents at some of our facilities, I've been tasked with the job of doing surprise inspections. The facilities have not been notified. Have you heard about the recent problems we've had with employee work conditions?"

She shrugged her shoulders but replied, "Yes, I saw it on the news."

"Okay, then you know how much trouble we got into. I'm sure your employer takes good care of you, and these inspections are all about making sure our people are being taken care of, but they must remain a surprise to be effective."

"Okay, I understand that. I think it's great to see a company that takes that so seriously. I will badge you to 16 in the elevator." With that, I was walking toward the secure elevators with my new ally.

I stopped and asked, "Alicia, some elevators require badges for both directions. What kind of a security system do you have in the elevators?"

"Oh, silly me. I almost forgot, yes. We just had this new type of elevator security system installed, and you need a badge to do both. Let me grab you a visitor one. Wait here." She ran back to the desk to grab me an unsigned badge and then sent me on my way.

I exited the elevator on the 16th floor, and to both my left and right were glass doors. I could see a secretary sitting to my right, and she was looking at me with an increasingly curious look. As I walked up to the desk, I knew she would ask me some questions, and I wanted to preempt her, so I said, "Hi there. I'm Paul from corporate." I pulled out my badge and showed it to her briefly, but I wasn't sure how accurate it was, so I pulled my pen out and pointed to the clipboard. "This is office 43211, right?" I asked this as I pointed to a work order.

"Um, yes. Paul, why are you here? You're not on the schedule," she said, looking very confused.

"I wouldn't be on the schedule—this is a surprise inspection. After last month's problems with OSHA, we need to make sure that our work space has been drastically improved. You got that internal memo, right?"

She nodded her head yes and said, "Yes. I was asked to print it and make sure everyone had a physical copy."

"Good. Well that marks my first check box off." I turned to the second page and checked off a box before I said, "Thank you! You made my job start off great! I want to write your name next to it as one of the employees who followed directions. What is your name?"

"Beth. Beth Simons."

"Excellent, Beth. As observant as you are, I am sure you saw some areas that need special consideration here. Where should I start?"

She looked toward one area and said, "I think we are all compliant here, but I'm not sure. I don't want to get anyone in trouble."

"I get that, Beth. Thank you for being so honest. I'm going to start my walk-through. I'll let you know personally when I'm done." With that, I was in the office space unsupervised.

Open-Ended Questions

Just as it sounds, an open-ended question is one that doesn't direct the receiver in any particular direction but instead allows them to answer solely from their opinion. Open-ended questions generally can't be answered with a simple yes or no. An open-ended question allows the target to decide how much information they will provide. This is empowering and validating for the person involved, and it can help build rapport. An open-ended question is something like, "What is your favorite restaurant in town?"; as opposed to, "Is there a good restaurant close to this hotel?" Both are valid questions, but one elicits information that will enable you to profile the target more thoroughly. The words you use within a question elicit emotions, and those emotions affect the answer you get. An open-ended question encourages the target to engage their knowledge, attitudes, beliefs, opinions, and feelings.

The success of these questions is largely dependent on the way you, as a professional social engineer, employ active listening and direct the questions to obtain useful information. This is important to understand, so when you are formulating your pretext, you can start to plan what type of questions you would naturally use. Remember, the goal is to keep the target talking openly about relevant details that can assist in the end goal of completing the social engineering engagement.

PRO TIP The motto "just keep them talking" is not really relevant to social engineering. We don't want our targets to just talk—we want them to talk about information that's relevant to our needs.

In OpOfficeSpace, I was able to use open-ended questions multiple times, but one you may recall is when I asked Alicia the security guard about the elevators. She not only answered the question but went on to tell me about the new security system installed in the elevators. Using an open-ended question in this situation allowed me to gather not just a badge but critical intel on their security systems.

Closed-Ended Questions

Closed-ended questions elicit brief and narrow answers. Usually, they can be answered with one or two words. Skilled interrogators often use closed-ended questions to verify facts they've already obtained. In addition, closed-ended questions are excellent to use for reading nonverbals. When a closed-ended question is asked, our bodies answer before our mouths do. Most of the time, our body language gives an honest answer even if we state a lie. We might shrug or shake our head no but say the word "Yes."

I have used closed-ended questions many times with my kids. For example, I might say this to one of them: "I told you that 11:00 p.m. was bedtime. Did you actually shut down the computer and go to bed at 11?" The head shakes *no* but the child says, "I think so. I didn't see the exact time."

A benefit to closed-ended questions is that they ensure the social engineer is able to elicit details and secure specific bits of information. When you're using closed-ended questions, it's a good idea to start off with basic questions before getting to anything too deep. The basics of who, what, where, why, and how are good places to begin.

In OpOfficeSpace, I used closed-ended questions with Beth the receptionist when I asked her if she had gotten the memo. She not only nodded her head *yes* but she also verbally answered "Yes." However, when I used the same type of question with Alicia about seeing any news regarding to the problems in ABC Corporation, she shrugged and replied, "Yes." This incongruence tells me she wasn't really sure if she knew about this. Because of my perception of her confusion, I could add some facts that might not have been completely truthful.

Leading Questions

I was sent a link to a web page that contained a video. The page started off with something like this: "In this study, only really observant and smart people can count the number of times the white shirts pass the ball."

I sat there thinking, "I'm a social engineer—one of the most observant humans on the planet. I got this!" I clicked Play.

I never blinked, and I counted every pass. I stared at the screen the whole time. When the video was done, I was presented with some options for the pass count. When the correct number came up, I exclaimed to the screen, *"That's it!"* with serious pride in my voice.

Then the video went on to say, "But how many of you saw the man in a gorilla costume and a tutu dance across the court and exit the other side?"

In utter disbelief, I exclaimed, "There was no gorilla!" After all, I'm a social engineer and one of the most observant humans on the planet, right? There's no way I could miss something that obvious.

I replayed the video from the beginning, and, to my amazement, a six-foot man in a gorilla costume and tutu came on the court, did a twirl, and exited the other side.

How had I not seen that?

The answer is simple: leading. I was led to focus on one thing—the pass count of people in white shirts—and my brain blocked out everything else.

So, how can a social engineer use leading in question form? In the OpOfficeSpace scenario, I was able to lead the target to thinking about possible repercussions of not complying with my request to get into the CEO's office. I did this by combining a statement with a leading question: "I understand that I'm not on the schedule, Beth, so how do you suggest we explain to Mr. Smith that I could not fix his computer after he comes back from his holiday?

In addition to leading questions, I often use misdirection when I am accessing a building. I have a clipboard with a camera embedded in the front. There is a large (quarter-size) hole with a lens protruding and another smaller hole with a microphone. I constantly worry that a target will see it. I put a work order or other paper on the front of the clipboard, and with a nice metal pen, I tap on that paper while saying something like, "Yeah, you see here? I'm supposed to check the serial number of the motor to see if there's a recall." So far, no one has ever seen the camera, because I lead them to look away from it.

As a professional social engineer, you have to plan ahead to be able to use leading questions. Build them into your pretext. Plan what you will do in order to lead targets away from the things you don't want them to notice.

In OpOfficeSpace, I didn't want Beth to take too long staring at my badge. If it wasn't a match for a real badge, she would have noticed, so I quickly used my pen and a work order to lead her to where I wanted her to focus. This was powerful, and allowed me to not only redirect, but to add legitimacy to my claims.

Assumptive Questions

Another way a social engineer can collect intel during elicitation is to use assumptive statements and questions. You can use these types of questions when you have some knowledge and can make an assumption to confirm that knowledge with a question or statement.

This is another technique I have used with my kids to find out details that aren't clear. For example:

Me: So, when you were at the party, did Tammy show up?

My child: Not 'til later that night—you don't have to worry, Dad.

That brief exchange let me know my son was at the party, so I could continue to probe in that direction to get more information.

As a professional social engineer, assumptive questions can be used upon the initial approach in order to bypass certain conversation-stoppers. A conversation-stopper is just what it sounds like: a statement or statements that are made with the intent to stop someone from moving past a particular person or area.

In OpOfficeSpace, I used assumptions with both Alicia and Beth upon initial approach. I assumed I belonged where I was and that they should have known why I was there and that they should have allowed it. I didn't use arrogance or anger—just an air of belonging, as if I knew where I was going and exactly why I was there.

Summary

A conversation is like an onion—both have many layers. As you peel back one layer, you can get deeper and deeper to the center.

Each elicitation technique is an important part of a conversation. Learning how to use each can help you become a master at conversation and a superb social engineer. The goal of elicitation is to extract information in a normal-sounding conversation. If you practice these skills, that is exactly what you will be able to do. The fascinating thing is that this is not limited to verbal conversations—these same skills work whether you are having a conversation over email, chat, text, phone, or any other means.

Just as a chef decides what tools and ingredients to use to make a dish, you can sprinkle a few questions into your conversation, add a dash of deliberate false statements, and mix in a healthy dose of mutual interest to elicit the information you need.

As you begin to master this skill you will be serving up perfect dishes of elicitation and conversation. With that arrow in your quiver, the last one you need is the one I describe in the next chapter: reading nonverbals and body language.

8

I Can See What You Didn't Say

It is our responsibility to learn to become emotionally intelligent.
These are skills, they're not easy, nature didn't give them to us—we
have to learn them.

—DR. PAUL EKMAN

When I wrote my first book, *Social Engineering: The Art of Human Hacking* (Wiley, 2010), I was relatively new to the world of nonverbals. But I had started a relationship with Dr. Paul Ekman and learned from him as my mentor. Dr. Paul Ekman started his journey to understand nonverbals in the late 1950s, and for the last 60-plus years he has been leading the field of research into nonverbal communications.

Dr. Ekman helped me refine not only my work, but also how I communicated. That led to my second book, *Unmasking the Social Engineer: The Human Element of Security* (Wiley, 2014), which delves deep into facial expressions, body language, hand gestures, and every aspect of nonverbals. I even cover the part of nonverbal communication you don't see: the hijacking of the amygdala.

If you followed, read, or listened to any of my work before, it is probably not too hard to believe that when it comes to Dr. Ekman, I pretty much react like what you see in Figure 8-1 when I am around him.

I have a few goals with this chapter. First, I want to make sure I uphold Dr. Ekman's high standards of ensuring everything I say can be backed up with research. Second, I don't want to just duplicate either of my previous books, especially if you have read one or both of them. In this book, I present nonverbals from one key area that can literally change your life as a social engineer: the understanding of baseline changes between comfort and discomfort.

Figure 8-1 What most people imagine I do when I see Dr. Ekman (not far from the truth).

PHOTO SOURCE: `https://commons.wikimedia.org/wiki/File:Elvis_Presley_-_TV_Radio_Mirror,_March_1957_01.jpg`

In this chapter, I smash any preconceived false notions you have had about certain body language tells and show you what exactly to look for as a socia engineering professional.

Nonverbals Are Essential

Before I get to the meat of this chapter, let me help you see why it's important to understand how to read nonverbal communication. Of course, the best way to do this is to tell a story.

When I was working with Dr. Ekman on *Unmasking the Social Engineer,* his role was to make sure that what I was saying was scientifically accurate, made sense, was logical, and was approved via his decades of research.

I had written a chapter about one study that had been done on mirror neurons. The study basically stated that the researchers believed there was a group of neurons in the brain that had the role of mirroring the nonverbals they see from other people.

Based on research from Dr. Ekman, we know that when we feel an emotion, we have an involuntary reaction, and that reaction is displayed by microexpressions. In addition, when we make facial expressions, we create the emotion attached to that expression.

I made the connection that if mirror neurons make us mirror someone's expressions—which are accompanied by emotions—we can control emotional content of our targets.

While I was writing *Unmasking the Social Engineer*, there was a scientific debate going on over mirror neurons and the research behind it. Consequently, Dr. Ekman wrote me a very nice email in which he basically said, "Do you want your book to have outdated or disproved research in it if this research gets quashed?"

I responded with, "But, but, but . . . I already have, like, 40 pages written all about it. And the chapter is due in five days." I hoped Dr. Ekman would basically respond, "Okay, that's cool."

Instead, he said, "Well, then I guess you have five days to read this research here on the amygdala and write a chapter on that." And with that, I had about 60 pages of information on something I could barely pronounce to research, understand, and write about.

Of course, Dr. Ekman helped me greatly, but there was a lesson or three in this for me.

» It is important to understand *how* things work if I am going to truly help my clients.

» It is important to adapt and grow with new research.

» Sleep is really underrated.

While writing that chapter on amygdala hijacking, I again saw a connection in the research between planting emotional content and controlling a target's response. If the amygdala processes emotional stimuli before the brain has a chance to "turn on," and I can cause the target to feel slight sadness or fear, then I can take advantage of their empathetic response.

In other words, mastering the use of pretexts can help me elicit the emotions I want in my subjects; I can make them feel how I want them to feel. Now we are getting to the point, finally, of why understanding nonverbals is so important.

When I'm about to break into a place as part of a job, or I'm about to do some vishing, I feel some pretty intense fear: fear of failure, fear of being caught, fear of messing up. Let's examine the emotion I feel.

How does fear affect me physiologically?

» My eyes are open wide and my eyelids are tense.

» My mouth pulls back in an "eek" shape, and I take in sharp breaths.

» My muscles tense and often freeze as I prepare for fight or flight.

> »   My heart rate elevates.

> »   My sweat production increases.

Now, let's discuss what my physiological state should be to elicit the desired emotional response from my target (which, as I previously mentioned, would be slight sadness to elicit empathy:

> »   My eyes are soft and not tense.

> »   My lips are turned down at the corners.

> »   My head is lowered.

> »   My muscles are not tense.

> »   My breathing becomes shallower.

Do you see the difference? If my pretext is using the emotion of sadness, but my body language is showing fear, what happens to the target? I would guess that the majority of people will never think, "Wow, this person is using a sadness-based story but showing fear. That is incongruent emotional content, which makes me feel uneasy." However, we all have internal radar that tells us when we feel (or should feel) like raising the shields and being more defensive. If I showed fear but tried to elicit sadness and empathy, my target's radar would throw up that shield.

A truly phenomenal study titled "Chemosensory Cues to Conspecific Emotional Stress Activate Amygdala in Humans" (www.ncbi.nlm.nih.gov/pmc/articles/ PMC2713432) proves this in an . . . uh . . . interesting way.

The researchers collected sweat pads from folks who had exercised. Then they collected sweat pads from a group of people who had jumped out of a plane at 13,000 feet in a tandem skydive. Then the researchers tested a group of subjects by attaching an fMRI to their heads and having them sniff each of the sweat pads. (Gross, but true.)

When this test group sniffed the sweat pads from the group who had jumped from a plane, the subjects' fear center, namely the amygdala, was triggered. When the subjects sniffed the pads from the exercise group, no fear was triggered. So, the old adage that you can smell fear is actually true.

Now that we know that other people can sense our fear, let's think about what I need to do as I get ready to approach a target. I have two choices:

> »   Learn to control my fear so I can display the proper emotion.

> »   If that is not possible, build a pretext that uses my natural emotion.

THINK ABOUT THIS

At DEF CON 25, we had Tim Larkin as our guest in our live episode of *The Social-Engineer Podcast*. Tim told a story about a Muslim woman who was walking toward a group of young men. The men didn't say anything to the woman, but something about them made her feel uneasy. So, she did the smart thing, and turned and started to walk the other direction.

However, she left her earbuds in, therefore taking away her advantage. One of the young men ran up behind her and cold-cocked her in the back, which knocked her out.

This is a sad and grotesque story, but it speaks to the point about how our internal radars work even though we sometimes try to quiet the warning signs. I always say *don't* ignore that radar—listen to it because it can save your life.

Understanding this can help you have a better grasp on your emotions to know what you're displaying and learn how to use, read, and then react properly to emotions and the nonverbal products of those emotions as a professional social engineer.

Before I get into the details about nonverbals, you first need to understand how to interpret emotional baselines.

All Your Baselines Belong to Us

Being able to read someone's emotional content can truly enhance your communication ability. I want to focus on how observing changes in baselines help the professional social engineer.

Let me first define a baseline. Simply put, it's the emotional content you see being displayed at the moment you start observing. You are not looking to understand their lifelong baseline. So, breathe—I'm not asking you to stalk your targets for months or years before each test.

Look at Figure 8-2. Amaya did something that wasn't too great, and her mom is letting her know.

What do you observe? In Figure 8-2, what is the emotional content of my wife, Areesa? Do you see the tight jaw? The pointed finger and terse lips? She's signaling anger.

And what about Amaya? Her arms are folded, her chin is up in the air, and her face expresses irritation. She is closed off and not really in a listening mood.

Now look at Figure 8-3 to see what Amaya looks like after that "discussion" ends and Areesa and Amaya have parted ways.

Figure 8-2 What baselines do you see here?

Figure 8-3 What change do you see here?

Amaya looks a bit saddened and self-comforting. Maybe she's even reflecting on the argument.

Now look at Figure 8-4. Amaya and Areesa just got done enjoying a nice cup of tea and talking about their fun day of shopping.

What baselines exist here? Both look happy. They're leaning into each other and enjoying the conversation.

The three photos show the same people in different circumstances and displaying different baselines. Herein lies a very valuable lesson. A baseline is not a person's personality definition. It's not a psych profile. It doesn't cover the long term. The baseline is merely the emotional content being displayed at a specific moment.

Being able to read a person's emotional state at the moment you approach that person is vital for you as a social engineer. Your approach to target Areesa from Figure 8-2 to Figure 8-4 would have to vary greatly if you want to succeed.

Many times, I've have heard people say that they can be taught to tell the difference between lying and truth in a matter of seconds.

Dr. David Matsumoto, Dr. Hyi Sung Hwang, Dr. Lisa Skinner, and Dr. Mark Frank wrote an article titled "Evaluating Truthfulness and Detecting Deception" (`https://leb.fbi.gov/articles/featured-articles/evaluating-truthfulness-and-detecting-deception`) in which they make a very important point: "It is not the mere presence or absence of behaviors, such as gaze aversion or fidgeting, that

Figure 8-4 What baselines do you see in this one?

indicates lying. Rather, it is how these nonverbal cues change over time from a person's baseline and how they combine with the individual's words. And, when just the behavioral cues from these sources are considered, they accurately differentiate between lying and truth telling."

Do you clearly grasp their assertion? There's not some mystical tell that always indicates a lie or truth. How a person's cues change over time indicates the content of the emotion and way we should decipher it.

Be Careful of Misconceptions

People often hold some preconceived misconceptions about certain body language "tells" that you need to understand and get rid of before you venture down this road. If you don't, you'll end up making some bad assumptions.

Let's analyze some examples together. Look at Figure 8-5. What do you see?

Figure 8-5 Is Amaya upset or not?

For years, people have been told that folded arms are a clear indicator of being closed off. That is not necessarily true. If someone changes from an open display to a closed-off position as I approach, that *might* be true, but some people routinely sit or stand like with their arms crossed because it's comfortable and not because they are closed off. On both sides of Figure 8-5, Amaya's arms are folded, but her facial expression and position of her head indicate which emotion she feels.

Now look at Figure 8-6.

Figure 8-6 Is she irritated, about to lie, cold, or comfortable?

You can't see it in this still picture, but Amaya's leg was bouncing at about 500 beats per minute. Is this a sign of deception about to occur? Or maybe she is not comfortable? It's hard to tell. Some people just have busy legs or move a lot. Again, notice when a movement like this starts and observe how often it starts or stops to figure out what it means. Look at the whole picture in Figure 8-6: Amaya's body position, her leg bounce, her hand on the back of her neck. When you consider all the elements, you might decide that Amaya is looking uncomfortable.

My son Colin's leg is like a perpetual motion machine. I've always thought that if we could attach it to a generator, we could produce power for our home. He's not deceptive; he just moves a lot. Here is an example of how I used this knowledge about Colin's habits:

I said, "Hey, Colin, how did the party go the other night? Did you have fun?"

Colin, with his leg drilling a hole through the earth, would say, "Yeah, it was okay. Nothing too much."

Now, in this case, I knew there had been a fight with Stewart, and I wanted to get details. I would say, "Oh, cool. Who was there again?"

Colin listed all the people there, but he left out Stewart. Hmm. I replied, "Oh, so Stewart wasn't there? I thought he was going."

Now Colin's leg stopped dead, "Yeah, he was there too," he said, as his leg started moving again.

"Oh. Is everything okay with Stewart?" I asked.

With his leg now firmly planted on the ground, Colin said, "Yeah, fine." This time, there was a pause before Colin started to move his leg again.

The indicator that there was a problem was not that Colin's leg was moving, but that it had stopped. From there, it was a matter of a few seconds before I had the whole story.

> **PRO TIP** Don't write about your methods to get your kids to talk until they are old enough to have either figured it out or you no longer use those tactics. In our house, it is like a constant battle of wits to see who will win. So far, I am way ahead. If we were keeping score, I'd say it's now PARENTS: 5,981,387 to KIDS: 5.
>
> P.S. My daughter disagrees with this score and says the numbers are reversed.

Now take a look at Figure 8-7 and see what you can interpret.

Face rubbing, scratching, or other types of manipulators can be indicators of discomfort, but sometimes people just have an itchy face. Notice when it starts and why.

Figure 8-7 Is this comfort or discomfort?

I can use my son Colin for this example, too. He had asthma and allergies. There were many times when his skin itched all over. When it was pollen season, Colin was always touching or scratching his face. In this case, the fidgeting wasn't because Colin was lying but because of his allergies.

If we play into these misconceptions, we can fall into a trap of assigning emotional content where it doesn't exist. That can be dangerous because you can start to react to emotion that isn't there. You don't want to treat someone as if they are closed off when they are just cold, or assume that someone is being deceptive when their behavior is the results of having allergies.

The best way to combat this error is to approach each situation without using preconceived judgments, even if you're approaching a target you've interacted with before. Reserve your judgments for after the initial 15 to 20 seconds of the encounter.

When it comes to body language, I try to focus on the changes from baselines and then look for a change that indicates comfort versus discomfort. In *Unmasking the Social Engineer*, I wrote extensively about facial expressions and body language, so if you want to learn more about that subject, you can check out that book.

For this book, I want to give you just the basics of understanding the difference between comfort and discomfort. Once you have a clear grasp of what those indicators look like, you will have a map that tells you what to look for and how to decipher what you see.

Know the Basic Rules

This section covers four good rules for you to keep in mind when reading body language. If you apply these, you will see a massive difference in how you read and interpret body language.

These rules are not meant to be "math" in the sense that you must do 1 + 2 + 3 + 4, but they all must be done if you want to master reading nonverbals.

Rule 1: Focus on the What—Not the Why

This rule is straightforward: Don't make connections between the what and why without having all the information.

I often start off my nonverbal training day with helping students remember one thing: "Just because you can see the *what* does not mean you know the *why*."

Think about this: While I'm speaking to the class, I say something as I make eye contact with you. I notice you fold your arms, your eyebrows go down while your eyes remain open, and your jaw tightens. I notice tension in your arms and hands. All these signs point to anger or discomfort.

I can assume you're feeling angry or uncomfortable about me or something I said. However, maybe you're reacting to pain you just felt because of surgery you had last year. Or maybe you have a stomach cramp that made you angry. Or maybe you weren't even paying attention, and you thought about something that made you mad.

Regardless of the reason for your body language, how do I connect the *what* to the *why*? As I discuss in Chapter 7, "Building Your Artwork," it's all about questions. In a classroom scenario, it's not appropriate for me to stop my lecture to enquire about why you looked angry.

Rule 2: Examine the Clusters

When you start to practice engaging with targets, it's easy to look at one particular body-language movement or facial expression and think you can understand what is being communicated. However, focusing on one cue is dangerous. You need context and other body language cues to indicate what is really being said. Look for matching nonverbal clusters that indicate what emotion is being displayed.

Consider this scenario: You're talking to your spouse and telling them that you disagree with a decision. As you're stating your opinion, your spouse folds his or her arms. Does this automatically mean they are shut off, angry, or not liking what they are hearing?

Expand your view a bit. Do you see anger on your spouse's face? Do you see a change in the placement of their hips and feet, so that they're now pointing away from you? What are the other emotional "clusters" that can help you to pinpoint if the arm-folding was an isolated movement or part of a larger emotional tell?

Rule 3: Look for Congruence

Look for congruence between verbal and nonverbal communication. If someone shakes his head *no* but says the word *yes*, those two indicators are telling you that things are not congruent.

When you identify a lack of congruence in the information you perceive about someone, rely on the nonverbal messaging to indicate what is truly being said. Examining the nonverbal clusters and looking for a lack of congruency between nonverbal communication and the verbal communication. will help you get very close to accurately reading what the target is telling you.

Rule 4: Pay Attention to the Context

Let's say I look out my office window and see my daughter sitting outside. She has made herself small, sitting almost in a ball. Her arms are folded across her chest, and her chin is down. Her head is tucked low into her folded arms. All of these are signs of sadness and discomfort.

What I didn't tell you is that it's only 35 degrees Fahrenheit outside, and she was not wearing a proper jacket.

In context, you understand that Amaya is cold. Without the contextual detail about the temperature, she seems sad and uncomfortable. To avoid misreading the nonverbals, you must understand the context of the situation your target is in.

In addition to these four rules, there are some body language basics you need to know before I get into details about each emotion.

Understand the Basics of Nonverbals

There are some basic things that you should understand as you start down the path of nonverbals. These basic characteristics are applicable to all humans and not tied to a specific culture, gender, race, or religion. Understanding these basics will help you to understand how our bodies communicate exactly what we are feeling regardless of what we are trying to display.

External stimuli come into our brain through our five modalities, assuming one is not damaged: sight, smell, taste, touch, and hearing. These stimuli are processed by our brains, and the stimuli can trigger one of the seven base emotions: anger, fear, surprise, disgust, contempt, sadness, or happiness. The emotion that is triggered creates physiological responses in both our faces and our bodies.

For example, when a person is confident, they make themselves bigger, which elevates testosterone and decreases cortisol in the blood, according to a study titled "Postural Influences on the Hormone Level in Healthy Subjects" by researchers R. S. Minvaleev, A. D. Nozdrachev, V. V. Kir'yanova and A. I. Ivanov. (https://link.springer.com/article/10.1023/B:HUMP.0000036341.80214.28). The researchers wanted to test whether certain yoga poises increased or decreased cortisol, testosterone, dehydroepiandrosterone (DHEA), and aldosterone. For our purpose, let's focus on cortisol and testosterone.

The researchers found that just by holding certain poses that are associated with confident behaviors, a person's testosterone increased by more than 16% and their cortisol dropped by 11%. Coincidentally, testosterone is known to increase behaviors that would be associated with a confident person. So, almost as a self-fulfilling prophecy, it appears that holding confident poses releases chemicals that help you feel and act more confident.

NOTE Cortisol is a hormone that regulates a wide variety of processes in the body, including metabolism and immune responses. Cortisol is often called the "stress hormone" because of its connection to the body's response to stress. Researchers have found that high levels of cortisol are linked to anxiety and depression.

In essence, what is important for you to understand is: It appears that comfort-based nonverbals assist in creating happy, confident, and strong chemical and physiological reactions, whereas discomfort-based nonverbals can create stress, anxiety, and negative emotion–based reactions.

It is important to understand how certain nonverbals can affect both you and your target. As a professional social engineer, you are influencing or manipulating the emotional content of your target. Do not take this lightly.

Because the effect of your pretext on your target can be short-term or long-lasting, it is important to plan your pretexts carefully. Remember the motto: Leave them feeling better for having met you. Whenever possible, try to use pretexts that trigger emotional content that will not have a long-lasting, damaging effect on your targets.

How can you determine if the pretext you choose might have long-lasting negative effects? Try to determine what emotion you are basing your pretext on. Fear, anger, disgust, and contempt are so strong as negative emotions that you risk a greater chance of leaving the target damaged for having met you.

For example, there is a difference in a phish that says, "Thank you for your recent order of this 55-inch TV," and one that says, "Your account has been hacked and your bank account has been emptied."

Understanding that nonverbals and emotions can affect the target profoundly should help you determine how to use these emotions during your social engineering gigs. To this effect, one of the most profound lessons I learned from Dr. Ekman is that not only does having an emotion trigger a nonverbal response, but if you were to force the nonverbal on yourself, you can trigger the emotion. This concept was backed up by numerous researchers, including in a study titled "Inhibiting and Facilitating Conditions of the Human Smile: A Nonobtrusive Test of the Facial Feedback Hypothesis" (www.ncbi.nlm.nih.gov/pubmed/3379579). Researchers Strack, Martin, and Stepper tested Dr. Ekman's hypothesis from the 1970s and 1980s and were able to show that if you create the expression, you can trigger the emotion. They did this by asking subjects to put a pen in their mouth to trigger muscular usage that simulated a smile. They were able to prove the same thing that Dr. Ekman stated in his research: Creating the facial expression (even by force) creates the emotion associated with it.

The key point to remember is that if you create an emotion, or you cause the target to express that emotion, you can leave the target feeling that emotion. You have to exercise caution when using this super power.

Comfort vs. Discomfort

It is important to learn how to communicate effectively, and part of that communication is nonverbal. There are some researchers who have developed statistics about how much of what we say is nonverbal. I have heard 80%, 85%, and even 90%, but one of the things I learned from Dr. Ekman was that, even though we can all agree that a large percentage of communication is nonverbal, the method of communication (spoken, written, in person) affects the way nonverbals are used.

What our bodies and faces show during normal communications can be overwhelming to people who can recognize the emotion being displayed. During normal communication, a person's body and face can display a myriad of emotions, and trying to interpret them can be overwhelming. For this reason, when you first start out as a social engineer, it's best to focus on the nonverbals that are the easiest to interpret: comfort and discomfort.

For this book I am trying something I haven't tried in my other books. I'm coming at this topic from the angle of the emotion and then discussing whether you, as a social engineer, would want to trigger this emotion in your targets. I explain how to look for signs that could indicate the comfort or discomfort displays that are associated with that emotion. I've divided this section by each emotion and described some of the indicators of that emotion in the face and the body. This is not meant to be an exhaustive list of every movement, but it provides a foundational basis for you to build on as you practice and begin to master this skill.

In addition to studying this section to learn how to read body language in others, you should use this information to learn how your body language can affect your targets. If you are displaying the emotions that I describe in this section, then you can trigger those emotions in others. Decide what emotions you want to trigger, and then practice the nonverbals for those emotions. Also learn to recognize the emotions and triggers that you do not want to elicit in others.

Anger

Anger is a strong emotion that has been labeled as a gateway emotion. What this means is that many times, anger leads to other emotions, feelings, or actions. Those actions can range from using expletives or angry words and escalate all the way up to exhibiting violent behavior.

Physiologically, anger makes us tense, tight, and ready to fight or defend. Muscles tense, the jaw tightens, and the person might clench their fists—all in a preparation for a fight or defense. As the person gets closer to taking a violent action, you might even see their chin lower in a protective measure to protect the neck.

Although things are tense and tight, you might notice a person who is experiencing anger try to make themselves larger. For example, an angry person might expand their chest, square their shoulders, and widen their stance. In addition, their breathing deepens and their heart rate increases.

Someone who is angry has the following facial characteristics:

» The brows will furrow, but the eyes don't squint. They open wide.

» The jaw tightens.

» The teeth clench, or, if the mouth is open, the person is often not saying pleasant things.

You can see all of this represented in Figure 8-8.

Anger can also be displayed in the rest of the body. Figure 8-9 shows me with a tight jaw and clenched fists. In addition, my chest is puffed to make me look bigger.

Figure 8-8 Anger in the face

Figure 8-9 Anger in the body

All of this points to anger. (FYI: This is the very picture I will hand to any boy that shows interest in Amaya.) If you notice any of these signs as you approach a person, it might be best to avoid that individual.

Another version of anger is shown in Figure 8-10, in which Amaya is displaying subtle anger. Her glare, tight jaw, and slightly furrowed brow are all signs of anger.

Most likely, you can figure out that anger is a discomfort nonverbal. It's one that I particularly do not like to elicit in my targets. Consequently, I watch for signs of this emotion and try to not use it in my engagements.

Many times, if I am too aggressive in my approach or if my pretext is too negative, I can catch signs of anger. It is a great warning sign to back off and to soften my voice or body language to alleviate some of the anger feelings in my target.

Figure 8-10 Subtle anger

Disgust

Disgust is also a very strong emotion. Disgust can be felt toward a person, place, or thing. Oftentimes, something that makes us have a very strong disgust reaction sticks with us for a very long time after we've been exposed to it.

When I was a young boy, my parents raised chickens. I would love to run out to the hen house, grab a couple fresh eggs, and make what I intelligently called "egg in bread." It was simply a piece of buttered bread in a pan with an egg in the middle.

One day, I grabbed my egg and cracked it open in my super-heated cast-iron pan. What came out was not a fresh egg but a half-formed chick. As it hit the pan, it started to flop around as it died. The sight and the smell made me heave into the sink. Because I was so disgusted, I forgot to shut the burner off, so the poor thing roasted, and the smell of burning chick filled the kitchen.

The disgust emotion that was triggered was so strong that even a decade later, the smell of a cooking egg would make me instantly feel sick. Eventually, I did get over that, but disgust is such a strong emotion that if you trigger it in your target, you might not be able to recover.

Think about the things that can trigger a disgust emotion in your targets: body odor, bodily functions, food on your face or in your teeth, foul language, word choice, and so on. It's important to carefully analyze your approach and yourself before you approach so you don't cause your target to feel disgust.

Disgust is exhibited a few different ways. On the face, it is a bilateral expression, meaning that both sides of the face show the same expression, as illustrated in Figure 8-11.

As we were prepping for the pictures, my dog had done something nasty in the living room. I couldn't pass up the opportunity, and I captured a picture of Areesa cleaning up. Notice how the sides of her nose are raised, which blocks both the olfactory sense as well as the line of vision. In essence, she's physiologically blocking the things that are causing her disgust.

In the body, a person demonstrates disgust by blocking or turning away from you. Look for signs of a lack of interest or repulsion.

Notice the leg position of Amaya in Figure 8-12. Where is her interest? It's definitely not in her dad (as sad as that makes me). And although she's not showing a

Figure 8-11 Disgust

Figure 8-12 Disinterest

strong sign of true disgust, her body language is showing signs of discomfort and disinterest.

Because disgust is such a strong negative emotion, I tend to not use it during engagements. However, I have been asked about using it to create a tribe of people who are disgusted at the same thing. Although this can work and be very powerful, it can also lead to some dangerous results if not handled properly.

Contempt

Contempt is a unique emotion. The *Oxford English Dictionary* defines contempt as, "The feeling that a person is worthless." Dr. Ekman offers a simpler definition, stating contempt is the feeling of moral superiority.

According to Dr. Ekman's definition of contempt, it can be felt only toward a person, and it is the only unilateral expression, which means it's shown on only one side of the face. At first, contempt may appear to be a smirk, or even the start of a smile, as shown in Figure 8-13.

Figure 8-13 Contempt can be confused with happiness.

Contempt is characterized by one side of the face being raised—for example, the corner of the lips is raised on only one side as in Figure 8-13. It is not uncommon to see this accompanied by a chin raise, even if it's only slight.

Because contempt is a feeling of being superior to another person and can often be a gateway into anger, you may see the following types of body language with contempt:

» Feeling superior to another person can make someone feel confident. That feeling of confidence can be displayed in several ways, but often-times, the person takes up more space by making him- or herself bigger.

» If the contempt has led to anger, you might see the same body language as I described in the previous section. However, before those anger nonverbals are fully displayed, you may notice a tightening of the jaw and more aggressive posture.

In my opinion, contempt has little to no use in a professional social engineering engagement. I can see how a nation-state might use it, and I have seen how it is used by terror organizations to recruit and then convert people to their cause, but for most standard social engineering engagements, it wouldn't lead to a desirable outcome.

> **NOTE** Terror organizations will often use the anger that people feel toward their governments or certain ideologies and convert it to contempt by feeding that anger. Once the target is feeling contempt for, or morally superior to, the object of the anger, the terror organization gives them the "solution" or "action" that can be taken. It is unbelievably divisive, but it works amazingly well.

Fear

Fear has many purposes, such as it alerts us to danger, but it can also be exhilarating and enjoyable when controlled. Some people even enjoy being scared or feeling fear.

Fear of disappointment, fear of failure, or fear of making the wrong decision can be useful for a professional social engineer, but I generally steer clear of stronger uses of fear. Pretexts that literally threaten or scare a person—such as those that cause them to fear for their jobs, lives, or families—trigger such strong emotion that when they find out they were being tested, they can be left with disgust or contempt, followed by anger.

Fear has some clear physical characteristics:

» The eyes are open wide to take in the whole scene.

» The body tenses, and there is usually an audible gasp of air.

» The mouth is open, with the lips pulling back toward the ears as if the person is saying "eek."

You can see these characteristics in Figure 8-14.

In the body, fear has manifestations similar to the facial expressions. The body pulls back, tenses up, freezes, and prepares for fight or flight. If you startle your target, you might see the person react as depicted in Figure 8-15.

Figure 8-14 A classic fear expression

Notice how Amaya has reeled back with her whole body tensed. Her mouth is in that "eek" position. This type of fear can be intense because there's no physical way for her to flee. She's cornered in her chair.

Figure 8-16 shows another aspect that we see in fear when displayed by women—covering the suprasternal notch.

Watch for subtle body-language indicators that can clue you in to how the target might be feeling. If you see signs of fear, you can then decide whether the fear being displayed is appropriate and how far you are willing to go to use it. As I mentioned before, I use fear as a professional social engineer, but I steer clear of the type of fear that can leave the target feeling threatened or in harm's way.

Figure 8-15 Startled fear in body language

Surprise

Surprise is often confused with fear because it looks so similar. With surprise, the eyes open wide, as they do in fear. The body generally freezes and the mouth also drops open. But instead of opening with an "eek" shape, the mouth opens in more of an "OHHHHH" shape. You can see this in Figure 8-17.

Surprise can be useful to a professional social engineer, but, as with some of the other emotions I've mentioned, it depends on how you use it. I don't suggest hiding in a closet and then jumping out to surprise your targets, but a surprise audit, visit, or reward might work to elicit the right response. In one engagement, which was solely a vishing engagement, I used a surprise reward to get some amazing results. The call went something like this:

Target: Hello, Beth speaking. How can I help you?

Me: Beth, this is Paul from HR. I have some great news. You may not have heard, but we entered your department into the drawing for a brand-new iPhone, and your name was picked!

Figure 8-16 Covering the suprasternal notch indicates fear.

Figure 8-17 Surprise, which can often be misinterpreted as fear

Target:	Come on! You're kidding! This is amazing!
Me:	I know. I love these calls. We're giving 10 away, and these calls have been a lot of fun.
Target:	Yeah, I never win anything. This is amazing!
Me:	As you know, we have a few Beths here at XYZ, so I need to verify some details with you to ensure that I have the right Beth. Can you spell your full name for me?
Target:	*E-l-i-z-a-b-e-t-h S-m-a-r-s-t-o-n.*
Me:	Excellent. I need your employee ID to enter it into the system.
Target:	T238712P.
Me:	Okay, you're the right Beth. Now I need you to go to a site where you'll be asked to log in with your domain credentials, and you'll tell the site where you want the phone shipped, etc. Go to iphone .company-website.com. *[This was a website we set up that did nothing; none of the buttons worked.]*
Target:	Okay, the site came up. I see our logo, but when I click the Enter button, nothing is happening. What do I do?
Me:	Hmm, I am on it now. When you click Enter, it doesn't go to another screen? I see another screen right now.
Target:	No. I'm trying a different browser. *[Tried every browser she had.]* Figures; I win something and can't even claim it.
Me:	No, we won't stand for that. Look, I'll claim it for you. Do you want me to enter your information?
Target:	Really? Would you do that?
Me:	Of course, I would. *[Feeling as guilty as a snake.]* It's asking for your full name, which I have. . . ." *[I say each letter as I fake typing it in.]* Okay, hitting Next. It wants your employee ID—you gave me that, so I'll enter that now.
Target:	Thank you so much. This is so cool.
Me:	Okay. It wants your domain login, which I assume is just E.Smarston?
Target:	No, I actually have it as B.Smarston. For Beth . . .
Me:	Okay, great. Now the last thing I need is your password.

Target	*[without even pausing for a second]*: I do really good with long passwords. It's "JustinandBeth99"!
Me:	Excellent, that worked. It says you'll get an email within 24 hours with further instructions on what to do to claim the phone. Congratulations, Beth!
Target:	Thank you so much!

With that, we had a full compromise of the network. Yes—for all of you who are preparing your hate mail—that was manipulative and used a pretext that made the target a little upset when she found out about it later. But, remember, I didn't threaten her; I didn't embarrass her; I didn't cause her harm. I used a surprise to trigger a happiness-based emotion, and that led her to give all sorts of information to me without thinking.

From a body-language perspective, there are a few things that you may notice that indicate surprise. These are shown in Figure 8-18 and Figure 8-19.

Figure 8-18 Surprise may cause a person to lean back with raised facial expressions.

Figure 8-19 Shock, a form of surprise, might be indicated by a person covering their mouth.

In my opinion, surprise is a good emotion for a professional social engineer. With the proper planning and execution, it can lead to large victories for you.

Sadness

Sadness is a very complex emotion. It also has a huge range, as it can span from feeling slightly blue to utter despair. As a social engineer, there are a few ways that you can use sadness:

» Noticing sadness in a target and then using that emotion to elicit a reaction

» Creating a situation that will most likely cause the target to feel sadness and lead to them to react the way you want them to

» Displaying sadness in your own nonverbals to elicit an empathy-based response

Some of these methods employ a more manipulative approach than others. It all depends on how you employ these emotions and what the resultant emotional state of the person you use this on.

Sadness has a few facial indicators, which are demonstrated in Figure 8-20. On the face, sadness is shown by

» The corners of the mouth turning down

» The eyelids drooping

» The corners of the eyebrows coming together and going up

In some extreme cases of sadness, you can read the emotion from just one part of face.

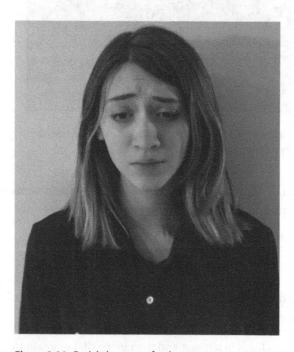

Figure 8-20 Facial elements of sadness

Sadness can also be conveyed by a person's body. Sadness makes us want to protect, comfort, and become smaller—the opposite responses of feeling confident.

Some examples of self-comforting nonverbal displays are shown in Figure 8-21, Figure 8-22, and Figure 8-23.

This is a short list, but you get the idea. These nonverbals can help you see that the person is feeling definite discomfort.

Figure 8-21 Self comforting hug

Figure 8-22 Eye blocking

Sadness, in all of its complexity, can be very useful for a social engineer—both in learning how to read it and displaying it. However, I caution you to temper how you use this emotion and to what level you use it in your pretexts.

I never want to leave my targets with an overwhelming feeling of sorrow or grief, but using the proper level of sadness can elicit a strong empathetic response. In a study conducted by Jorge A. Barraza and Paul J. Zak titled "Empathy towards Strangers Triggers Oxytocin Release and Subsequent Generosity," (https://nyaspubs.onlinelibrary.wiley.com/doi/abs/10.1111/j.1749-6632.2009.04504.x), the researchers showed that there was a 47% increase in oxytocin release when empathy was triggered, even when the empathetic feeling was between complete strangers, whereas sadness can create a lack of serotonin, dopamine, and oxytocin in the brain. As a professional, I try to stick to the empathy side of sadness instead of the worry, grief, or depression side of the spectrum.

Just think about how many times this tactic is used in marketing and charity drives. From homeless children to abused animals, the goal is to trigger an empathetic response to encourage you to more easily decide to part with your money. This doesn't mean those organizations are being dishonest or manipulative—they just know how our brains work, and it helps them achieve their goal.

Figure 8-23 Slumped body language

Happiness

Happiness is one emotion that we can all agree is very useful to all human interactions. When we feel happy, content, at peace, or relaxed, we are more prone to make more altruistic decisions. We tend to like the people, places, or things that make us feel this emotion.

For that reason, it is easy to see that, as a social engineer, happiness would be one emotion you want to master reading and eliciting. The first thing that can really help you to see if you are doing a good job and creating happiness is learning to identify the difference between a real smile and a fake smile. The one thing that separates a real smile from a fake smile is the activation of the orbicularis oculi muscle. When triggered, this muscle raises your cheeks and forms what we call "crow's feet" around the eyes.

In the mid-1800s, a French researcher named Guillaume Duchenne postulated that a real smile could be faked. He was studying neuroscience with the use of a very invasive form of electroshock. He administered shocks to stimulate muscle movement (www.thevintagenews.com/2016/05/07/44782-2).

Due to the pain involved, Duchenne did not get too far with this research, but his research into how emotions were displayed through facial expressions showed that the face is a roadmap to emotion. Around 1855, he developed a method to use electroshock stimulation to trigger muscular response, and he wrote about his findings in *Mécanisme de la physionomie humaine*. The result was what you see in Figure 8-24.

Figure 8-24 A fake real smile

Reading about this research can help you understand why happiness produces the facial expression known as smiling. But as a professional social engineer, you need to learn to recognize other body-language indicators of happiness.

How is the emotion of happiness displayed by a person's body language? If happiness releases strong neuro chemicals and creates a confident environment, then we can expect to see certain body expressions, too. Look for body postures like those shown in Figure 8-25, Figure 8-26, and Figure 8-27.

Figure 8-25 Notice the open, confident arm position.

Figure 8-26 Open ventral displays indicate trust and happiness.

NOTE   Ventral is the underside of an animal—or the vulnerable side. In humans, this means our wrists, jugular, and areas of our body we would naturally protect from attack.

On the face, we look for the eyes to be engaged in the smile in addition to the mouth forming a closed- or open-mouthed smile (see Figure 8-28). Many times, people who feel happy also lean in toward the object of their happiness.

Other signs of happiness might include things like raising the toes or bouncing on the balls of the feet. When people feel confident or good, they tend to make themselves bigger or bounce more.

Happiness is one of the emotions I look to use frequently as a professional social engineer. Appealing to a person's ego is a great way to create happiness that can

Figure 8-27 Open ventral displays are often associated with welcoming or cordial greetings.

lead to an emotional decision. For this to work, though, the ego appeal must be realistic, believable, and appropriate to the level of rapport you have built at that moment.

I find that, if it fits my pretext, approaching a target with open ventral displays and a warm smile with a proper head tilt can go a long way in making the target feel comfortable with me.

Look for ways to create a happy environment in your social engineering pretexts, and you will be rewarded with good results.

Figure 8-28 Happiness on the face shown by a genuine smile and head tilt

Summary

Nonverbals are a complex and huge topic that I realize can't be covered in a relatively short chapter. As I mentioned in the outset, my hope is that by going through a high-level overview of this information, you could walk away with a few different things in your arsenal. Understanding how emotion works will benefit you for many pretexts. The more you understand about what someone is saying without using words can help you to understand their communications much more clearly. Here are the main ideas that I hope you take away from this chapter:

Foundational Tools   As a starting point, this chapter can help you learn what subtle things to look for in the face and body for each emotion.

Better Understanding   I hope you have a better idea of which emotions will work for you and how to not only see those emotions in others but display them yourself.

Defense   Understanding how emotions are conveyed through facial expressions and body language can also be very helpful for you as a defense mechanism. Realizing how these emotions can and are being used will make you more aware when they are being used against you.

Enhancement   As a professional social engineer, it is essential for you to always be learning and enhancing your skill set.

I want to tell you one more story about social engineering that might help solidify the ideas of this chapter. During one DEF CON, I had an interaction with an employee that helped me see how important it is to be observant of nonverbals all the time.

The conference is always a busy time for me and my team. I feel like I rarely get a break or even a few minutes to myself during those five days. I just flip the switch "on" and leave it there as I feed off the energy and positive vibes from the crowd.

This is powerful for me, but it can also make me unaware of others' feelings. I bounce around, barking out orders and making sure things are getting done. At this one conference, I had given a few orders to some of the employees to get things packed up. It was our last day, and we were rushing to get everything organized so we could go out and have our final team dinner at our favorite sushi place.

Things were going smoothly; everything was running 100% perfectly. We needed to do the closing ceremonies, and then we could finally decompress. I was trying to be more aware of others' emotions, and I noticed one person's face registered not just fatigue but utter exhaustion. Another person was expressing some serious distress.

To the first person, I said, "Hey, if you are really tired, you know you can request to sit out of this part—you don't need to come to closing."

"What? *Really*? I could have opted out?" he asked with utter surprise.

"Yeah, bro—I just thought that was a given. Sorry I didn't mention it before."

"I had no clue we could opt out. I thought it was mandatory," he said.

"Well, it's only mandatory for Michele. The rest—you can opt out."

Then there was a huge sigh of relief from my employee.

When I approached the next person, I needed to be delicate. I couldn't call her out without creating problems in front of others. The emotion I was reading on her was a mix of sadness, anger, and fear.

I approached her privately, pulling her away from the group, and asked if she was okay. I won't describe the interaction in detail, but there were a lot of tears. She was feeling stress because she felt like things got dropped or ignored. And she was very stressed due to the lack of downtime.

So, I learned a new lesson. During that last day of the conference, I was being particularly observant and attentive to my team's emotions. However, I realized that I should have been using this skill throughout all five days of the conference to notice issues before we got to that level of stress.

Let me apply this story to social engineering: Be observant, but not just during the engagement. Look for "flags," but also be observant during all communications. Be observant for changes in the baseline and for emotional leakage that can help you see what a person might be feeling before, during, and even after your interaction.

Being able to read nonverbals is a powerful skill. When you add the ability to use nonverbals to elicit emotions in your targets, you have achieved almost superhero level.

This concludes the chapters in which I outline the majority of the skills I use as a professional social engineer. In the next chapter, you'll learn how you can apply these skills to social engineering penetration testing. What vectors can these skills apply to? That is the very topic of the next chapter.

9

Hacking the Humans

If money is your hope for independence you will never have it. The only real security that a man will have in this world is a reserve of knowledge, experience, and ability.

—HENRY FORD

As a quick recap, I have covered what has changed in SE over the last seven or so years: OSINT and how to use it, communication modeling, pretexting, rapport building, influence, manipulation, elicitation, and nonverbals. From a communications stance, this is a great foundation of knowledge, but because I'm a professional social engineer, I need to tell you how to apply this information and use it in an SE context.

From a malicious social engineering angle, there are four main vectors that I see being used in attacks: phishing, vishing, SMiShing, and impersonation. There are also combinations of those attacks that trap us.

In this chapter, I discuss how you can use the skills I discussed in each of these vectors. Then I go over (briefly, I promise) the always-fun topic of reporting. And finally, I discuss how to break into the business and close some clients.

Before I get into any of that, however, I have to discuss the principles of the pentest. This will set the foundation for how you approach social engineering pentests.

> **NOTE** One of the things I don't discuss in this chapter is how to use these skills from the malicious side of the fence. This whole book is focused on how to become a professional social engineer with the goal of "leaving them feeling better for having met you." Malicious uses of the skills I've talked about *do not* leave anyone feeling better for having met you.

An Equal Opportunity Victimizer

The other thing I want to mention from the beginning is that social engineering vectors are not things that work just on dumb humans. They work on all humans. With the right emotional trigger, in the right situation, the right pretext can get any one of us to fall prey.

I'm often asked if I have ever been maliciously social engineered. Unfortunately, the answer is, yes. The right trigger at the right time made me fall for a phishing email. Fortunately, besides some embarrassment, there was no major loss for me, because I knew how to quickly react and what to do to fix the problem. I had a M.A.P.P. (which is the topic of Chapter 10, "Do You Have a M.A.P.P.?").

I am not a fan of slogans like "There is no patch for human stupidity." Yes, I acknowledge that there are many problems from a security perspective that are results of laziness or even stupidity, but that doesn't mean that only stupid people fall for these things.

There was a case where a college professor received a 419 scam phish (which is also known as the Nigerian prince scam). The professor fell for it 100%. He fell for it so hard that he stole money from the university treasury after he depleted his life savings. Even after he got caught and the FBI was involved, he accused the agents of trying to take his leads so they could reap the benefits of the millions he was about to see in his accounts.

> **NOTE** A 419 scam, otherwise known as a Nigerian scam, obtained its name from the article of the Nigerian Law (Article 419) that deals with fraud. Nigerian scams generally start with "I am a prince with millions of dollars . . ." but lately have converted to being about a widowed woman who needs help. Either way, these scams seem to continue to work on people who want to hold on to hope that a small investment might lead to huge payouts.

Sounds stupid, right? Well, that is an easy answer. Instead, I look at the situation and consider what caused this man to be so invested in the attack. Here are some thoughts to consider:

» He was having serious money problems, and the scam gave him *hope* of financial freedom.

» His feeling of *greed* was triggered by the massive number he thought he would see transferred to his bank account.

» Once he *committed*, he wanted to remain *consistent* with his decision.
» He felt he was *helping* a person in a third-world country to a better life, while also helping himself.

By examining the situation from this angle, I could more easily understand how the professor could be so invested in this scam that he ruined his life, committed theft and fraud, and deceived his wife—all for the hope, greed, and desire to remain consistent and committed to helping himself and another person.

I can't tell you how many times a CEO or other high-level person has told me they would *never* fall for my scams, only to be really angry when they find out they are the source of the remote access during the pentest. Anyone can be a victim of an attack, regardless of their position in an organization.

The Principles of the Pentest

Pentesting, a shortened form of the term *penetration testing*, is where a company hires a professional to try to penetrate the company's network. The end goal is that a pentest should help expose and patch any problems before malicious attackers can use them.

Over the years, pentesting has become a standard security tool, and many compliance boards require companies to conduct pentests at least annually. As of right now, there are not many government compliance laws that require companies to include social engineering in these tests.

For that matter, a company that just wants to check off a box that a test has been done to meet compliance requirements is usually a pretty poor client to have. They are doing it because they are made to do it, not because they want to. Think of it this way: When your kids clean the kitchen because they want to surprise you, they do a better job than when they are forced to do it as a chore.

There are a few written standards regarding pentesting, as well as regulations that can help pentesters learn some best practices for performing the tests. In 2009, I started to write a framework for social engineering, which is now the backbone of www.social-engineer.org. It's called "The SE Framework," and many organizations around the globe use it as a standard when planning out services for their annual SE engagements. However, there is still not a clear set of standards for SE pentesting. I think that's mainly because social engineering is so dynamic, it's nearly impossible to plan each stage.

There are some steps or stages that comprise the normal path of an SE attack vector, which are illustrated in Figure 9-1.

Information is the lifeblood of the social engineering attack. So, it makes sense that OSINT or information gathering is always first. You can't really plan attacks until the research is done.

After you gather your OSINT, you can easily determine what pretexts may or may not work. Knowing how a company uses social media, communicates, is geographically located, and other details about their inner workings enables you to develop some good pretext ideas.

After those ideas are developed, you can start planning the attack vectors. Will you send a phishing email? Or will you vish them for more info or credentials? Will you use a mobile-device attack? Will you go in person to the site? Will you combine those vectors? You can answer all these questions as you start to plan out the attacks.

From there, you launch these attacks, collecting the results from all the steps and reporting to the client everything that took place. However, a pentest doesn't always move through strictly linear steps. You may be doing OSINT, come up with a great attack vector, and then want to do more OSINT to see if you can find some supporting data.

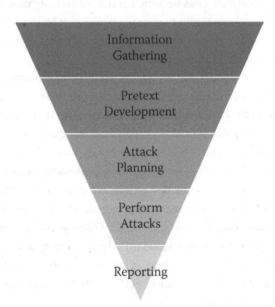

Figure 9-1 The SE stages

No matter how you approach it, the principles of the SE pentest should include these points:

» Do you want to record phone calls? That is illegal in many states without consent—and don't assume that a client hiring you is the same as them giving you "consent" to do as you wish. Do you want to record video of your break-in? Make sure that is signed off as approved.

» Do not just assume that the client should know exactly every step of a social engineering pentest. Spell out the services you want to offer so it is clear. This also gives them the option to ask about each step of the pentest before you move forward and potentially create a problem.

» Make sure you obtain written permission to record calls you will make.

Many states are two-party consent, in which case, you will need to obtain the company's consent so you don't run into legal issues.

» Detail the exact Google search string or tool that was used so the client can duplicate the steps if needed.

I have heard some pentesters say they fear they are arming the client to do the pentest themselves. In all the years I've done this, however, there's never been a time that a client did not use my services again because I overeducated them.

» The story is as important as the results.

For example, you might tell the client that there was a 90% click ratio and that 47% of the people you called gave you their domain creds over the phone, which are scary statistics for sure. But you also must explain each step of the process, the way you developed that attack vector, and who shut you down and why—because all those details are important parts of the story for the client.

» Don't live-tweet or post on social media about your successful exploits of your clients. *(Seriously, when I see people do this I cringe.)*

Imagine going to your doctor for an invasive test. He probes you in places you'd rather not be probed. It's uncomfortable, maybe even a little painful, and certainly embarrassing. He finishes the test and excuses himself from the office for a minute. You pull your phone out to check some apps and see a tweet from him that says, "You should see the size of the tumor on this fat slob I just had to exam." LOL" He didn't mention your name, and there are no photos of you, but how does this make *you feel*? Do you like the doctor? Do you feel as if he is on your side? If I was the patient, this would be the last time I would use this doctor.

Apply that to live tweeting about how easy it was to break into a client's place or how bad their security is. It's embarrassing and unprofessional.

These five principles are good general guidelines to apply to your professional engagements. Before I get into rules that can help you with each vector you might use as a pro SE, I have two more guidelines: document *everything*, and be judicious in your choice of pretexts.

Document Everything

The client is paying you to dig deep, and even if you don't use the OSINT you found in your attacks, the client still needs to know what you discovered. Inevitably, there will be times in your work that you will find truly sensitive material. The question is, how do you handle it?

In one test, my company was hired to pentest a high-level executive in a financial institution. During our searches, we found photos that she had willingly posed for when she was in her 20s, which were now being used on the photographer's website as promotional material. Sadly, some of those photos were stolen by pornographers and were being used to promote their sites. How do you handle this as a professional social engineer?

We determined that this information was too damaging and embarrassing to use as a theme for a spear phish. So we tabled it, performed our pentest, and then requested a special meeting with the executive in question. We offered to help her get these photos taken down off the websites they were on and to not report them to her company. She was truly appreciative and to this day remains a friend of mine.

Be Judicious with Pretexts

There have been more times than I can count when I found something truly embarrassing on a client. I personally chose to never use these as the pretext themes. Some of you are probably thinking that I'm wasting good opportunities. However, remember my goal is to "leave them feeling better for having met me." Also, I want to be able to provide education, which is hard to accomplish if I just humiliated someone. Consequently, I'm judicious and sensitive about what I'll choose to use in a pretext. With that said, remember that I previously recommended that you always report what you find—so even when you don't use embarrassing information, you should tell the client what you found.

I had a client who asked my company to do some spear phishing. One of their employees had used his company email to go on a "hook-up" site and post some comments to some very attractive and unclothed women, telling them he was coming into town on a business trip and wanted to meet. Put aside anything you feel about his scruples for offering to cheat on his wife or the security problems of using his company email publicly on a site like this. Would a phish from one of these ladies have worked? I can almost guarantee it 100%, but we didn't use it. Again, a professional social engineer's goal is to educate and assist rather than humiliate to win.

Phishing

Phishing is defined as the act of sending malicious emails that pretend to be from reputable sources. The goals of phishing can be broken down as follows:

»   To deliver malicious payloads that give access to remote attackers

»   To gather credentials

»   To gather other bits of intel for further attacks

The goal of the phishing email determines its content, pretext, and delivery method. As a professional social engineer, you might be asked to send a few different types of phishing methods.

Educational Phishing

Sometimes, clients don't want to test the network resources of the company—they just want to test the human side. One effective way of doing this is to send an educational phishing email, which means that when a person interacts with the message, no malicious code is delivered or remote access obtained. It just pings back to a site to report that the phishing message was clicked. The stats are used to help a client see how susceptible people are to the attack vector of phishing and where education might be needed.

With this type of phishing, the goal is to use curiosity, greed, happiness, or healthy fear to get people to click. To do that, you base the pretext on OSINT into a specific target or the whole company. My team and I have sent this type of phishing emails to one person and to hundreds of thousands at one time.

Here's an example that illustrates why it's important to follow the principles from the previous section: I wrote a phish for a client that looked just like a legitimate LinkedIn invite. I sent it to a client's 7,000 users. It had a very high click ratio—about 73%. I was floating pretty high, and everyone, including me, was impressed with the success of this phishing endeavor.

Another pentest engagement was coming up, and I was able to reuse my successful LinkedIn Invite phish. I sent it out the following week to 10,000 users, and clicks were barely trickling in. When the campaign completed, the click ratio was only about 4%. I couldn't believe it. After all, it was a *genius* phishing method, right? I asked the client to try and find out from their users why this phishing attempt had failed so badly.

It turns out that the fail was my fault. Company 1 was a manufacturer with employees in the 35-to-55 age group. Company 2 was a retailer, and the average age of employees was 19 to 29. When Company 2 asked its employees if they had seen the email and why they didn't click, they replied with comments like, "Yeah, I saw it, but only old people use LinkedIn. I use Facebook."

<facepalm> Because I was high from the success with Company 1, I didn't stop to think that it's not a one-phish-fits-all situation. Each company needs to have a customized phishing message. This experience also solidified my disapproval of phishing Software as a Service (SaaS) solutions that rely solely on templates.

Even when your purpose for the phishing attempt is educational, it still requires the steps in the pyramid in Figure 9.1. Starting with OSINT, prepare a phish that appeals to the target audience and achieves the desired goal.

Pentest Phishing

Pentest phishing is basically the same as educational phishing except for one big difference: the end goal. Instead of being geared toward education, pentest phishing is aimed at obtaining remote access, credentials, or some other type of compromise.

Pentest phishing generally uses pretexts that involve fear, greed, surprise, or even sadness. I use these emotions because in a phish used on a pentest, I need more than just the click. Often, I need the target to open a document and click past warnings and/or enter credentials. Because these steps take more of the target's time, I need to keep the target in alpha mode for longer, so the emotional triggers need to be stronger.

One example of this was a company I pentested that had a very strong love for all things Apple. Almost all of this company's employees used MacBooks and talked about their brand-new iPhones. The pentest took place around the time when a new version of the iPhone was launching. The phishing email that I sent to the company's employees had a pretty picture of the new iPhone on it and a message that appeared to come from human resources:

> [Name of Company] *is going to reward 10 lucky employees with a brand-new iPhone and 1 year of your service plan covered 100%. The drawing will take place next Friday at 3:00pm. To enter, all you need to do is go to this intranet page and enter your corporate login and password, and you will be automatically entered:* https://iphone.updates-company.com
> *Good luck!*

We bought the domain `updates-company.com` and created a mock intranet page that had two text boxes and a button, as well as the corporate logo. I sent the phishing email to 1,000 people, and received 750 corporate login credentials.

The right emotional trigger at the right time to the right people leads to massive success.

Spear Phishing

Spear phishing, and all its variations, is a very personalized form of phishing. After deep OSINT into both the target and any family I can find, I generally will pick something very personal from the list to use as my pretext. Many times, the OSINT that I find and use comes from postings that a family member puts on social media.

In one case, I found that a target and a group of his friends had gone to Las Vegas for a guys' weekend. The large number of photos his friends posted of their escapades that weekend led me to pick this OSINT as the pretext.

My phishing email came from the hotel where he had stayed, and here's what it said:

> *Mr.* [Name of Target],
> *On July 3–8, you stayed at our hotel. Upon checkout, our cleaning staff found an item that might be yours. Can you please check the attached picture and tell us if this item is yours?*
> *If the item is yours, please go to* <u>this link</u> *and fill out the form so we can mail it back to you.*
> *Sincerely,*
> *Hotel Staff*

Now why did I choose to put the link even though I knew that the malware-laden attachment would show no picture? Because there is a chance that the person who received the email will claim the item regardless. The form asked for the following information:

Full name

Mailing address

Phone number

Email address

DOB (for proof of being over 18)

The last four digits of the credit card that the target used to book his room

This pretext was very successful and led not only to a full compromise but a whole lot of additional OSINT I used for further attacks.

Even when I use personal information for a spear phishing pretext, I don't use OSINT that can be damaging to the person. For example, in this same phishing pentest, I would *not* have used a pretext like this: "We located some pictures of you with a prostitute while you were in Vegas. Click here to pay a ransom."—or anything even remotely close to that, even if that was the fact. If I did uncover that type of data in the OSINT, I would report it directly to the target and ask how he or she wanted us to handle this matter.

Phishing Summary

I don't know about you, but I am averaging more than 200 or 250 emails per day from all my accounts. The last time I checked, my job was *not* to solely check email.

CRAZY FACT

According to a report by **The Radicati Group** (www.radicati.com/wp-content/uploads/2017/01/Email-Statistics-Report-2017-2021-Executive-Summary.pdf), there was an average of 269 billion emails sent per day during 2017. That is 3.1 million emails sent every second of every day. Another fun fact: I think half of them come into my inbox (okay, that may be a very slight exaggeration).

Because email is the way we do business, communicate globally, keep in touch, send letters, and even shop, it is also the vector most widely used for social engineering attacks. As a professional social engineer, it's necessary for you to learn how to craft professional-looking emails that are based on solid OSINT to truly test your clients' susceptibility to this vector.

Vishing

In 2015, the term *vishing* was entered as a word into the *Oxford English Dictionary*. I tried to claim responsibility for the popularity of the word, but no one believed me. (I'm partially kidding.)

Vishing is a mash-up of *voice phishing*, which is phishing over the phone. This vector is much more common now than it was even just a couple years ago, and my theory is that its popularity is because it's such an effective attack.

Here are a few reasons why I would choose to use vishing for a pentest:

» Credential harvesting

» OSINT

» Full compromise

I will discuss each of these so you have a clear picture of how they differ.

Credential Harvesting

Many times in a pentest, my team and I have technical plans for compromise, but we try vishing or phishing to see if we can gain credentials that will give us an easier way in to the network.

In one case, after doing OSINT online, I had 10 to 15 numbers that I wanted to try to use for credential harvesting. I developed my pretext based on some other OSINT. I found the target company was using a third-party outsourced IT company to manage their move from one operating system to another. It was a massive upgrade, and it involved not just the OS but all the other software they relied upon that would need to be updated along with it.

My pretext was that I was Paul, from Secure IT (a totally made-up name for this book), and I wanted to check on the company's employee upgrade status because we were seeing some problems with traffic from their machines. It went like this:

Target:	Good morning. This is Steve. How can I help you?
Me:	Hey, Steve. This is Paul from Secure IT. I wanted to . . .
Target:	*[interrupting]:* Oh, you guys! Do you know how much work I have to get done? And your new fancy upgrade is screwing up my life!
Me:	I understand, Steve. That's why I called. We noticed there was a bunch of malformed packets coming from your IP address, and I think it might be a DNS poisoning problem due to the stack overflow. *[My voice trailed off at the end as I prayed he was nontechnical.]*
Target:	My computer is poisoned? What the living hell are you talking about, Paul?
Me:	I'm sorry. I do that—just spout off all the tech jargon. I'm really sorry. What this means is that during the install, there might have been a problem that is causing your slowness. I can walk you through a few steps to see if we can fix it. Do you want to do that?
Target:	Listen, Paul. I would rather you just send a rep here to fix it—I don't really understand all that stuff you said.
Me:	I get it Steve. I don't have a rep available to send for at least four or five days. But there is another option where I can help you remotely. If you want, I can log in and fix it remotely.
Target:	Sure, if you can make this machine work again, I'm all for it. What do you need?
Me:	I'm all ready to log in and make the adjustments—I just need to get your username and the password you use to log into your machine.
Target:	*[with no hesitation]:* SMaker, and don't forget the capital *S* and *M*. My password is a good one, so don't steal it: Krikie99.

And with that, I had the keys to the kingdom.

When it comes to credential harvesting, I find the job is easier if I can find some OSINT that helps me build a believable pretext using details of something relevant and real to the target. Also, in addition to vishing for domain credentials, I have vished credentials for VPN, email, secure storage, specific databases, and even door codes.

Vishing for OSINT

Sometimes, during a pentest, I do not have enough details to complete an attack or I want to verify some details before the attack. In one case, I had a spear phish and vishing attack planned for a target, but we had located several phone numbers and email addresses that could be his.

We developed a quick pretext to determine which of the numbers where real. We found that the target traveled frequently between Canada and London. We located the number for a Hilton Hotel in London and spoofed as that hotel and then called the numbers we had for the target one by one.

Target:	Hello?
Me:	Hello, is this Mr. Alfred Gaines?
Target:	Um, yes. Who is this?
Me:	I'm sorry. This is Paul from the Hilton in London. I wanted to take a minute to thank you for your recent stay with us. We have a short survey about your stay if you have only 30 seconds. . . .
Target:	Stay? What are you talking about? I haven't stayed at a Hilton in London in a few months. How did you get this number?
Me:	Sir, I'm very sorry for the confusion. This is Alfred Gaines phone number 846-555-1212, right?
Target:	Yes, that is correct, but you might have the wrong record for my recent stays.
Me:	Okay, would it be okay if I email you the invoice and you tell me if that is you?
Target:	Sure you can.
Me:	Excellent. Can I send that to a.gaines@hmail.com?
Target:	Um, well, I would rather use my other email address. That one is one I don't check often. Send it to gainesat@gmail.com.
Me:	Okay, no worries, sir. We will send that right out.

This gave us confirmation of the phone number, email address, and a clear vector that the target will fall for thanks to this vishing call.

My team and I have used this technique many times to verify data we have found and to uncover new pieces of intel. I find this form of vishing very effective because the target is not given much time to decide whether to help. Also, most companies have not properly educated their population on this vector. That combination creates a big risk for companies.

Vishing for Full Compromise

It's possible to perform a full compromise using only vishing. The principles remain the same, and with the right pretext and supporting evidence, a professional SE can easily obtain even the most sensitive of details.

In one case, my team and I were tasked with testing a large financial institution using vishing as our vector. The goal was to call in as C-level employees to see if we could gain access to their usernames and passwords or any other part of their systems or data.

Our pretext was going to be a female executive that was traveling to Hawaii for her honeymoon and that while she was in the airport, her boss called and said he couldn't find the report that was *essential* for the Monday meeting . She knew it was on her desktop but had forgotten the login for remote access.

We loaded a YouTube clip called "airport background noise" and started the call. I was listening in, muted, as support to provide quick thoughts or ideas as a silent partner. It went like this:

Target:	Support. How can I help you?
SE agent:	*[heavy sigh and stress in her voice]:* Can you hear me okay? The noise in this airport is so loud.
Target:	Hi, yes, it is loud, but you are coming in clear. Who am I speaking to today?
SE agent:	Oh my, I am so sorry. *[another sigh]* This is Jennifer Tilly, SVP of Finance. I'm heading to Hawaii for my honeymoon, and my direct called me to say the latest budget report is missing from the directory. He needs it for the Monday meeting, and I need to log in and get it to him, but I forgot my login.

Target: Okay. Let's see if I can help you. First, I need to verify your identity. But before that, let me say congratulations on your marriage, and I hope you have a great time in Hawaii.

SE agent: Thank you so much. I'm so excited. This is my first time in Hawaii, and I get to go with my best friend and new husband.

Target: Bless you. It warms my heart to hear people talk like that. Ms. Tilly, can I get your ID number, please?

SE agent: You know what is crazy? Since I was promised no work for two weeks, I didn't bring any of my laptops or IDs with me. I can't remember my own birthday half the time, so I don't think I'll remember my ID at all.

Target: *[trying to be helpful]:* Well, maybe if you try. It starts with 17—you only need to remember five more digits. *[This piece of intel was very important.]*

SE agent: I'm really drawing a blank. I don't know if I'm missing something like 98231?

Target: Well, there is a nine and an eight in the number, but, let's try something else. Can you tell me your manager's name?

SE agent: Sure, it's Mike Farely.

Target: Okay, great. And can you confirm your email?

SE agent: j.tilly@companyname.com

Target: Perfect. Okay, so here is what I can do, I can reset your password and send it to you on your mobile device; then you can log in and get that report over. Let me just . . . *[sound of typing and clicking in the background]* Ms. Tilly, I'm sorry, but I do not see that you have remote access installed as of yet. So even if I reset this, you won't be able to get in.

SE agent: Oh, no. This is just terrible. I'm going to be gone for two weeks, and my flight boards in just under 30 minutes. How can we fix this? Please help me! *[sounding near tears with high anxiety in her voice]*

I had just typed a message to the SE agent to suggest to her that we needed to see if we could get the target to install remote access for us on her machine and give us the one-time code when the conversation continued:

Target: Well, we can put in a request for remote access to be installed, but that will most likely take a few hours or even until tomorrow.

SE agent: You have been so kind, and right now, my husband is not too happy. We're supposed to be sitting in the lounge together sharing some champagne, and I am trying to deal with this work issue. Is there a way we can rush this?

Target: You know what, Ms. Jennifer? You're going to have an amazing honeymoon; let me see what I can do. Will you be okay if I put you on hold for a few minutes?

SE agent: Sure, just not too long. We're supposed to board soon.

With that, we could hear the target in the background saying to his coworker: "This poor woman is heading to her honeymoon; we need to help get her onto her machine. I'm sure we can do this fast, right?"

We couldn't really hear the commentary from the other person, but we got the sense that everyone was really rallying to help Jennifer. A few minutes later, the target put the phone on hold to make another call before he came back to the call with the SE agent:

Target: Ms. Tilly, well, I have a wedding present for you—an agent is installing remote access right now for you. In just 10 more minutes, we should get you on the machine.

SE agent: You are just the most amazing person I have met! My husband will be so happy, and this is the best present! Thank you!

Target: When I get the notice from the agent, I'll text you a one-time code, and then you can get in to the access.

SE agent: Oh, I can't do that. I didn't bring my work phone with me, so I won't be able to check that SMS.

Target: Oh, no, Ms. Tilly. We cannot get past this portion. I don't know what to do.

SE agent: This is just terrible!. This will teach me a lesson for being so dumb. I should have brought my phone. Now I will have to cancel this

> flight and delay my trip. Well, that is sad, but you have been truly amazing and helpful. Thank you so much.

Target: *No!* We will not have you miss your honeymoon; that is not acceptable . . . *[in a very low whisper]* Listen, I will send your phone the code; then when it is issued, I will give you the password over the phone, okay?

SE agent: You would do that for me? I may cry.

Target: Now, none of that. We have to get you on that plane not thinking about work at all.

With that, we had remote access, a password, and the ability to compromise the whole institution if we wanted.

PRO TIP You may notice that I tend to go with emotional pretexts that can offer the target the ability to "save" or "help" me. There is a science behind this. Giving someone the ability to trust you while you trust them with that role creates a very strong bond between two people. It releases oxytocin, and then that bond makes the target want to be consistent in their desire to help you, regardless of how insecure that decision might be.

Using vishing for full compromise can make the job of the pentester much easier. Many times, it is important to understand that vishing for compromise may require starting off with OSINT vishing before moving to more and more detailed pretexts.

Vishing Summary

Vishing is a powerful vector that can be devastating in the wrong hands. Because it can be used for almost every aspect of the social engineering attack, it is a potent weapon.

For a professional social engineer, it is imperative to not be afraid of the phone if you want to succeed. Learn to embrace it, even if it is not your favorite method of communication. Having skill on the phone and learning to build rapport, gain trust, and then elicit information without being able to see your target makes you more successful.

SMiShing

This is a short section because SMiShing is not widely used by attackers or professional social engineers. In 2017, Wells Fargo was breached, and after that breach, we saw a larger number of SMiShing attacks. Many of them looked very much like what you see in Figure 9-2. Most SMiShing messages are simple, but they're effective and generally geared toward loading malware on the mobile device or stealing credentials.

Over the last two years, mobile operating systems have been the targets of malware and other attacks in the hopes of gaining access to a victim's device. With the move for companies to also allow BYOD (Bring Your Own Device), we've seen an increase in mobile device breaches as well. Mobile breaches, which do things like reading emails, remotely turning on the camera or microphone, and using the mobile device as some sort of remote access point, have been the fear of many organizations.

For that reason, it is important for a social engineer to understand how to use SMiShing in their practice. Here are a few rules that make SMiShing much different from phishing:

Brevity is key. A SMiSh needs to be short and sweet—no build up, no opener and closer, just the facts and a link.

Links. In my opinion, it is always better to have a domain that looks similar to the attack you are launching, but if that is not possible, then shortened URLs are way more acceptable in an SMS than in an email. Hovering to check a link is nearly impossible on a mobile device, so the user needs to have advanced training to see bad links.

Figure 9-2 A popular SMiShing message after a breach

Don't skimp. If you are trying for credential harvesting, don't think that you don't need branding or the web page to look legit because the target is using a mobile device. To ensure you are fully testing targets, make sure to spend the time to make everything look real.

Don't make it too many steps. The target is on a mobile device, so if there are three or more steps, you'll lose your audience, and they'll not be motivated to continue.

As we see the increase of BYOD and home-based employees, it will become even more important for the professional social engineer to understand this vector and how to test a population with it.

Mobile phones are here to stay, and they're getting more and more robusy and integrated as part of our mobile work life. This will make it even harder for our clients to detect attacks.

Impersonation

Impersonation is one of the most dangerous vectors, but it's also one of the riskiest for SE agents to employ. Therefore, it's the least used vector out of the four. Impersonation is the physical impersonation of an employee of the target company or someone in authority who can be trusted (law enforcement, utility worker, and so on).

For myself and my team, impersonation is the most fun vector to help clients with, but the risk is quite low for us. With an actual attack, there is quite a large risk to impersonation, and that means it requires the most planning. In our pentests, we have a "get out of jail free letter," which means we can't really get in trouble for our exploits, whereas the real bad guys, if caught, spend lots of time in prison.

IMPERSONATION SE VECTORS VS. RED TEAMING

A red team generally goes in at night (although it can be at any time) and focuses on trying to breach the physical security—elevators, locks, security cameras, and so on. An impersonation SE vector focuses on the people part of physical security. So, instead of picking a lock, we are convincing the person with the keys to let us in. Instead of shimming that door, we are getting someone with the badge to let us through. A red team focuses on the security hardware, while impersonation from SE focuses on the people.

Planning an Impersonation Pentest

A social engineering pentester needs to keep in mind that *all* senses of the target are engaged when it comes to the impersonation vector. Whereas phishing engages only sight and vishing involves just hearing, impersonation needs to address almost all the senses (although it might not involve taste too much).

For that reason, it's important to thoroughly plan the principles of the pentest, as described in the following subsections.

Info Gathering

Information gathering is an important part of a physical onsite impersonation assessment. I often ask students to give me a pretext that will guarantee entry. Think about this for a second. Do you have an idea?

Students often suggest something like UPS delivery. My follow-up questions help them think through their initial statement: "Okay, great—but then what? How many of you have seen a UPS delivery guy roaming the building? They don't usually get past the front desk or the mailroom."

OSINT is essential for developing a plausible pretext for impersonation. On one of my jobs, I found out that local construction was causing spiders that normally come out in spring to come out a bit early. It was so bothersome, it made the local news. My pretext was spraying for the spider infestation, and it worked amazingly well.

Pretext Development

I touch on pretext development when I talked about gathering information, but don't make the mistake of trying to plan your pretext *before* you do the OSINT. Also, after you pick your pretext, you need to consider some other things: clothing, tools, your look, and so on. In addition, consider whether the props should look new or used. You have to think about all the things that make the pretext believable. Cover your bases.

Recently, I was breaking into a couple of banks with one of my employees, and I had learned by doing OSINT that the bank had just completed a PCI compliance test. We found the name of the company that had done the test, so we came fully dressed, badged, and carded up as the PCI compliance company. This got us right into the ATM testing center with no problems. From there, we were into two different computers, even obtaining the credentials of other employees in the cube.

When a manager approached and asked who our internal contact was, we didn't have a name. That was an oversight on my part, and it was a fail that led to us being caught. Yes, you can argue that by this time, we had compromised the network and had close to 30 minutes in the ATM testing center with access to multiple computers, but that one piece of data would have saved us and given us more time.

Attack Planning and Performing

Once you have the pretext, you need to understand what the goals are when you get into the building. Another way of saying that is you need to know what you *cannot* do. Are you allowed to get a remote shell? Are you allowed to compromise a server? Are you allowed to take a device from the building? Don't make the terrible assumption that just because you were hired to play a bad guy, you have free rein to do whatever they would do. That would be a pretty bad assumption.

Plan out what the attack should look like from start to finish, and then make sure you have the tools on hand and tested to accomplish those goals.

Once the plan is complete, make sure that your GOOJFL ("get out of jail free" letter) covers all that you want to do, and if it doesn't cover everything, get it included.

Perfect practices make perfect.

Reporting

Remember, the most important part of an engagement is telling the client what you did, how and what needs to be done next. Before you even start, make sure you have permission to record audio and video. Or if you don't have this permission, figure out how you will ensure that you capture the full story for the report.

For me, it is important to tell a story with this kind of attack. I want the client to feel like they can see, hear, and feel the full attack and get a sense for what worked and what didn't. I find it very beneficial to be overflowing with praise for their successes and matter-of-fact for mine.

My goal in the report is to "leave then feeling better for having" read it. To do that, I can't be embarrassing or overly flamboyant or at all derogatory.

The principles stated here thus far will help you with your physical onsite engagements. I find that a lot more planning needs to go into this part of the job. Still, there may be some more questions on the information to include in a report. The following are my thoughts on the handling of some sensitive data.

The Legality of Recording

Remember, I am *not* a lawyer, and nothing I say should be construed as legal advice. You should definitely have a lawyer to run these things by.

For my company's engagements, we do the following:

» Research the state and/or country laws for audio and video recording before the job.

» Get permission in writing from the client to record both.

» Never, ever, ever, ever, ever (did I say *never ever*?) use these recordings in a speech or training without permission.

And even if you get permission, you should sanitize the recordings so there is *nothing* identifiable. By "sanitize," I mean take out all names, workplaces, and any other identifying words.

» Make sure all recordings go to the client for their education.

» Ensure that storage, transportation, and usage are always secure.

It is important to understand the risks of what you are doing and know also how you plan to use what you collect. In one job I asked a woman to enter her user ID and password in a nearby computer. As she was complying with my request I not only recorded her face but captured her credentials on camera. To save her embarrassment, I blurred out her face from the video. Of course, the client could have told me that they wanted the unblurred video—it's their choice and right to do that. But I presented the blurred video first, and the client didn't argue. If the video is used for educational purposes, I will not feel like the woman has to relive her embarrassment forever.

Considerations of Sanitization

While on a job, I was recording everything using my pinhole camera that was hidden in a clipboard. I slipped into a server closet as I was trying to evade security, and I stumbled upon two people engaged in . . . well . . . not something you would think they would be doing at work. (Yes, sex, if you didn't guess it yet.) Stumbling on that made me forget I was supposed to be an SE for a second. The couple in the closet got mad and yelled at me, and I ran out. Later, I realized that I had almost 60 seconds of a sex tape filmed thanks to their lack of professionalism. This is obviously not something I could send in to the client, and I had to think about how I wanted to handle this.

Eventually I decided that the company had paid me a pretty penny to help secure them, their network, and their people. What I witnessed was a breach of company policy and, for all I knew, could have been a honeypot. How liable would I be if I did not report it and then heard the company had been breached and I could have stopped it?

PRO TIP In the world of espionage, a honeypot is a person who goes undercover to seduce another person into giving up sensitive information. It has also been used to describe a system (computer) that is set up to collect details from unsuspecting users.

I decided it was my obligation to report this incident. And, yes, it did result in the gentleman being fired. Why wasn't the woman fired? Well, she didn't work for the company—the guy had brought in someone from the outside to a server closet to partake in activities that should have been saved for the privacy of home, a hotel, or anywhere but a work environment.

You must decide what part of what you record you will sanitize. I sanitize when someone has taken an action that is not illegal—If they just fell for the social engineering attack, but they weren't malicious toward company rules. My focus is always trying to ensure that education is the first step rather than firing.

However, if I find someone downloading pornography, engaged in sexual activity, stealing, accessing data they shouldn't, or heaven forbid, engaging in any form of child exploitation, they shouldn't expect any kindness from a professional social engineer who's trying to protect his or her clients.

Equipment Procurement

There are lots of places where you can find "spygear." From Amazon to specialty shops (one of my favorites is online at https://spyassociates.com), there are many locations to get this type of gear. Keep in mind that you get what you pay for. The $25 pen cam will be poor quality and shaky, whereas the $600 button cam with DVR recording capability will most likely be a lot better.

Do a little research before you make a purchase. I always do the following before I place an order:

» I check the return policy and ensure I don't have to ship the item to a foreign country if it breaks.

» I read reviews of both the product and the company to ensure I am getting the best bang for my buck.

NOTE It might take you some time to get comfortable enough to worry about filming angles while also being a good social engineer. For that reason, I try to have a couple cameras going at one time, so I get at least one good angle.

Impersonation Summary

With the right planning, the execution of this complex vector can be made much easier. Remember that impersonation is different from red teaming, and you need to do good solid planning to make sure you test the physical security protocols thoroughly.

It's important for you as the SE pentester to understand the scope of what you're doing so you can hit all the goals the client wants. Especially since the end goal is to include a section of the report that outlines how to fix the problems found. That section will be more useful if you, as the SE, understand not just the what (you did) but also the why (it worked).

We are seeing more and more breaches involving the physical side of security—USB drops, physical theft of devices, and even worse, violence in the workplace. For these reasons, it is essential for a professional SE pentester to have mastered the impersonation SE vector as part of their practice.

Reporting

Early in my career, I was hired to break into seven warehouses. I had a 100% success ratio. I was even able to get into one warehouse twice in the same day by using different pretexts.

It was a great feeling, and I had the whole thing recorded and ready for the client. The project lead told me to start writing the report and sent me a template document. The template document was blank with the exception of some headers.

I think I stared at it for hours—starting, then stopping, then erasing, and then starting again. After dozens of hours, I had completed what I felt to be a masterpiece of reporting history.

I envisioned that the reporting team would receive it, read it, and throw palm leaves in the streets for me as I entered the building. I sent it in and waited for the glowing praise.

A day later, the phone rang, and the call went something like this (I've tried to make it more family friendly):

"Hey Chris, what is the steaming pile of garbage you sent to my inbox? Is this a joke? Is this some kind of laugh you are having? Do you think this would ever pass as a report? It's coming back with redlining for repairs. Get it done *now!*"

When I got the report back, it was no longer black and white—it was red, green, and white. It seemed as if there was not one paragraph that didn't have major edits.

It took me two weeks to fix the document, and it was the worst experience in my reporting career. However, at the same time, it was the best experience I've ever had. It taught me what a good report looks like and feels like. My initial report contained a storyline that made me look amazing and cool—like James Bond on steroids. However, it was missing some key elements that might be helpful for the client.

This part of the chapter isn't a seminar in report writing, but I have some principles to share with you.

Professionalism

Professionalism is the art of being a professional. Think about going to your doctor, someone who you hope and pray is professional. How would you feel if you stepped on the scale, and he said, "*Whoa Nelly!* Anyone got a fish for this whale?" before patting you on the back and saying that he was "just kidding."

I can't imagine many of us would enjoy that. Similarly, our clients don't want to hear things like, "We pwned you so bad!" or "Wow, did this guy actually put this on the web?" or "All your warehouse belongs to us." (I might know something about that last one from experience.)

Remember that this report will be read by many people, and the best environment for change is one in which people feel happy rather than embarrassed or humiliated. Your language, descriptors, and the way you relay facts should all exhibit professionalism.

Grammar and Spelling

Grammar and spelling are a personal pet peeve of mine. It is *attack vector*, not *attach vector*. It is *rapport*, not *report*. You get the point. You should always factor in the time to run a spell-check on your report and then have a trusted person proofread it.

Even with those checks, you still might leave a few errors behind. Mistakes happen. Don't expect perfection, but don't send in a report that has so many errors, you leave the client thinking that you just didn't care about this piece of the work.

All the Details

I have heard pentesters in the past say they leave out certain details—such as how they found OSINT, the exact Google search string they used, or some other artifact—because they feel if they give the client too much information, the client won't need the social engineering services anymore.

To me, that is just plain silly. I heard the same argument when I wrote my book, *Phishing Dark Waters*, in which I outlined the exact methodology and process for making a phishing program. However, the reverse occurred: Many companies are using that book to build an amazing phishing awareness program, as well as many who read it and wanted my help in setting up the program for them.

Don't get too worried about giving your clients too much. Most of them will appreciate your knowledge and be impressed by your finds. They'll want to stick with someone confident enough to give them all those details.

With that said, if you find super-sensitive items, be sure to communicate with your point of contact to clarify what should and should not be included the report.

Mitigation

Mitigation is maybe the most important part of the report, but it's also the most overlooked. Do you want your doctor to tell you that you have a terrible disease, then wish you "good luck" and leave the room; or say, "See you next physical . . . I hope."? Of course not. You shouldn't do this to your clients, either. Instead, give them some mitigation that's actionable.

If the mitigation steps are what I call platitudes and nonsense, what does it mean to your clients? For example, let's say you've done a vishing test for a client and achieved an 80% compromise ratio for the month. Which of the follow mitigations options do you think will help the client more?

» **Option 1:**

Social-Engineer recommends that you continue testing your population and using positive reinforcement to elicit the proper responses to vishing attacks.

» **Option 2:**

Social-Engineer analyzed the data from this month's vishing campaign and noticed the following two points that could be used in further education:

> » *Female callers tended to do better using the same pretexts as male callers. This may point to more education being needed on how to recognize elicitation.*

> » *When presented with a fake employee name, only 12% of your population tried to verify the name, and there were even a few who continued to give information after not finding the name. This demonstrates the need for more education on how to properly verify a caller.*

Social-Engineer would like to schedule a call to discuss how these can be implemented into an educational program as we continue testing.

Obviously the second option is the best, but too many times (and I admit my team has been guilty of it too), reports include non-actionable statements that really don't help the client and act as filler.

Even after doing this for years, it is a constant battle to make sure complacency doesn't set in, and I am giving 100% effort on this point for my clients.

Next Steps

In addition to mitigation (fixing the problem) clients often want to know, "Now what?" Including next steps is an essential ending to the report. It allows the client to know what they should do and expect moving forward.

I don't mean you should simply state, "See you next pentest." You need to follow the same rules of mitigation as I previously discussed. Give your clients enough detail to feel armed with a clear path to progress.

Many of my clients are monthly service clients, so the path forward is already known, but that doesn't mean I can rely on that solely. The client will still want to know if we should alter things or adapt to enhance the program.

When you put all these steps together, you will have amazing reports that will truly help your clients and leave them and you feeling better.

Top Questions for the SE Pentester

As I conclude this chapter, I want to cover some of the most commonly asked questions I get as a professional SE pentester. I'm sure there are tons of other questions, but these are the most common. I hope these will help you whether you are presently in SE as a career or working toward making it a career.

How Can I Get a Job Being a Social Engineer?

This may be the most asked question of my whole career. After you've decided you're going to go for it, what do you do? Well, you have to start somewhere, and this is why this answer is so hard. Maybe you have been working at your current career for the last 10 years. You have expertise and skill in that area, and you have the pay to match. Starting a new career as a social engineer means not only starting over in expertise and skill, but maybe in pay as well. My best advice is that you be willing to do the following:

» Step out of your comfort zone.

» Start over.

» Learn whole new skill sets.

» Take a pay cut if necessary.

If you can do these things, you can expect a nice career in social engineering. *But* (there is always a *but*, isn't there?) you can't just expect that SE companies will be calling you to offer you a job. There are only a handful of us social engineers out there, and you still have to prove yourself different from all other candidates. These things will take some work on your part.

> **NOTE** Remember that being a professional social engineer is not all about breaking into banks and getting shells through phishing. There is a lot of office work and reporting that needs to take place. Being a professional social engineer is not just about being able to talk to others or being able to think quickly and clearly under pressure—it's about the whole package.
>
> Where are your weaknesses from this list:
>
> » Elicitation
>
> » Smooth talker

»   **Quick thinker**

»   **Good report writer**

»   **Professional speech**

You need to identify them, so you can then improve upon them.

If you get the chance, go to `https://youtu.be/RGnzf66-a4A` **to watch a speech I gave at DerbyCon7 about this topic. (Warning: It begins with a prank that my friend Dave Kennedy pulled on me, but hang in there—I get back on topic soon after.)**

How Do I Get My Clients to Do SE Stuff?

Let's say you are already a pentester and doing some social engineering work, this section gives you some ideas about how to get your existing clients to hire you for more SE gigs.

Don't Offer Them Some of the Services for Free

Some people have suggested that if you give clients some free services, those clients will see the benefit of what you do and pay you for more work. I have an anecdote that explains why this tactic doesn't work the way you expect it to.

When I started in the tech industry and was building computers, I tried launching a free seminar on how to stay safe as a small business. In this seminar, I provided more than 60 minutes of real actionable tips on antivirus, networking, file sharing, and more. At the end, there was a 5-minute sales pitch on why companies needed to use me as their provider for all this.

I partnered with a local chamber of commerce and offered the speech for free. We set up three of these of seminars, and the number of people signing up was *huge*. I was getting 20, 30, or more people signed up for each seminar. I was already seeing dollar signs and feeling like I won.

The day of the first seminar rolled around, and I went to the room, set up my projector, and laid out my handouts and all the give-aways I had paid for out of pocket. Five minutes before the start time, there was only one person in the room. At two minutes before start time, there was still only one person in the room. The starting time arrived, and no one else had shown up. It was quite awkward. I started giving my speech to the one person. After five minutes, he said, "Hey, this is really weird. Do you want to just go get lunch and talk?"

I was lost—I couldn't figure out what happened. After the same thing happened on the second seminar I just canceled the third. Someone suggested, "Hey, next seminar charge people $50 per head to sign up. Tell them they will get more than $50 worth of stuff free but make them pay."

I was very reluctant to even try. I thought that if they hadn't come for free, there was no way they'd pay to attend. However, when I charged for the seminar, I had 10 people sitting in the room, and each had paid $50.

WHAT??? It didn't matter that the attending numbers were smaller than my original sign-up numbers. What did matter was that the 10 that came, actually paid for the privilege to come.

Later, I sat with the business friend who'd suggested that I charge for the seminar, and he explained that when people pay, even a small amount, they add a value to it. If someone signed up and paid but didn't end up attending, they would be out the nonrefundable $50. That became a powerful incentive to attend.

When I was just starting my SE career, it was as if I had not learned anything about offering things for free. I was getting offers to give speeches all over the globe, and I was charging them nothing. I found that many times, people would cancel or not commit until the very last minute.

A friend of mine, Ping Look, told me to stop charging nothing and to start charging a fixed amount. I was very reluctant to listen to her, but I reflected on my previous experience and decided to try it.

Amazingly enough, people were more than willing to pay the higher amount. They also seemed to value me more. This changed the way I did business, and from that point on, I didn't ever give things away for free.

The moral of this long story is this: Don't think that giving away your talents for free will make people value you. It won't work. You can find the balance of offering a high-end service with some discounts or offering a three-month contract with one month free. It's okay to get creative about what you charge, but know that working for free just devalues your expertise.

Fail Fast and Move On

If I meet a potential client who is reluctant to engage my services, I offer to begin with one spear-phish on a corporate-level person in the company to demonstrate how effective it can be. Usually when that decision-maker sees the danger and benefit, they are ready to put a budget forward for these types of services. One small engagement is often all it takes to lead to more engagements with a company. But sometimes that is not enough, and a company doesn't want to engage in further social engineering services.

If nothing you do is working to convince a company that you can help, what should you do? Walk away. Realize that it is better to fail fast and walk way than to try to make a square peg fit in a round hole.

If a company cannot see the need to have SE as part of their security regimen, then you probably don't want them as a client. They will be frustrating to work with and eventually will not find value in you.

I had a client that was with me for four years. When I first started with this company, they were almost the perfect client. I had an amazing point of contact, and that person was raring to go. The program was so successful that the client saw massive changes. The woman who was our internal contact running the program was offered a job by a much larger company that wanted her to run its security program. She jumped at the chance, and I understood why. A new woman was hired to take her place.

From the first day working with the new woman, it wasn't the same. The new point of contact was easily offended, took this way too personal, was not willing to take the risks, and didn't want to take the program to the depth her predecessor did. Consequently, the program floundered. People reverted to their old ways, and although the phishing statistics still looked great on paper, the program was stagnant.

Six months before I parted ways with the company, I had told my team we would lose them as a client, and we sure did. They are only the second client we have ever lost this way, but I think it was for the best. They didn't want to take the program in the direction it needed to go, so it was frustrating for them and for us.

With only a set number of hours in a day and clients we can handle, I would rather spend it with clients that want to see the change. Don't be afraid to walk away from deals because they aren't the right fit.

How Much Should I Charge?

I often hear this question, but it's something that I considered not even putting in this book because the answer isn't easy or simple. However, since it's such a popular FAQ, I try to cover this topic as best as I can.

First, you need to understand what hourly rate you *can* charge as a consultant. I did a little research and found several sites that give suggestions for what rates are acceptable for consultants in the security field for different areas around the globe.

The rate depends on a several factors, such as years of experience, expertise in the field, how well-known your company is, and what services you offer.

For the sake of easy calculation, say I decide my rate should be $100 USD per hour. I work out my fees by deciding (based on experience) that phishing 1,000 emails per month is going to take me 20 hours per month. I spend three hours on

OSINT and seven hours on reporting, which means I will invest a total of 30 hours per month. My rate calculation will look like this:

30 hours per month × $100 per hour × 12 months = $36,000 for an annual contract

This is not a hard-and-fast rule—it's just a method I use to gauge my price. I may alter the rate based on things like

>> The size of the company

>> Multi-year contracts

>> How I feel about the client (very subjective)

The point is, the preceding calculation can help get you close to figuring out your rate, but it might not be exact. At least it gives you some guidance on how to start charging for your services.

> **NOTE** These are just a few of the questions I get asked often. There are many others—too many to put into one book. I promise if you email me through the website www.social-engineer.com/contact-us/, I'll do my best to answer you or help you find an answer.

Summary

I read a report that said only a minority of the companies in the United States actively provide training on phishing awareness through monthly campaigns.

If only a small percentage of U.S. companies are providing training, and my company grew by 300% in the last three years, what will happen when 20%, 30%, or 50% of U.S. companies start actively training?

The fact is, there is a huge need for professional, quality social engineering pentest professionals. I cannot do all the work myself, so I might as well help as many people as I can get in the space to give the best quality services they can to all the companies that need it.

I don't think there will be a time when humans are no longer in the workforce. Consequently, human vulnerability will always exist. In addition, people have to deal with a never-ending barrage of attacks on their empathy centers, fear centers, and logic centers. These attacks can wear us down and can cause us to make bad decisions.

We will always need SE professionals to help companies learn how to stay secure against these attacks. I think there will be a huge increase in artificial intelligence and technology that helps combat these attacks, but there will never be a time when we do not need humans to help other humans.

Maybe you are reading this book because you want to break into the social engineering business. Or maybe you are reading this book as an existing professional looking for new tips and tricks. Or there can be a number of other reasons that you may have picked this book up. For any of those reasons you want to really focus on the next chapter that will help you prepare a M.A.P.P. .

10 Do You Have a M.A.P.P.?

I'm a very big believer in controlling what you can, forgetting what you can't, and not wasting mental energy on things that don't deserve it.

—Josh Citron

I feel a book that is focused on creating professional social engineers would not really be complete without this chapter. You can blend all the attacks, the psychology, the physiology, and the report-writing to achieve something, but without a M.A.P.P., a giant piece of the puzzle is missing. What is a M.A.P.P.? It stands for *Mitigation and Prevention Plan.*

Why do you need a mitigation and prevention plan? How do you help your company or your clients develop one? What can you mitigate and plan about social engineering attacks? I answer these questions in this chapter.

When I started gaining momentum with my clients, I realized something important. My goal needed to be something really odd: to be so good that I would eventually work myself out of a job. Yeah, you read that right. I needed to help my clients learn how to defend against SE attacks to the point that they eventually would not need me.

You know those pentesting companies that advertise that they *always* have a 100% success ratio? Well, how demoralizing is it for a customer to be writing you the check knowing they will never get better. Or that no matter how good they get, the social engineer still will always win? The message in that is there's no hope. Nothing they do will ever block all the holes in their security. Eventually you might be able to understand why customers say, "Why bother trying to protect ourselves?"

In my epiphany, I decided that I had to help my customers plan how they would mitigate attacks and how they would get so good at catching these attacks that eventually all they would need is maintenance. If you are a professional social engineer like me, then you need this chapter to be successful. If you are a company, this chapter will help you plan your M.A.P.P.

This hit home with me when I realized I needed to change my health. I had tried a bunch of things on my own, which failed miserably. In the community of white-hat hackers, I had seen a few who'd made some serious health changes. I spoke to one and asked how he did it, and he put me in touch with a man named Josh Citron.

Josh wanted to do a video chat for our first conversation. I really didn't want to—I imagined that he was in super shape, and the last thing I wanted to do was video chat with my fat-self on camera with him. To make matters worse, I looked him up on the Internet, and it was not too hard to find some pictures of him. He is some sort of beast-man-chimera that can lift small vehicles and still run six miles.

Now, imagine that if in my first meeting with Josh, his opening words were: "Okay, Chris. Here's the deal. If you do everything I say, and if you listen to every word and never cheat and keep paying me . . . well, you'll never win. You'll stay fat and probably won't get stronger—ever. So, let's get started!" I probably would have looked at Josh like he was *nuts*! Or if he had scornfully looked at me on that video chat and treated me poorly because all he saw was a fat slob, I most likely would have not continued with him.

However, Josh told me that if I did everything he said, I would see gradual changes, and when I hit my goals, we would move to a maintenance-only program. Because he also treated me with dignity and respect, I was ready to rock and roll.

Josh helped me make a M.A.P.P. that would mitigate risk of bad habits and build new and better habits. It wasn't some radical diet of cutting out anything that tastes like food and eating only salads and sadness. I made habit changes, enhanced my decision-making, and gained knowledge to make the best possible decision in all situations.

That process can be applied directly to developing a social engineering and security M.A.P.P. I've developed four steps that, when followed, will create this M.A.P.P. and all the benefits that come with it:

» Step 1: Learn to Identify Social Engineering Attacks

» Step 2: Develop Actionable and Realistic Policies

» Step 3: Perform Regular Real-World Checkups

» Step 4: Implement Applicable Security-Awareness Programs

Here is what I promise: If you follow these steps, you *will* see the change you want in your population. It won't happen overnight—in fact, depending on things like turnover, corporate culture, and so on, it can take a few years or more—but it *does* work.

Are you ready to get started?

Step 1: Learn to Identify Social Engineering Attacks

When I was younger, I wanted to learn how to fight, so I took a martial art. I remember the first day I met my trainer. As a test, he asked me to block the punches he threw at me. It seemed to me that, out of thin air, he created fists aimed at every part of my head and body. I was unable to block a single hit.

Fortunately, he wasn't actually punching me—he was giving me light taps, but he landed every single one. Jump forward one year: I had become successful at blocking a large majority of all the hits coming my way. What had changed is that I had learned to identify what an attack looked like and felt like, so I was able to not only identify but learn how to react to it.

Step 1 seems self-explanatory, but it is not. How many people in your company do you think can define phishing, vishing, SMiShing, and impersonation attacks? How many people do you think realize how dangerous the name of your dumpster vendor can be in the hands of an attacker? How many people in your employee population do you think know what malware, ransomware, and Trojans are?

Don't get me wrong: I'm not saying that every employee needs to be a social engineering Bruce Lee, but each person needs to at least understand what the fight may entail. This first step of understanding what attacks are, what they might look like, and what they can do to you is vital.

You might be sitting there asking, "But how do we do that?" That's a great question. Imagine if I had walked into that dojo, and the trainer had said this to me: "Okay, you want to learn to fight? Get on the mats with this fifth-degree expert who has been fighting for 20 years and go at it." I would have run out of the dojo. And if he just put me in front of a computer for 20 minutes and showed me a CBT (computer-based training video) on martial arts and then put me in the ring, I would have had a similar response. (Put down the pitchforks. I'm not saying that computer-based training is totally useless, but relying on it as the main portion of your program is a mistake. CBTs have a specific role, which I talk about later in this chapter.)

What I received from my trainer—and what you should expect from a social engineering expert—was to be taught how to recognize and *take* a "hit," in the form of a social engineering. I was given the proper training on stance and body position, and then I was put on the heavy bag and the light bag. When the trainer felt I was ready, I sparred with a person who didn't want to kill me; he wanted to help me learn.

This first step of learning how to identify and know that these attacks exist will put your team light-years ahead of the average person. Help your employee population to understand the value of the information they possess—that emails can be used to breach the whole company; that phone calls are used to get passwords and other sensitive details; that if their mobile device is breached, it can be used to attack their home and work networks; and that just because a person is smiling and friendly, you can't ignore the badge policy.

Helping your employee population understand the possible attacks can enlighten them enough to make them more aware. Because I do this day in and day out, I sometimes forget that not everyone knows these attacks exist.

I was sitting with a friend who was telling me how his grandma gave over a large sum of money through MoneyGram because someone had called claiming to be her grandson and needed bail money. I said, "Oh, no. She got hit by the grandma scam!"

He asked, "The what?"

I explained how this type of attack is sadly all too common. His reaction was one of anger, and he said, "If you knew these things existed, why didn't you warn your friends?"

Wow, he was right. I had just assumed that everyone read about these things, but they don't. Would my warning have saved them? Maybe not, but the lesson is still there.

Think back to my experience with health and fitness coach Josh, the trainer. After that initial video-chat meeting, I had to send him my daily log every week for a while, and there had been days of failure. Do you know what Josh *never* did? He never scolded me like a child, never guilted me, never gave up on me. Instead he'd say, "Okay, let's do better this week."

Apply that and learn from it. Don't assume that the knowledge about these attacks is just common sense. When someone doesn't have the knowledge, it doesn't mean they're just stupid, lame, and deserve to fail. Instead, have empathy and think: "Okay, we can do better next time. How can we do that?" That will really help you make the next step more successful.

Step 2: Develop Actionable and Realistic Policies

One of the things Josh started me off with is learning what a real portion of food looked like. He would tell me how much protein, carbs, and fat I should consume in a day and leave it up to me to make the decisions. So, I could consume it all in one meal, but I would have been really hungry later.

Josh also taught me not to rely on my eyes. He once told me to put on a plate what I thought were the right amounts of several foods. Then I was to weigh it. *WHOA*, it was way more than I would have ever guessed. This rule, or "policy," helped me to learn a valuable lesson about changing my decision-making habits.

In the security world, *policy* may seem like a bad word. Most people hate making policies, enforcing them, and/or having to follow them. I have found that policies often get a bad rap because they don't make sense or are not clear in their intent. Other times, policies are so restrictive that they seem to create an adversarial relationship with the population.

Finding a balance is not an easy thing to do, but it is essential to succeed in creating a secure environment that is filled with a security-awareness culture.

What makes a good policy—one that is not too restrictive and yet actionable and realistic? There are a few aspects to a good policy that will help you in building solid rules for improvement.

Take the Thinking out of the Policy

Too many times policies are so broad and general that they can leave way too much thinking, or decision-making, in the hands of a person who has not yet been educated on what these attacks are. Now, I'm not saying you should treat your people like they're dumb. Just know that the less time the employee must spend thinking about something, the better. Simple is best.

Here's an example: My company did some vishing work for a large financial institution, and more than 80% of the time, we were successful in getting very personal details on the targets. We played on their empathy and trust and exploited those things.

To this company's credit, they had really nice employees working for them, and we didn't want that to change. How terrible would it be if the mitigation advice was, "Make your employees more paranoid and untrusting"? What this company did was astounding. They made a real, actionable policy: "You are not allowed to give any information out to unauthenticated users."

And they didn't stop there. They defined both what is valued information and how to authenticate users properly. Then they did one more thing that made a huge difference: They disabled the employees' ability to move past this first stage if the questions were not answered properly. For example:

Attacker: Hi. This is Joe Smith. I need my account info. I have my account number, but I forgot my password. Can you help me please?

Agent: I sure can. Before I do, though, Joe, I need you to verify your identity with me. Can you . . ."

The agent would be instructed to ask a series of questions, enter the answers into text boxes, and only the correct answers unlocked the agent's ability to move forward.

I followed up the policy with some education, and then we tested again. When the agents were armed with this great policy, solid education, and knowledge, they became unstoppable. They were still kind people—in fact, there were at least a dozen times that an agent was truly sad that he couldn't help me and worked his or her hardest to find a way but wasn't able to. The policy and the education made it possible for the agents to stay protected without having to think about what to do.

Remove the Ability for Empathy Bypasses

This guideline doesn't say "remove empathy." I would never suggest that. However, you need to remove the ability for empathy to motivate a bypass.

I have a good friend in the UK, Sharon Conheady. While she was in the late stages of her pregnancy, she did an SE job. She used her pregnancy to work the empathy angle.

Sharon filled a large box with heavy looking items. As she walked toward the door, playing up her struggle with the box, multiple men ran to her aid. They not only carried the box to the server room for her, but they never even thought of checking her ID or badge. After all, criminals can never be pregnant, right?

These chaps did the right thing in helping a pregnant woman. You would never want to stop people from showing that kind of concern. Instead, the company instituted a policy to educate the staff on how they should always help those in need but then check for a proper ID badge before escorting the person anywhere in the company.

Just saying, "Check all IDs," is not enough, because when empathy kicks in, that good ol' amygdala shuts down logic centers so that people make decisions solely on emotional thoughts. The education, reminders, and clear instruction help remove the empathy bypasses and ensure secure process.

Make Policies Realistic and Actionable

I have seen with my own two eyes policies that read, "Do not click on malicious links." How does that sound to you? If you are saying, "Yeah, that's great—I'm gonna use that," I want to you put this book down and slowly use the back cover to slap yourself in the face.

Now that you are done, read on.

That kind of policy is bad because it's not detailed enough for the employee. How do they know what a malicious link is? Do they know that support-microsoft .com is not the same as Microsoft.com?

The policy doesn't include an *if* clause. If you click the link, then what? This policy needs a further piece that says something like, "If an email, phone call, or live person is interacted with, and you feel like something right did not occur, please report all these instances to xxxxxxx@company.com."

But wait, there's more! Now you need to tell your employees *how* to report it properly—forwarding the email, sending in the caller ID info, and so on. What details do you want reported? What are the consequences for reporting?

A realistic policy helps the employee see the situation from all angles and doesn't leave them with questions. In working with one company, I helped develop education around a new policy for phishing. It went something like this:

> Phishing is a threat to our company and you personally. Malicious attackers want to get your information, and they can do it through email-based attacks. They may use malicious documents that come with extensions like EXE, PDF, XLS, or DOC. Or they may send you links to websites that are not what they say and contain malware or other dangerous programs.
>
> If you receive an email from any source that you are unsure of, before you take an action report it to abuse@company.com by clicking FORWARD on the email and entering that address in the TO section.
>
> Someone from that department will reply within 24 hours to tell you if that email is safe.

> *If you did click a link or open an attachment and you feel it might have been malicious, it's not too late. Report the email to the abuse department.*

Of course, there was more information in the policy and links to internal training and other resources. You get the idea, though. A good policy is realistic and gives clear direction on what actions to take and not to take.

Returning to my martial-arts story, this step is like the trainer showing me how to stand, how to hold my arms and hands, and where to look and explaining *why* each of those things is important. A good policy helps the person know not just the what; it also explains the why. If done right, eventually your employee population will react with muscle memory about these things.

And when that happens, you are ready to move on to applying the third step.

Step 3: Perform Regular Real-World Checkups

Every week, I send a sheet to Josh that outlines my calorie intake, exercise, sleep, weight, and a bunch of other details. Each day, I record those items, knowing he will see them. This real-word checkup keeps me on track. It also helps me keep the goal in mind, and it alerts Josh to inconsistencies or problems.

One time when I was traveling a lot, I stopped tracking and tried to guess. When Josh saw that the facts and figures didn't really jive, he asked me a series of questions, and we got to the bottom of the problem so we could correct it and move forward. This real-world checkup made the difference between an effective program and an unsuccessful program.

This is exactly what Step 3 is for your security program. You have given your people education on what these attacks are. You have provided training to your employees on what to do when they encounter these attacks. You have set up policies to help them make the best decision possible when they run into an attack. Now, how well did all this information stick? Will muscle memory kick in when the employees are tested? The only way to find out is to choose the right security consultant partner and get in the ring with them.

Choosing your consultant partner is important. If you're reading as a social engineer who's hoping to become a company's vendor, it's important for you to know what a smart company is looking for. Remember, it's not just about always being 100% or having done the most amazing hacks—it is more about your knowledge and how you apply it to helping companies improve.

How can you know if the partner you're looking at is the right fit? Here are a few suggestions:

Ask good questions.   Don't be afraid to ask for stories of previous jobs or how the company recommends a certain situation be handled. Does the answer align with your core values?

For example, I was consulting one company, and they asked how I'd suggest they handle those people who would fail our testing. My answer was honest and simple: I told them it was essential to educate the people about what they had done wrong, retest them after education, and then determine if they were a threat to the organization. But systematically firing people for failing was a terrible idea. That answer aligned with their belief system, and it was a good match. During the first discovery meeting with a company that has hired me for SE work, I have often been asked for exact attack scenarios that I planned to use. I usually tell them that I need to do OSINT before I can develop any themes but then offer them something I did at a similar company as an example.

Just go into the meeting with good questions if you are the company seeking a partner and good answers if you are the company answering those questions.

Have qualified referrals.   Fimding companies that allow you to use them as referrals can be hard, because a lot of clients don't want to broadcast the social engineering services that have been done for them. Many large organizations have been breached through their vendors. In my case, I've found three or four clients who have allowed me to use them as referrals for prospective clients. If you can get referrals, I think this is a really important part of the puzzle. It helps to find out from a third party what it's like to work with the company you want to hire.

Keep in mind that no vendor is going to give you an angry client as a referral. The goal is to get a glimpse into how they work with their clients and what quality they offer.

Clearly define the rules.   As a client, nothing is worse than thinking a pentest will only go one layer deep and then finding out that the pentester went five layers deep, so now you must explain to your boss what happened. The best way to ensure there are no problems is to have a clearly defined set of rules for the test, so no boundaries are overstepped. Clearly defined rules are like the protective gear that boxers wear during sparring matches.

As a client looking for a pentester, you may have a few requirements that you like to use when picking a vendor, but these three are a good starting point to ensure you chose the best partner to spar with.

Once you have picked a partner, start testing and then use the results to determine what services you need and how frequently you will be tested. A good partner can help you determine what is needed and will also be honest about your needs (rather than basing it on dollar signs).

Some services are best done monthly, like phish testing. Other services work better as annual services or semi-annual services, such as penetration tests. There is no one-size-fits-all solution—it largely depends on what your needs are and how you want to accomplish your desired goals.

Another factor is how well you apply Step 4.

Step 4: Implement Applicable Security-Awareness Programs

Josh will post videos of himself doing certain exercises, running, and engaging in other healthy activities. The videos he posts are little pieces of education that help his program make sense for the people he trains. This is like applying security-awareness programs.

Maybe you're sitting there thinking: "Didn't you just cover security awareness? Is this a repeat point?" Well, no; not really. All the preceding steps are part of your security-awareness program for sure, but this step is specifically about how well you apply the previous three steps to create real actionable and applicable awareness programs.

Let me tell you another story to help illustrate. I had a client for whom we did a barrage of tests. My SE team committed a good amount of time to OSINT, then followed that up with both vishing and phishing attacks.

We found that when it came to vishing, the people in the company had almost uncanny ability to stop us. They rejected giving us names, would not give out extensions, and would not even confirm whether someone was in the office. But when we phished them, we found some serious vulnerabilities.

We looked at what they had been doing and found they had a robust plan for education on both vishing and phishing, but their vishing education covered all the bases. It taught employees about the attacks, gave them realistic scenarios with actual actionable policies, and tested them routinely in a safe environment.

However, their phishing program consisted of only a few computer-based video modules per year. I could have sold them on a brand-new vishing and phishing training program, but they didn't need it. Instead, I worked with them on their phishing program and encouraged them to change *nothing* about their vishing program. In other words, I helped them make their awareness program applicable to the company's specific situation based on what they had done in the previous three steps.

The next client will *not* be the same, as the next will be different, and the next and the next—all will be unique. That is why creating applicable programs takes some serious work and cannot be relegated to templates or modular approaches to security.

By making security-awareness programs applicable to your client's specific needs, you can help their employees learn not only what not to do, but also what they should do when and if something bad happens. Applicable security awareness helps employees make sense of and support the policies and programs that are established.

Here's another example based on my experience with being coached by Josh. When Josh tells me to cut down on a certain type of food or increase a certain activity, I can fully support him in those changes, even if I don't like them. Why?

» I see the positive effect of these changes.

» Josh fully explains what it is he is doing so it is clear to me.

» He gives me actionable tips for success when I hit challenges.

» When I fail (because I do), Josh doesn't scold me like a loser (which is what I feel like). Instead, he treats me like a person who needs a little more help and tries to come up with a more foolproof plan for next time.

This program has helped me generate some serious momentum in improving my health, and an applicable security plan can do the same for your security. Don't assume because *you* have finally gotten it, everyone in the company will also have gotten it. They may need some more time to come along.

Tie It All Together

Think back to those dark ages before your cell phone had every feature known to man, including a fully loaded world map with GPS. Can you remember back that far? I can.

I remember using a hard-copy map for directions. Just like Step 1—learning to identify attacks—I had a starting point on my map. I looked for the fastest route that avoided toll roads and backroads, all while taking me closer to my destination.

Then, like Step 2—having actionable real-world policies—I made sure I stayed on the highways, so I knew I could maximize my speed.

Then, like Step 3—regular real-world checkups—I would periodically check the road I was physically on and compare it to the map to make sure they matched.

Finally, the last piece was the actionable awareness program (Step 4), which is just like the final point of using a real map; I made it from my point A to my point B safely, securely, and in the time I had planned.

Having a map in real life got me all around parts of the United States. Having a M.A.P.P. in your security program can do the same by helping you to think through your mitigation and prevention plan.

Doing just one step will not be sufficient, the same way as just having a physical map in the car will not get you from point A to point B. You need to have a plan and then act on it to make it work.

I can't promise that each of you will turn into the "Josh of Security," but the four steps can flex your security muscles in a positive way. (See what I did there?)

The rest of this chapter describes a few other things that can help you create your M.A.P.P.

Gotta Keep 'Em Updated

Let's say that you have mastered the four steps. Can you put a stamp on your door that says "hacker proof"?

Well, you can, but only if you want to be laughed at while getting hacked. Generally, following the steps will make sure you're *not* the low-hanging fruit and help keep your human network hardened against attack. That's a good place to be, but there is always the chance that someone in your company could fall for a phishing, vishing, SMiShing, or impersonation attempt. If that happens, what can help you stay even more secure?

Making sure you are up to date on your computer updates. I can't tell you how many times during routine security audits I have found companies using browsers, PDF readers, mail clients, or even (gasp!) operating systems that are three or four versions old. Those older versions can contain lots of vulnerabilities. Keeping your systems up-to-date can protect you from the potential breaches that occur if you get hacked and have older software on your network.

I write this knowing full well that this is much easier written than done. I realize there may be legacy systems in place that require time, effort, and money to upgrade. However, remember that as of 2017, the average security breach cost a company $3.62 million USD. And that's just the average! In 2017, there were some breaches that cost $10–300 million USD.

I am not naïve enough to say that updates would have saved each one of these companies from a breach, but I am trying to make a point. You can incur the cost before a breach (to protect yourself from it) or after (when you're paying for the fallout). But if your idea of security resembles Figure 10-1, we might have to have a more serious discussion.

Burying your head and *hoping* the predators don't see you will not make it true. Decide when you want to pay: before the breach or after. I vote for before—although it might cost time, money, and stress, it protects your clients and reputation and saves you the embarrassment of being breached.

Figure 10-1 This is *not* security.

Let the Mistakes of Your Peers Be Your Teacher

Go to Google, type in the words **network breaches**, and then click the News tab. On the day I did this, I was greeted with what you see in Figure 10-2.

Each of these stories contains details about a breach, how it occurred, what caused it, and what vulnerability was exploited (whether it was human, hardware, software, or all of these). Understanding attacks that affect other companies can help your company stay safe.

Delaware doctors, hospitals increase security as medical data ...
The News Journal - Dec 18, 2017
Dr. Jan Lee, CEO of the Delaware Health Information **Network**, said she realizes the "double edged sword" of electronic health records. About 90 percent of practicing Delaware physicians are using electronic health records, she said. "We're not naive....it is a real concern," she said about **breaches**.

Hackers hit major ATM **network** after US, Russian bank **breaches** ...
AOL - Dec 11, 2017
FRANKFURT (Reuters) - A previously undetected group of Russian-language hackers silently stole nearly $10 million from at least 18 mostly U.S. and Russian banks in recent years by targeting interbank transfer systems, a Moscow-based security firm said on Monday. Group-IB warned that the attacks, ...

8000 Tallahassee Utility customers' data at risk after **breach**
Tallahassee.com - Dec 28, 2017
A PayPal owned company that processes utility payments for the City of Tallahassee notified about 8,000 customers who used remote location kiosks to pay their bills that a data **breach** may have compromised their personal and financial information. The 40 or so kiosks are operated by TIO **Networks** USA, ...

The dirty dozen: 12 top cloud security threats for 2018
CSO Online - Dec 21, 2017
A data **breach** might be the primary objective of a targeted attack or simply the result of human error, application vulnerabilities, or poor security practices, ... Once in place, APTs can move laterally through data center **networks** and blend in with normal **network** traffic to achieve their objectives, CSA says.

Crime, fraud and investigations 2018: Cyber security
Lexology - 12 hours ago
Reporting companies can expect to be asked to conduct investigations into cyber security **breaches** and report to the ICO. ... worldwide, to the "Petya" infection of a major law firm's global IT **network** and hundreds of thousands of customer details being seized from Wonga and Three Mobile amongst others.

Virtual College

What DHS employees need to know about OIG data **breach**
FederalNewsRadio.com - Jan 3, 2018
In order to prevent future **breaches**, DHS OIG has further limited the number of individuals who have back-end access to its case management system and added new **network** controls to better detect unusual activity from approved users. "The Department of Homeland Security takes very seriously the ...

Federal Cyber **Breaches** in 2017

Figure 10-2 Just a sampling of the current news

When you see that a current exploit is being used against a certain firewall and has breached companies, it's time to check whether that firewall is in your network and if it is patched. When you see that business email compromise (BEC) phishing scams are on the rise, it is time to harden against those with education and proper policies. No matter what the cause of the breaches you read about, it's a good lesson to start cataloging the current threats and comparing that to your infrastructure to see where there are weaknesses.

There are lots of companies out there that sell threat-modeling services to help with this, and you may want their help. Otherwise, it's a good practice to start modeling on your own and determine where you can enhance, harden, and bolster your current programs and protocols to remain vigilant against attacks.

Create a Security Awareness Culture

I am going to use Josh and his training with me as an example again to illustrate this point. After working with Josh for a while, it became easier to identify behaviors and situations that would put my progress at risk. For example, not counting my calories throughout the day or trying to guess at a portion rather than weighing it were generally minor behaviors that could lead to a lack of proper gains. On the other hand, going to an all-you-can-eat pizza buffet and trying to convince myself I would stop after two slices would be a major setback.

Josh has helped me realize that the decisions I make throughout the day can create in me a health-conscious lifestyle. I don't need a 24-ounce porterhouse steak when a 6-ounce filet will do just fine. If I want to get a dessert, I need to make sure I make better decisions in early parts of the day, so I don't blow my whole program. So on and so forth.

What does this have to do with creating a security-awareness culture in your organization? Everything!

With proper training, reminders, and rewards, you can create a culture where your employee population knows that the minor decisions they make can have long-lasting effects. And they will realize how major decisions can be devastating if they make the wrong choice.

In my work with Josh, the reward is weight loss, feeling better, looking better, and having overall better health. That reward is a good motivator for me to keep going with the program. Not every employee will feel the same reward for "catching the phish" or "reporting the vish." It's not because they don't care or hate the company—it's just that some people are so busy they may view training programs as a time-wasting necessary evil.

Those folks will be the hardest to convert, but conversion is possible. In one company I worked with, a department manager made it very clear that he hated the testing we were doing. As a result, his department of 450 people seemed to be one of the largest threats to the company. Malware, phishing, and other attacks often caused problems in this department.

The manager realized his people were not complying. He was frustrated, and he wanted to use a methodology of shame and embarrassment by calling out the worst offenders. I have never seen that methodology work effectively—normally, it creates an adversarial relationship between the manager and team. In those cases, compliance, if it is given at all, is a result of fear, anger, or resentment. In a meeting with the client, I asked about trying a quick game with their call center team. I said I would send them a plush fish doll, and I wanted them to announce that the first person to *not click* and *to report* the phish each month would get the fish at his or her cubicle. That person would be labeled the "King Phisher" for the month.

Now, you might be sitting there thinking that this sounds like ridiculous idea. You're right, it is. But after two months, you wouldn't believe the race among 450 grown adults to have that stuffed animal at their cubicle. It became a badge of honor to be the "King Phisher."

The results were more than just increased interaction with our program. Because the employees were actively looking for the phish, reporting went from a mere average of 7% to more than 87% in a few months. Clicking went down from about 57% to less than 10% in that same time. And the most rewarding outcome was that actual malware that was found on the network dropped by more than 79%.

This simple change created a security-awareness culture. The employees started to make better decisions, they saw the change, and they were motivated to keep the change.

What will make that change for your organization? I can't tell you exactly what you need without speaking with you, but here are a few ideas that I have seen work over the years:

Rewards I have seen everything from the plush fish doll mentioned earlier to raffles for gift cards and other rewards for taking the right action for X number of months. Of course, rewards can get expensive if your group is large, or it can lack motivating force if the reward is something not useful or too insignificant. In one organization, they tried to give away one $5 gift card per quarter to those who stayed in the ideal behavior group for the whole quarter. The gift was too small to be a motivator. The reward needs to motivate, but that doesn't mean it has to be a brand-new 60-inch flat-screen TV or a year's salary. It just has to be something that represents how much you appreciate the actions and attitude you are asking for.

Positive Reinforcement   I have seen companies create intranet lists of folks who have stayed in the ideal behavior group for X months. Some call out "Star Employees" in their intranet pages for those who have caught the phish for X months in a row. Positive reinforcement works much better than shame and embarrassment, and it motivates continual desired behavior for the right reasons.

Extra Training   Before you start burning my barn, let me explain what I mean by "extra training." I have seen many companies have great success with sessions they call "Lunch and Learn." They bring in pizza or some other type of food (if you invite me, please have salad or something healthy so Josh won't get mad at me), and they have a short speech or video or presentation about some security topic that benefits those who attend. Sure, those who attend may do so at first for the free food, but the sessions I have attended always ended with many people being able to take at least one bit of useful information away. It is also a great opportunity for you to reinforce the concepts and actions you want the employees to take.

Top-down Reinforcement   This one seems to have almost mystical powers, as if you put a spell on your population. When the CEO lets the group know they are also getting phished with the employee population each month and how he or she fared, it gives a very clear message of "we are in this together . . . for reals." In one organization I worked with, the initial reaction to the phishing program was less than ideal. In one extreme case, a woman who took all the wrong actions when receiving the phish was so angry, she demanded that I get on the phone, and she spent 10 minutes chewing me out. She told me what an awful person I am and how I need to reevaluate my life course. A few months later, the CEO of this massive organization held an all hands corporate meeting. In that meeting, the CEO mentioned the phishing program; he explained that he got phished like everyone else, and he was learning that he needed to be more aware. As if some mystical talisman was waved over the population, anger ceased to exist, aggression toward my SE team was lessened drastically, and we saw a much larger percentage of compliance. Sometimes the population feels they are being singled out to be made to look dumb. This can cause an adversarial relationship, and getting the top management of the company to support the initiative can really help.

Here are two more points that you should keep in mind:

»   **Be Patient**

Don't assume because you are now training them all correctly, your employee population will just jump on the bandwagon right away. It may take time and continual effort to get your employees to see your vision and have your passion for it.

»   **Manage Expectations**

Does this sound familiar? It should. Not only can this help build rapport, but it can help you to create a culture of security awareness in your company. Just because you can catch the phish or identify the vishing call or pick out the person who doesn't belong doesn't mean every employee will be so fast to do the same.

By being patient and managing your expectations, you will help your employees come in line with the new education.

Summary

As difficult as it may be at first to believe you can do this, you can create a culture of security awareness. You may look at what "shape" you are currently in and think it's going to take too much effort or time. However, the effort is worth it. The rewards of having a culture of security awareness far outweigh the risks.

In one email that Josh sent to me, he said, "This is a lifelong journey, not a 3- to 12-month one. Making habit changes is *hard*, but we are all works in progress."

That doesn't mean you should keep doing the same thing over and over and hope it gets better. It is important to fail fast and move on. Try something in this chapter, and if it doesn't work, don't keep doing it. See that it isn't working and try something new.

Josh constantly changes my program, sometimes weekly. It is rare for the program to stay the same for more than a month. I'm not saying you need to adjust this often, but there is a lesson in this. For my program to work, I have to check in with Josh weekly to give him the full picture of what my previous week looked like.

He then takes into consideration my travel, diet choices, exercise quantity, and even my level of personal problems for the week. All of that information helps him see if there are changes that need to be made to keep progress on track. I'm sure he does a lot of analysis and has a process for the decisions he makes.

This directly correlates to how you can apply this chapter to your SE awareness program. Make sure you have a full picture of your organization—from the physical side of testing to the psychology of your employee population. Try to understand what stresses they may be under and how that can affect their decision-making. Once you have this full picture, it becomes easier to plan your security program. Develop a clear path forward, initiate the program, and then watch how it progresses.

I can't tell you that this will make you hacker-proof. I can't even predict the percentage of success you will see. However, I can promise that you will see change. I can promise you that you will begin to create a culture of people who not only know what types of attacks are out there, but can defend against those attacks.

How can you apply all the knowledge in this book to become a social engineer pentester or as a company looking to defend against social engineers? The final chapter helps tie this all together, and I promise I won't even mention Josh. (Sorry, Josh. Your 15 minutes are done.)

11 Now What?

It's easier to limit yourself, but if you do, you will never reach your true potential.

—Chris Witty

When I think back over the last eight or nine years, there is no way I could have predicted what was coming. I would never have guessed I would have a successful business doing what I love as well as a nonprofit that helps safeguard children from harm.

The adventure has taught me, molded me, and helped me develop into what I am right now. It wasn't all perfect, and I still have lots of room to grow, and I think that's the point I want to make clear in this chapter.

There is no silver bullet or magic wand for social engineering. You can't read these pages and think if you add a little rapport, a dash of influence, and a sprinkle of nonverbals, and then blend all that with a dollop of trust, you can become the perfect social engineer. It takes work, self-reflection, and then more work.

Inevitably, people ask me how to get into the industry and how to become a career social engineer. The answer to this question has many facets, but in this chapter, I tell you what I look for in potential social engineers.

Soft Skills for Becoming an Social Engineer

I have met so many people who have amazing skill, but they couldn't handle the job. They literally just could not move forward in this industry. And I have met some folks who didn't have a lick of confidence in themselves but turned out to be amazing social engineers.

There are four marked characteristics in those two groups that I think can help you if you want this as your career path. I truly feel they are essential to your progress:

Humility

Hands down, the one thing that the people who excel at this field have is humility. Often, being humble or meek is considered a weakness, but I ask you to take a moment and think about one person in your life who you feel is truly humble. Do you have that person in mind? (P.S. If you said yourself, you're doing it wrong.)

Now answer this question without thinking: "How does that person make me feel?" For me, it is a combination of happy, respected, and important. Isn't that more powerful than being considered as someone who knows everything and cannot be corrected—in other words, someone who's *not* humble?

When I had the privilege of working with Dr. Paul Ekman, I got to experience this firsthand. Because he has such a powerful intellect, I expected working with him to be hard and demanding. However, I found him to be truly humble, to be open to other's opinions, and to be willing to allow creative freedom. When I needed correction, he was firm but also insightful and directing.

Every person I have seen excel in the social engineering field and that I have loved to work with has a measure of humility and a willingness to be corrected.

Motivation

I view a job as something you can do by going to work each day and accomplishing your tasks and then forgetting about it when you end your day. If you want a job, being a professional SE is probably not a good choice Being a professional SE is more of a career. It will change who you are during work and non-work settings. However, the skills involved don't all come naturally, so you need the motivation to learn, grow, and keep improving if you're going to be in this industry.

Extroverted

Now wait! Before you throw the book in the shredder and scream, *"I am an intro-vert!"*, please know that I'm not saying you need to change. I'm suggesting that you tap into a little bit of extroversion and learn to switch it on for the job.

You might remember from Chapter 3, "Profiling People Through Com-munication," that I'm a strong *D* (direct) type of a communicator. *D*s are generally known for "telling" and not inviting. It is where I'm naturally inclined to go, but when I started speaking and training more, I realized that direct communication was not as good as an Influencer (*I*) for those tasks. I practiced some of the ways that *I*s communicate and started to use those skills during training. The result is that I'm less exhausted, and the students love the training more.

I suggest that you practice one skill at a time, until it becomes a tool that you can spontaneously pull out toolbox when you need it. As painful as it may be for you to say, "Today, I'm going to start a conversation with two complete strangers," I suggest you do just that. After a while, that task will become much easier, and you'll need to step up the challenge.

Over a short period of time, you can move to another aspect of communications until you are able to turn those skills on and off at will.

EXTRA INFO

According to the Meyers Briggs research (www.myersbriggs.org/my-mbti-personality-type/mbti-basics/extraversion-or-introversion. htm?bhcp=1), an extrovert actually can be energized by being in social settings, whereas an introvert is exhausted by the same situation. It goes on to state that an extrovert is outgoing, comfortable in groups, has a wide range of friends, jumps into action too quickly, and can lack attention to detail.

An introvert, on the other hand, is reflective, comfortable being alone, prefers to know just a few people, spends too much time planning, and can be slow to move into action.

Willingness to Try

Fear of failure is one of the biggest causes I have seen for people not being good at this job. It can even be immobilizing for some. Those who have excelled at the path to becoming a professional social engineer have been able to step out of the comfort zone and realize that sometimes failure is the best teacher. Those who have a willingness to try new things seem to be able to fit into many different tribes and adapt to situations more readily. I have noticed that those who are afraid of new cultures, foods, people, and experiences often find this job most stressful and exhausting.

It Really Works!

I have seen someone who thought he could never be a social engineer apply the four characteristics and become an amazing SE. I remember when I met him the first time. He walked into my classroom, sat in the back of the class, folded his hands in his lap, and put his head down.

I realized when I met him that he was an extreme introvert. I was curious why he was sitting in *my* SE class of all places. Did his boss make him come? Did his company mandate that he needed to be there? I started my normal process for the beginning of class: I start each day with a good dose of Clutch (the best rock band on Earth). When the first chord on the first song started, this student, Ryan, lifted his head up, and I saw a marked sign of comfort on his face.

I said to myself, "Okay, good. He's a fan of Clutch." I introduced myself to him. In a short conversation, I found out that his boss did not make him come, and there was no mandate—he simply wanted to challenge himself to step out of his comfort zone and try something new. I still sensed that he fully expected it to be too hard.

Over the next four days, I saw Ryan demonstrate an amazing willingness to try everything I asked him to do. He was motivated to not give up on any task. He even became more extroverted as the week went on. The biggest thing I noticed was that he would routinely come to me and ask for more advice, criticism, and critique on his evening homework.

When the class ended, Ryan was awarded the most-changed student award by the whole class. I told my team, "I'm going to hire Ryan in the next year or two."

However, hiring him would prove to be no easy task. Ryan was a changed man. His present company saw the changes and rewarded him. He went from being the lead pentester to moving into leading the charge with all SE attacks. He was vishing, phishing, and breaking into places. And above all that, he was good at it.

It took me three years to hire him, but now Ryan takes the lead in all the SE work for my company. He is still introverted. He still loves to plan (too much, in my opinion), but he is motivated, willing to try new things, able to turn on his extrovertness (yes, I made that word up), and still routinely asks for advice, help, and counsel.

I know that someday I will be working for Ryan—I'm sure of it. If he can be successful in the SE field, so can you. You just need the four principles I just described.

Technical Skills

Maybe one of the questions I'm asked most frequently is about what type of tech-related courses an SE needs. There is no simple answer to this question, but let me try to point you in the right direction.

Technical skill is important in this career because you will be interacting with technology all the time. Understanding how to use simple technology, such as USB keys, booting machines, and connecting to a VPN, can go a long way in helping you with your pretexts and after you gain access.

With that said, is it a necessity for you to be an expert exploit writer? Not at all. Here is my quick rule for how you can determine how technical you should be. Will you be a one-person shop or working with a team of people? If you are a one-person shop, then you might want to have some robust tech skills. If you do not have them, it will severely limit your service offerings.

On the other hand, if you are going to work with a team of people, you check and see that some of your teammates have the skills needed, so you can be weaker in some areas than when you're working solo. On my team, we have a great blend of technical and nontechnical people working together.

If you've determined that you want to have some technical skills, the following are some things I find important:

- » Basic computer knowledge
- » Basic office productivity knowledge (such as Word and Excel)
- » Knowledge of the different parts of a computer and how they operate
- » Ability to navigate in Mac, Windows, and Linux operating systems
- » Understanding of how a network works
- » Knowledge of how to set up a mail server
- » Photo-editing skills

If you're going to use exploitation in your pentests, you also need the following skills:

- » Knowledge of exploit frameworks like Metasploit and Empire
- » Ability to read and understand code
- » Ability to write some code

Education

"What education should I have to become a social engineer?" Every time I get this question, which is way more often than you would imagine, I tell the person I feel that I really am not qualified to be their guide in this aspect. After all, my college experience ended with me writing a war dialer and then being "asked" by the dean and police to leave the school.

> **FUN FACT**
>
> In the early 1990s, there were no computer-crimes laws, and most "hackers" were just curious people—not like the malicious hackers of today who are out to destroy things. I wrote a program, called a war dialer, that daisy-chained two 4,800-baud modems together; then dialed a number, played a few digits to tell the number to shut off for 5 minutes, and then hung up; and then did it all over again. I used something called threading, which allowed the program to call many, many numbers at once. This script shut down 60% of the county's phone systems for a day. That resulted in my being asked to leave the computer school I was in.

Despite my dubious educational background, I do have some opinions about what kind of education is beneficial. You do not need to be a master in these areas but I do suggest basic understanding of the following areas:

Psychology   The key is to remember that although you're *not* a trained psychologist or therapist, having a basic understanding of how humans make decisions is important.

Language, Grammar, and Writing   You can be the best social engineer on Earth, but if you can't write a good, clear report, then your efforts will never be recognized. A high quality course that can help you learn your language and how to increase your professional vocabulary has my vote.

Social Psychology   Learning how humans interact in social groups, what influences us, and how those groups affect us will make you a better social engineer for sure.

Now you may be asking, "Wait, that's it?" Well, like I said, I'm not your college guru. I'm just offering suggestions based on my experiences. If you don't have a formal education in these things, please don't think you will never be able to succeed. You can read books, visit websites, listen to podcasts, and talk to others who have the knowledge you seek in order to get a basic understanding of many of these things.

Remember that the end goal is not to become psychologists, therapists, linguists, or social psychologists. You just need to be knowledgeable enough to identify when you see a certain principle at play.

Job Prospects

If I could have included in this book a surefire way to always get a job, I think I would have a *New York Times* bestseller on my hands. The sad truth is there is no quick way to ensure this, but I can point you to a few paths that I have seen work.

Start Your Own Company

You can start to sell social engineering services to companies in your area. Today, starting this kind of company is not as hard as it was when I started. (You're welcome.)

When I started, I offered to give away five (yes, only five) phishing emails just to get people to try it. And yet potential clients still would reject the offer at times. Today, people want to see social engineering used in pentests and services. Media, the news, and the world at large have helped make companies aware of the threats posed by SE, so that makes your job easier.

Even with the changes of the past few years, there still are some hurdles on this path. Think about what you are asking a company to let you to do: "Please give me a list of your users and let me phish them or vish them. Oh, and let me break into your company and take stuff. If you want, I can get remote access and hack you while I'm at it."

Most companies will want to know who you work with, if you have references, who knows about you, and other details that make starting off really difficult. But don't sit down and cry just yet—there are things you can do to make yourself known.

Speak at a conference, or write a few blog posts or articles and get people to read them and comment on them. Having even a small public name in this space can help make your business a valid contender for providing services. I have seen a few people start a successful business by generating some buzz in the community even though they had no previous experience in social engineering. They came to DEF CON and entered the Social Engineering Capture The Flag (SECTF) contests I host there. After doing really well and winning, they went on to create successful companies that provide social engineering services. Building credibility helped them along their path.

Get Hired by a Pentest Company

Most pentest companies offer some form of social engineering services. One path I have seen work for some folks is to get a job at a pentest company. If you're just out of college or have no experience, you may have to start at the bottom.

Once you're in, though, you can make it known that you are willing to do the vishing, help with pretexting, and so on. When you do a great job, the company will give you more opportunities. If you're successful, you might quickly move up the ranks using this method.

However, this path can take months, or even years. You may offer to help, but your company might not use you for a while. You have to go in with a plan for how long you're willing to try.

My suggestion is that you take this path with patience and a willingness to learn new skills that may help you as you move up or move on from this company.

Get Hired by a Social Engineering Company

A quick Google search tells me there are quite a few companies that focus on social engineering, and only a few do it as their sole service offering. My company is one that solely focuses on social engineering, and we get many requests per month from people who want to work for us. I would love to hire them all (if they are qualified), but we only hire when we need people. (Logical, right?)

However, that shouldn't stop you from asking. You can reach out to these companies and tell them you are entering the field. Share things you have written about, spoken about, and/or done, and let the companies know you'd like them to let you know when there are any positions to be filled. Getting on the list of potential hires in these companies may land you that dream job.

Whichever path you choose to take, this field is going to need people. Social engineering is *not* going away any time soon, and the need for skilled people who want to make a difference will be there.

The Future of Social Engineering

Can I get serious for a second? Besides the reports that talk about hacking attacks—such as the Verizon DBIR report, CISCO's report, and others—social engineering is being used in some very dark places.

Every day, there are new reports about people who are leaving their families and homes to join terrorist organizations. How is this happening?

When you analyze these stories, you can see all the elements of social engineering I have mentioned throughout this book. People who join terrorist groups are angry, emotional, and looking for a tribe. Then a tribe comes along and gives them answers and motivation to "solve" their problems. The people feel needed, wanted, and accepted. The new tribe asks for small things at first, building trust and a close bond. This continues until the conversion is complete.

According to an article titled "The Geography of Foreign ISIS Fighters" by Richard Florida (CityLab, August 2016, www.citylab.com/equity/2016/08/foreign-fighters-isis/493622), more than 19,000 people have left their homes in Tunisia, Russia, Saudi Arabia, Turkey, and Jordan to join ISIS. In Western countries like the UK, France, Germany, and the United States, the numbers are lower (not more than 2,000 people have joined), but the same principles for recruitment are being used.

Another very disturbing trend is how these principles are being used by child predators to groom children. Using online chatting tools, predators start a relationship with a child by entering their "tribe." A predator will seek a child who is fighting with his or her parents or has a bad home life and then build rapport, actively listen, use open-ended questions, and suggest ideas and concepts that eventually become the child's ideas.

NCMEC (The National Center for Missing and Exploited Children) reports that in 2017, there were 465,676 missing children in the United States (www.missingkids.com/KeyFacts). In that same year, out of the 25,000 runaway cases the FBI assisted with, one out of seven children are victims of sex trafficking. Many of these children have been groomed by pedophiles.

I know this is all very dark, but I am trying to impress upon you that social engineering is not going anywhere. From corporate attacks, to personal attacks on your grandma, to terrorist grooming and child predators, social engineering is here to stay and is increasingly being used.

We need people to be on the good side to help defend, protect, educate, and empower others to understand these skills and learn how to defend themselves from these attacks. I don't promise you that it will be easy. I will promise you, though, that it is rewarding.

In the last eight years of my career, I have had a chance to work with dozens of companies around the globe that have seen drastic reductions in their susceptibility to social engineering attacks. One company reported to me that they saw an 87% reduction in malware on their network, and they directly related it to our phishing education.

Another company reported that their agents were successfully able to recognize, stop, and report an active vishing attack on their organization because of the training we had done with them.

One of my students told me that what he learned in my five-day course saved his marriage. Although saving marriages was never my intent in writing an SE class, it pleases me that this student was so affected by what he learned about communications, rapport, and influence that he applied it at home, and it helped fix his relationship.

I have also been partly responsible for saving multiple children from exploitation both with my corporate work and the work I am doing with my new nonprofit organization, the Innocent Lives Foundation (www.innocentlivesfoundation .org). Using the very same skills I teach every day to unmask those who prey on children is more than rewarding.

Finally—one last, very personal note—I have been able to teach my children these same skills, which makes them more self-aware, less susceptible to attack, and (in my not-so-humble opinion) some of most balanced and amazing people I know.

Learning how to use these skills is rewarding not just as a career but in everyday life. I hope that this book motivates you to want to learn more. If you have already mastered many of these skills, then I hope this book gave you at least one or two new ideas to ponder. If you are a skeptic or enthusiast, I hope this book fosters some healthy discussion about these skills and how to use them.

I welcome your input and opinions on this topic. I encourage you to make these skills part of your everyday tool box. Stay safe, and stay secure.

Index